Pra

"Fitzsimmons has hit a stunning three-pointer with this fascinating, engaging and thoroughly researched behind-the-scenes look at national powerhouse St. Patrick. *Celtic Pride* pulls back the curtain on the inner workings of the tiny Catholic school that produced Al Harrington, Kyrie Irving and Michael Kidd-Gilchrist. It is a must-read for anyone interested in high-level basketball."

—Adam Zagoria, author of ZagsBlog.com and *She's Got Handle - The Story of Nicole Louden's Triumph Through Inner-City Basketball*

"With rich detail, Fitzsimmons brings to life the colorful characters of Court Street, relating a tale of how Kevin Boyle built a no-frills program into a national power."

—Kevin Armstrong, *New York Daily News*

"This book gives you an inside perspective on arguably the best high school basketball program in New Jersey and the nation. Well written, with a Jersey flair."

—John Celestand, NBA champion

"*Celtic Pride* captures the close detail and attention that St. Patrick High School's basketball team received during the 2010-11 season."

—Alex Kline, TheRecruitScoop.com

"Brian Fitzsimmons not only captures the true essence of St. Patrick High School in Celtic Pride, but also a long list of figures who helped turn it into one of the nation's premier high school basketball programs. His extensive interviewing and tremendous attention to detail helped tell a story no one dared to take on until now."

—Josh Newman, Asbury Park Press

CELTIC PRIDE

How Coach Kevin Boyle Took St. Patrick to the Top of High School Basketball

Brian Fitzsimmons

iUniverse, Inc.
Bloomington

Celtic Pride
How Coach Kevin Boyle Took St. Patrick to the Top of High School Basketball

Copyright © 2011 Brian Fitzsimmons

All rights reserved. No part of this book may be used or reproduced by any means, graphic, electronic, or mechanical, including photocopying, recording, taping or by any information storage retrieval system without the written permission of the publisher except in the case of brief quotations embodied in critical articles and reviews.

iUniverse books may be ordered through booksellers or by contacting:

iUniverse
1663 Liberty Drive
Bloomington, IN 47403
www.iuniverse.com
1-800-Authors (1-800-288-4677)

Because of the dynamic nature of the Internet, any Web addresses or links contained in this book may have changed since publication and may no longer be valid. The views expressed in this work are solely those of the author and do not necessarily reflect the views of the publisher, and the publisher hereby disclaims any responsibility for them.

Any people depicted in stock imagery provided by Thinkstock are models, and such images are being used for illustrative purposes only.

Certain stock imagery © Thinkstock.

ISBN: 978-1-4620-6370-3 (sc)
ISBN: 978-1-4620-6369-7 (hc)
ISBN: 978-1-4620-6368-0 (e)

Library of Congress Control Number: 2011960249

Printed in the United States of America

iUniverse rev. date: 11/21/2011

For Grandma Wanda,
who was looking forward to this book more than anyone

♣

In loving memory of Neil Boyle Sr. and Neil Boyle Jr.

The Prayer of Saint Patrick

May the Strength of God pilot us.
May the Power of God preserve us.
May the Wisdom of God instruct us.
May the Hand of God protect us.
May the Way of God direct us.
May the Shield of God defend us.
May the Host of God guard us.
Against the snares of the evil ones.
Against temptations of the world.

May Christ be with us!
May Christ be before us!
May Christ be in us,
Christ be over all!
May Thy Salvation, Lord,
Always be ours,
This day, O Lord, and evermore. Amen.

PROLOGUE

Playing for Coach Boyle—it's just a blessing.
—Michael Kidd-Gilchrist

He gave a thumbs-up.

One of the four camera operators yanked off his headphones and rested them on his neck, nodding in approval of his coworker's motion after asking if he had filmed the thunderous slam dunk that rattled the backboard mounted to the ceiling of St. Patrick High School's gymnasium.

Award-winning filmmaker Marc Levin stood in the doorway with his arms folded, carefully monitoring one of the first practice sessions his production crew was capturing for a documentary that was in the works to be aired on HBO sometime the following fall.

Meanwhile, Kevin Boyle stopped the action after his players ceased their enthusiastic cheers. Another cameraman jogged over to the most fascinating figure of the crew's project with hopes of catching one of Boyle's colorful breakdown talks that carefully dissect a play and explain why it produced a certain result.

Speeches of that ilk instantaneously proved why Boyle, who was entering his 23rd year as head coach at St. Patrick, was looked upon as one of the most respected high school basketball coaches in the entire United States. That type of knowledge alone was enough to differentiate the Celtics from your average high school team. For more concrete proof of Boyle's status, one could've also gone downstairs under the gym in the coach's office to see a Gatorade advertisement with his face on it. Such was one of the perks of being a two-time National Coach of the Year. In other words, there were plenty of physical education and sports marketing teachers in the country, but only one like Boyle.

In this brief lesson, every word Boyle spoke reeked of urgency. His team, which entered the 2010–11 season as the eleventh-best team in the country according to the *USA Today* Super 25 rankings, had a plethora of lofty goals set in place to further etch the program's name into high-stakes high school hoops lore. It was a remarkable feat in itself that this school was able to construct a dynasty despite being nestled in a rough urban area off the ports in Elizabeth, New Jersey, with little to no financial backing.

St. Patrick costs $5,700 a year in tuition. In the Archdiocese of Newark, two schools (St. Vincent and St. Mary of Jersey City) charged slightly less than St. Patrick; oddly enough, St. Mary's was scheduled to close its doors by the end of that school year.

"We're a no-frills school. We're a college-prep school with no art or music. My teachers are overworked and underpaid, but we also get a lot of donations," said Joe Picaro, who had served as principal for nineteen of his forty years as part of the administration at St. Patrick. "And over the last forty years, I heard we're closing. I always react the same way. 'We are?' But I never look past the next year, because you never know what could happen, especially with the economy."

St. Patrick sits in the middle of Court Street, across from a large square park and to the left of an eerily beautiful cathedral. The church's gothic structure is molded after the Cathedral of Cologne in Germany, and its two towers, standing 212 feet above the ground, maintain their position as the most visible points of the city. During the nights, chain locks wrap around the rusted gates that lead to the stairway into the church; the closest one can get to standing near a white statue of Saint Patrick is by leaning over the pointed fence that runs down the block, past the high school, and ends at the St. Patrick Academy grammar school building.

St. Patrick High School consists of two, three-storied buildings, which offer a majestic, old-time image because years of erosion have smeared areas of the red bricks and dark gray cinderblocks.

In 1858, ground-breaking for St. Patrick's church took place in the section known by many as a "wilderness with cow paths." Fifteen years later Fr. Martin Gessner was assigned to the parish, in debt by some $65,000 due to the construction's pending expansion plans. Fr.

Martin spent his tenure at the Roman Catholic institution, consisting of mainly Irish parishioners, walking from home to home asking for donations. He tried to clean up the area, decimated by shoddy living conditions and saloons on every corner. Slowly, but surely, his vision transformed into positive action.

Fr. Martin had established the first St. Patrick school in 1863 with the help of a staff filled by Sisters of Charity. Twenty years later, an even larger school was erected, but as the parish continued to grow it was clear a new facility was needed. More construction resumed in 1886, and by 1907 the cornerstone for a new rectory and St. Patrick High School was laid. In turn, St. Patrick has become the oldest Catholic parish high school in the state, with a rich tradition of academic excellence.

"We have kids who come in as underachievers and leave as overachievers," Picaro said. "The success of people here is amazing."

Thomas Mitchell, a member of the St. Patrick class of 1910, played Uncle Billy in *It's a Wonderful Life* and Scarlet's father in *Gone with the Wind*. Buffalo Bill used to attend Mass at St. Patrick because his uncle, Fr. Cody, was the pastor.

"We've also had so many doctors and lawyers graduate from here," added Picaro, a buttoned-up old-school educator whose jokes and uncanny ability to carry a conversation for hours often overshadow how strict he could be. "I bet we've had 25 graduates that served as Elizabeth police officers, too. There seem to be a lot of graduates in the service areas, such as teachers. St. Pat's just produces these types of people over and over and over."

In December of 2010, the school was about to produce a basketball season unlike any it had ever seen. Across the street from the park, where a monument dedicated to Fr. Martin stands, Boyle and his Celtics were hard at work, drawing up their own construction plans.

Coming off a season in which St. Patrick was banned from the New Jersey state playoffs for out-of-season practice violations, yet still finished fourth in the national poll, the team possessed enough talent to win a Tournament of Champions title—the highest form of a state championship trophy in the Garden State—for the fourth time in six years. The team was also looking to prove that the graduation of superstar point guard Kyrie Irving, who enrolled at Duke University, wouldn't give rival St. Anthony of Jersey City a clear path to glory.

Finishing as the best team in the state and perhaps the country would have also closed the gap between St. Patrick and St. Anthony, led by legendary coach Bob Hurley, who became a 2010 Naismith Memorial Basketball Hall of Fame inductee.

Boyle had taken the Celtics to 17 consecutive Union County title games and walked away with 12 championships in that span, eclipsing state records on both accounts. He also had eight state titles and five Tournament of Champions trophies prominently displayed on his sterling resume.

What was missing? The answer chronically served as igniter fluid for the fires many rabid high school basketball fans lit on countless online forums: Despite finishing ahead of the Friars in nine of the previous 13 years, Boyle was absent of the same respect Hurley had accumulated and embraced over his four decades.

"(Boyle) made it clear he wanted what Hurley has, and he's kind of gotten vilified for it," said Mike Quick, a high school sports guru and current talk-show host for MSG Varsity. "Basketball really never gave him his due. He deserves to be looked upon as a great coach. You could put him in any public school in the state, and they'd win. His kids are always better. His kids will always win because he imposes his will."

A native son of Union County, Boyle was always known for his strong personality and quick wit. He was never one to mince words when asked any question regarding basketball; the former Division I collegiate point guard would spit out his uncensored opinions with the help of a heavy New Jersey accent and quick annunciations.

"I wanted to know what he was all about," Quick recalled about the first time he covered a St. Patrick game, "and I wanted to know why does he talk so fast? You could see he had a vision. You could tell that right away. You knew this was a guy who wanted to win and was such a competitor. It oozed off his words. And as I watched more and more games, I took notice of this coach and how he imposed his will in games. It was hard not to notice. I found myself watching the coach rather than the game."

That was Boyle in a nutshell; he was the gripping storyline behind a riveting tale, the asset whose character development provided the HBO documentary crew with more than a portly portion of gusto.

Boyle's teams often attracted more spectators to observe practice on any given day than most schools did for games. Some onlookers were present to make sure their son was working hard at all times. Many were crouched quietly on the three-tiered metal bleachers tucked in a corner, intently marveling at how even the most powerful program in the area, year after year, had to go back to the drawing board, time after time, just like any other.

Though it was around 7:00 p.m. on this mid-December evening, several students could still be found wandering the school hallways waiting for a ride home. Some didn't know where their transportation was coming from. Some feared it may not be coming at all. St. Patrick was the safe haven for young kids who called the inner cities home. It was also a welcoming sanctuary used to escape the rough streets for some, a place to take pride in their classmates who carried around a discernible celebrity status on the other side of the gymnasium doors.

In a way, the scene outside practice was akin to a line of fans waiting in anticipation to catch a glimpse of their favorite movie star at a public appearance. One teenage boy was sitting on the steps adjacent to the entrance, playing with the tags on his oversized black backpack. He looked up and asked me, "You're here to see Michael Gilchrist, aren't you?"

♣

I attended a Wednesday evening practice at Public School No. 28, a modern middle school with a much bigger facility than the high school several blocks away down First Street, which the team sporadically used. Just two days before the Celtics were scheduled to board a plane for Fort Myers, Florida to compete in the highly publicized City of Palms Classic and begin a long journey toward yet another state championship, Boyle was fuming.

Several players weren't fully executing the motions of help-side defense around the perimeter, a cardinal sin for any contender simply because it allows an opponent to run a fluid scheme in the half-court set, usually resulting in a basket down low or a wide-open jump shot.

"Instead of staying here, move here," Boyle bellowed, frantically waving his hands in the air while shuffling his feet to clog the free passing lane, "and get in his fucking ass!"

Defense is the most important teaching of many coaches, especially at the high school level. Without stopping the opponent, there's little chance another trophy would be added to the case sitting in the middle of the school corridor—even if this squad was armed with arguably the best teenage hoopster across America in senior forward Michael Kidd-Gilchrist.

At the City of Palms tournament, a lockdown approach would be the precious formula necessary to stymie the other national powerhouses such as Winter Park High School, which boasted a high ranking thanks to Duke-bound point guard Austin Rivers.

The Celtics weren't guaranteed a date with Rivers and the suburban Florida school in the tournament, but that was the last thing on the players' minds. After all, they were slated to face Winter Park later in the season.

At this point, they figured whichever foe they drew would certainly be itching to knock them from their current high status in the *USA Today* poll.

Several weeks before the season opener, a game in which St. Patrick cruised past a far inferior Westfield team by a score of 60–28 on December 17, Mike held a banquet in honor of signing his national letter of intent with the University of Kentucky. That day, he learned that his 42-year-old uncle, Darrin Kidd, had passed away after suffering a sudden heart attack. It was yet another tragedy in the life of Mike, whose father died on August 11, 1996 from multiple gun-shot wounds.

While speaking with reporters with a heavy heart, the rising senior, who changed his last name after the 2010–11 season from Gilchrist to Kidd-Gilchrist in honor of his uncle, made it a point to emphasize one goal. It had nothing to do with being awarded the coveted National Player of the Year. He surely did not speak about winning any type of scoring title. He made his one wish loud and clear.

"I will not lose this year. I will not lose this year."

You would never guess, judging by his charismatic smile and genuine nature, that Mike was a budding superstar, likely destined to cash in on millions upon millions of dollars in the near future. It was no secret he'd be the next in line of several St. Patrick products to dominate headlines in college and then reach the NBA.

He was a gentle kid trapped inside a lean six-foot-seven frame, blessed with loads of rare talent that had been leaving hundreds of Division I college scouts drooling since he was a freshman. For the last year many persistently claimed he could be a high lottery pick in the

2012 NBA draft, as long as he continued to terrorize opponents during his senior year in high school and freshman campaign at Kentucky.

"I kind of see Mike as the Kevin Garnett of high school basketball," Boyle said in his soft conversational voice, a stark contrast from the raspy snarls he unleashes when scolding. "He's a terrific all-around player who can play multiple positions. He can score from anywhere on the floor, rebound, block, defend, play in the post. You name it. He's the best you'll see at filling up the stat sheet. He's the reason we've been so good, and he's so good because of how unselfish he is."

The truth is, Mike, who was aiming to collect his third All-American honors, had generated a media blitz unrivaled by any high school player aside from kids named LeBron James or Kobe Bryant. Even his mother, Cindy Richardson, created a part-time job for herself as her son's de facto manager, making sure Mike wasn't drowning in the hype and being negatively affected by the extraordinary and daily attention from countless media personnel.

"I've never seen someone as humble as Michael Gilchrist," Picaro said of his school's biggest celebrity. "It's almost like it's embarrassing for him when he gets awards or does something special. I told him, 'Michael, don't change. Stay the way you are.'"

He certainly was the most vital returning player from the previous year's squad, which opened the season atop the national rankings. As a senior, Mike had been learning how to adhere to the spotlight as a true leader. For the previous two years, acting as the team's ambassador was a heavy task handled by Kyrie Irving, who went on to take the college basketball universe by storm as a freshman at Duke in 2010 before suffering a toe injury that cost him all but 11 games.

Thanks to Kyrie, Mike was afforded the rare opportunity to perform at an All-American level as Robin, as opposed to Batman.

Mike, in fact, claimed he learned a lot on and off the court from his partner in crime. It was evident Mike was trying his damndest to mimic Kyrie's mature demeanor and follow his former teammate's footsteps. Such practices persisted even when the guard packed his bags for Tobacco Road after the 2009–10 school year. All it took was a click of the television remote for a reminder.

"I'd see him on TV all the time," Mike said. "I'd just keep saying, man, that's my best friend right there."

Making mental notes of Boyle's in-practice lessons was probably the most treasured characteristic Mike copied from Kyrie.

Following several intervals of motion offense sets, Boyle interrupted Jarrel Lane, a smart point guard headed to the University of Maryland-Baltimore County the following fall, as he was about to lob an entry pass to six-foot-ten freshman center Dakari Johnson.

"Austin, I need to see your hands," Boyle complained to Dakari's defender, Austin Colbert, a slender six-foot-nine forward ranked among the country's Top 10 sophomores. "Deny, deny, deny!"

Mike paused to listen and followed with a shot of encouragement toward Austin.

Boyle had his team attentive, but there was still work to be done. If the Celtics were destined to compete for a fourth Tournament of Champions crown in six years, nothing short of perfection would be tolerated from their larger-than-life leader. It turned out that so much more was on the line—more than Boyle, or the HBO documentary crew, for that matter, could've hoped for.

By following this team every day at practice and games for multiple months, and by drawing from many interviews of people who were involved or familiar with Boyle and his teams since his first year on the sidelines, I learned the true essence of "Celtic Pride" in a season that would shake the high school landscape. It's more than the Jordan brand uniforms and custom-made sneakers, more than the headlines in every morning's newspaper and sporadic spots on national television.

It's a way of life.

Everybody immersed in the hoops universe is well aware that over the course of two decades, Kevin Boyle and his St. Patrick Celtics rose to the top of high school basketball. This book, however, illustrates how they actually got there.

One

Kevin expected nothing but their best. He'd take them on five-mile runs and run with them. He'd always beat them back. Some of the kids later made it a contest to see if anyone could beat him. No one ever did.
—Joe Picaro

Sandy Pyonin was taking a 10-minute break from working out with three high school basketball players. One was about to enter his junior year at a well-known New Jersey institution and the other two, both standing well over six foot six, were in eighth grade.

"See that one? He's going to be better than Kevin Durant one day," Pyonin said while wiping his sweat-drenched forehead with a towel.

He was asked where the two eighth-graders were planning to attend high school.

"No idea," he replied, giving off subtle hints he was offended by the question. "I don't pay attention to that stuff. I'm just here to help players get to where they need to be."

Pyonin had developed a reputation as the world's most prominent basketball trainer. Helping hundreds of Division I athletes and 32 NBA players over three decades made up a sterling resume no gym rat could ever match. He was confident, damn near cocky, but had the track record to back it all up.

One of the mysterious figures in the background of the hoops universe, Pyonin graduated from Kean University in Union, New Jersey, in the 1960s. He was unsure of what his career would become, but he soon learned basketball would take him on a path toward success. He got his start when a coach named Bob Leonard, who was the head of St. Patrick High School in nearby Elizabeth at the time, asked Pyonin to help him train some kids. From there, his business blew up.

Now, the gymnasium inside the Young Men's and Young Women's Hebrew Association on Green Lane in Union is Pyonin's factory, the laboratory of a mad scientist with a colossal influence on high-stakes high school basketball.

Black and white pictures and newspaper clippings line the left wall leading up to Pyonin's gym. He pointed to one and asked, "See him right there?"

"That's Kevin Boyle in high school," said Pyonin, who coached the curly-haired guard with high socks when he was a teenager tearing up the local AAU leagues. "He loved the game as a player, and he loves it as a coach."

Sandy excused himself politely and extended his hand before parting. "I have to get back to these guys. I'll say this, though. Anybody that gets close to Bob Hurley has to be one outstanding coach."

♣

Neil Boyle pulled into the driveway of his home in Roselle, New Jersey, and saw his son dribbling a basketball and hoisting up shots. This was the usual routine for Neil, who would change out of his work clothes after another long day as a business manager of an electrical company and join Kevin outside.

Stitched together by the love of basketball, Neil and Kevin treasured their bond. Neil was the Catholic Youth Organization coach at St. Joseph grammar school in Roselle, and Kevin was a young kid trying to mimic the trademark spin-and-shoot move New York Knicks legend Earl Monroe had perfected.

It was clear Kevin needed to grow a lot more and tone his skills in order to ever reach the level his father had been on as a player. Neil was a talented guard, blessed with a six-foot-four frame, and was a member of the 1954 graduating class at hoops powerhouse St. Patrick High School.

He possessed enough flair to garner some interest from college coaches but opted to give up the game in order to find a job and provide for his family. Part of that decision turned into enjoying the evenings outside with Kevin when he wasn't coaching.

"I always wanted to play with him," Kevin recalled. "I went to every one of his practices. As a kid you always want to spend time with your father, and he loved basketball. As far as I could remember we both loved it. It didn't matter if it was raining, or hot or cold or whatever, we played.

"I wanted to get better at it because I knew someone was out there getting better. I always dreamed of playing in college and maybe being good enough to play in the pros."

Neil was a Christian man who was a model father, always looking for new and innovative ways to get involved with activities at church and coaching basketball. Even after securing a better job and moving his family from Roselle to Clark, he surrounded himself with people in the community and encouraged his children to do the same.

Along with his best friends, Mike Brown and Jerry Hobbie, Kevin Boyle spent every night practicing.

"KayBee played ten hours a day," recalled Brown, a former Union Catholic standout who was a rival of Boyle's in high school and went on to play two years at Texas A&M. "If Jerry and I drove past the park, and he wasn't on the court, we'd make fun of him. He just loved basketball.

"Jerry's parents split and he moved to Iselin, but we always played at the same gym in Plainfield. Jim Spanarkel, Kelly Tripucka, anybody from this county, they were all there, too."

Eventually, Neil watched his son grow up to be a six-foot-two point guard who hoped to execute that Monroe spin move throughout his high school basketball career.

Kevin Boyle suited up for four years and started for three on the varsity squad at Arthur L. Johnson High School in Clark, which took the area by surprise in putting more check marks in the win column than usual.

"Since 1960 Clark has probably had about ten winning basketball teams," he said. "We won the county championship and were ranked among the Top 10 in the paper during my senior year, so that was a great accomplishment. It was special to be a part of."

Boyle scored 1,415 career points in high school, with 700 of those coming from the free-throw line. He was named Second-Team All-State by the Newark *Star-Ledger* and earned a hoops scholarship at Seton Hall University once Bill Raftery discovered Boyle.

Boyle did not play for Raftery in 1981–82, however, because Raftery quit prior to the season. The sudden news forced the administration to hire longtime assistant Hoddy Mahan to take over the Pirates prior to Boyle's freshman season.

The Pirates responded well to Mahan by winning consistently, until three players ran into academic problems and later were declared ineligible. Seton Hall went from sporting an impressive 9–3 record and beaming with confidence upon defeating Hakeem Olajuwon and Clyde Drexler's Phi Slama Jama Houston team to finishing a pedestrian 11–16.

"We lost two starters and our sixth man, so that was detrimental to the team," Boyle recalled. "But, selfishly, it was good for me because I played about 18 or 19 minutes a game and contributed as a good ball handler."

Mahan was released after that campaign and a new coach, named P. J. Carlesimo, was brought in to bring the Pirates back on top of the Big East. Boyle called the next season a "tough transition period" for Carlesimo, who coached them to a porous 6–23 record. Boyle played 14 minutes per game that year and was dealt a heavy dose of reality when Carlesimo evaluated the state of his team by speaking individually with each of his returning players.

"P. J. was honest with me. He said he saw me as a backup at this level," Boyle said. "I wanted more than that. I wasn't the best athlete, and he wanted quickness at the point-guard position at that time."

Boyle decided it'd be best to transfer to a smaller school, where he'd be guaranteed more playing time and more exposure. Sometimes being a big fish in a small pond is more gratifying and beneficial than being a small fish in a big pond. St. Peter's College was the choice for Boyle, who presented the idea to Carlesimo.

"We both agreed it might be in my best interest to go to St. Peter's," Boyle said. "He understood."

In Boyle's junior season, the Peacocks went 17–12 under head coach Bob Duquette. "We were pretty good," Boyle said. "I started 52 of 68 games on that team in my two years there."

It turned out the decision was a great one. St. Peter's provided a nurturing environment that enabled Boyle to showcase his talents as a smart point guard who played the game the right way. Boyle broke the school's single-season assist record as a senior, but his mark was eclipsed by the brother of Jerry Walker—one of Bob Hurley's prized alumni at St. Anthony—years later.

"(Thanks to Patrick Ewing), Georgetown was at the height of their success at that time," Boyle said. "And I got to play a lot, so it was a great experience playing against the best basketball players around. There was always great competition. The guys I played against were outstanding: Ed Pinckney, Hakeem Olajuwon, Clyde Drexler. You're talking about playing against guys who are among the greatest in the history of the sport."

After Boyle graduated with a degree in business management he competed in the United States Basketball League, "a summer pro league, for lack of a better term," and earned some money playing for the Jersey Jammers and coach Nate Archibald.

"A lot of those guys played in that league hoping to get a shot at the NBA or in Europe," Boyle said. "At the time I wasn't thinking about coaching."

Coaching eventually became an avenue that was presented to Boyle one night at a restaurant with a man who had played for Neil. He asked if the then-unemployed Boyle would be interested in coaching at St. Joseph of Roselle, like his father had.

"Sure," Boyle said.

One of Boyle's young players was a small boy named Jimmy Picaro, whose father was a disciplinarian administrator at Boyle's father's alma mater: St. Patrick.

"When any of my sons played sports, I would go and watch all the time," said Jimmy's father, Joe. "Jimmy's fifth-grade team had a nun coaching them. I don't think they even had an out-of-bounds play. So I volunteered to coach the sixth grade and help out a guy named Bob Carne. Then somehow, someway, they got Kevin Boyle to coach the eighth grade.

"So I used to go to all the games when Jimmy was in eighth grade, and Kevin had never played my son. I told Jimmy, you're the best at sitting the bench, jokingly. He was a peanut, and he was a bit inattentive. At the time, he couldn't care less about basketball and the whole thing. So at the time, he probably didn't deserve to play a lot. But I saw Kevin Boyle in action coaching, and even though this was his first stab at coaching, he had the kids playing hard. I just saw how well coached they were."

Well coached, yes. Talented, not so much.

Boyle lost the first game he ever coached, 88–11, and realized leading the team was going to be a work in progress.

Over two years, Picaro saw the steady improvement and was a fan of the type of energy Boyle brought to the table. "I think he was just overall pleased by the progress of the kids," Boyle would say.

Meanwhile, St. Patrick High School was suffering from a prolonged lull in success on the basketball court. In 1936, St. Pat's had the "Wonder Team" that kicked off a stretch in which the program tasted plenty of achievement that spanned over the next 15 years before a dry spell in the '50s. In the 1960s, the Celtics won championships, and in 1971 they won the state crown, further validating St. Patrick being synonymous with high school basketball.

Stan Saniuk, a former 1,000-point scorer for St. Patrick and the key player on the 1961 state championship team, was serving as head coach in the mid- to late 1980s, but he wasn't getting rave reviews.

"There were a lot of people politicking (Athletic Director Red Migliore) to make a change. People wanted change," Picaro said. "I thought, 'I can't fire him.' I asked Red, 'Will you do it?' We were, and still are, friends. But we had just finished a season in which we won only four games, and Stan wasn't doing an effective job. I'm a loyal guy, but under those circumstances I knew I had to ask him to resign."

Picaro approached Saniuk after the miserable campaign and said, "I'll give you the option, but I think you should step down."

"He said, no, no, no," Picaro recalled.

When Saniuk was finally released as coach of the Celtics, Boyle received word.

"They had the opening, and I decided to give it a shot," Boyle said.

Migliore couldn't get rid of him, couldn't shake the feeling of being followed. Just one week into his new title as commander of the American Legion, a group for veterans who were enlisted during conflict or war, Red realized this apparent stalker wasn't going away until he received an answer.

One day Migliore stormed into Picaro's office to rant about "some nut" that wouldn't leave him alone.

"This guy knew (Migliore) was the athletic director here, and he found out we were about to make a coaching change. Red would put

- 14 -

him off. Yet, he kept telling him how he'd put us on the map and eventually win the county and state and everything. Red just kept telling me, 'this nut keeps following me, and it's Kevin Boyle.' That's the truth of the matter."

St. Patrick had once owned a rich tradition in high school basketball, but the 1987–88 Celtics had won just a handful of games, so Picaro wanted someone with a fiery attitude and a craving for steady improvement to take over.

Reluctantly, Picaro and Migliore gave the nut a chance. They hired Kevin Boyle.

Jimmy Picaro's two older brothers were well aware that their father was the disciplinarian at St. Patrick High School, so enrolling there was out of the realm of possibility.

"Being shy, they were going to Roselle Catholic to be with their friends," Joe recalls. "In eighth grade, Jimmy took his high school admissions test, and my wife asked him to put down Roselle Catholic and two other schools. My son said he's not putting down Roselle Catholic. He's going to St. Patrick.

"My immediate thought was, 'I don't have to pay tuition.' But seriously, I told him he's got to do everything right, and I can't let him get away with anything. Kids would then think I would be showing some favoritism. I also thought about if one of his friends got detention, there might be a situation where he'd either side with his friend or side with me. He said, 'They better not bad-mouth you.' He was four foot eleven, so it's not like he was going to hurt anybody."

Jimmy wasn't scheduled to be a starter on the freshman team, but three kids were academically ineligible, so he became a starter by default. "That's when he really started to get interested in basketball."

On the varsity level, Boyle and his group of misfits kicked off the season with four straight losses.

In Boyle's second game on the sidelines, his team was up by one point in the final minute and a St. Patrick fan ran up to the ref to hand him glasses upon making a bad call. A technical foul was called, so New Providence hit the awarded free throws and got possession to ice a slim victory over the Bad News Celtics.

"Walter Mattheu would've turned this job down at that point," Boyle joked.

"Then, in the fourth game, when we went to 0–4, I was wearing cufflinks with my suit," he remembered. "I was kind of pounding my hands together because I was nervous and anxious and mad. So I'm jabbing myself, and the next thing I know, I have blood dripping from my hands. I didn't even notice."

"Red and I said we should put a suicide watch on Kevin, jokingly," Picaro said with a laugh, looking back.

"When I got here, this team was losing to Solomon Schechter," Boyle cracked, referring to a small school with little to no basketball history. "They played in the lowest-rated league in New Jersey and were losing to small schools such as New Providence and Bound Brook."

The state of St. Patrick High School's basketball program was a disaster, but it didn't take long for Picaro to feel good about his new hire.

"He righted the ship in-season with kids who had bad attitudes. He couldn't believe the lack of commitment," Picaro said. "The point guard in Kevin's first year missed a game because he had a date. Kevin couldn't believe it. But he changed the culture a lot by his example. He pulled them along. I told him, 'Until you have enough kids to field one team, you've got to deal with nonsense.' So, he couldn't kick that kid off the team because we didn't have enough bodies. He wasn't able to say, 'Do it my way, or you're out.'"

Boyle was making the best of a messy situation, one that forced him to play several jayvee kids in varsity games because there were so few students interested in playing. Forget talent; he was begging for anyone to show up.

"Kevin worked so hard that he eventually had these kids working just as hard," Picaro said. "Kevin expected nothing but their best. He'd take them on five-mile runs and run with them. He'd always beat them back. Some of the kids later made it a contest to see if anyone could beat him. No one ever did. In practice, too, Kevin would be taking charges and diving for loose balls. He would always demonstrate. It was all of that hard work that enabled him to build this program."

After the 0–4 start, Boyle and his sandlot-esque Celtics finished 13–12 and then recorded 13, 15, 17 and 19 wins in the ensuing seasons.

The former collegiate point guard showed vast improvement, and he was making a name for himself as a coach.

"We were finally able to compete," Boyle recalled. "We won the Mountain Valley Conference. It was a big step."

Thanks to a six-foot-eight forward named Charles Lott and a guard named Chris Clemons, St. Patrick resembled nothing like the doormat it had been for the last three decades.

As a sophomore, Jimmy Picaro was on the jayvee squad but hardly played. Then as a junior he sat the bench on varsity and started on jayvee. By his senior year, he started some games on varsity after he grew to about five foot eight. In addition, Jimmy was an All-Conference goalie in soccer and second baseman in baseball.

"He came a long way in basketball, and it's because Kevin Boyle got him to play," Picaro would say. "If Kevin had a peach to eat, a beer to drink, and a stack of basketball tapes in front of him to watch, he was happy. He had four different coaches in college, so he was able to absorb a lot of different views and knowledge. He's just a basketball junkie with friends everywhere."

One of those friends overseas helped Kevin land a point guard named Jorge Ortega for one year of eligibility. Back then, foreigners could only play one year at a United States high school. The very next year Ortega was ineligible. Later, the rule was changed.

When Ortega said he wanted to go to the States and play ball, one friend of Kevin's suggested he attend St. Pat's to get an education under the tutelage of a former player with a knack for maximizing potential from his players. Ortega enrolled at St. Patrick, birthing the growing trend of kids expressing interest in wanting to play for Kevin Boyle.

"Say what you want about speculation about recruiting and all that, but think about it. Is Kevin Boyle handpicking kids from Spain? Of course not," Picaro bellowed. "He just benefited from having friends everywhere."

"If I'm 16 and I'm at a St. Pat's game, I see sneakers and stuff. We're sponsored by Jordan, we play against the best players and the best teams at the best events," Boyle would say. "If you're a kid who takes basketball seriously and you think you could play here, why wouldn't you? So, you really think we need to recruit? C'mon."

Ortega had a great shot, was a great penetrator, and was an overall solid player. The year after Jimmy graduated, in the 1992–93 season,

Kevin won his first county championship by defeating Elizabeth, which was in rebuilding mode upon losing future Seton Hall University and NBA center Luther Wright, another graduate of the so-called Sandy Pyonin School of Basketball.

"Back then the Union County championship was bigger than the state championship because of the local bragging rights," Picaro said. "So when Kevin won the county for the first time, it was a big deal. Looking back to when he first started, the Tournament of Champions, the national rankings, it all seemed so far out of reach."

Boyle promised to bring St. Patrick to the top of the New Jersey basketball scene upon his arrival. He was far from becoming a man of his word, but he knew the tracks had been laid.

He had changed the culture at the school and expected to raise the bar higher year after year. Eventually Boyle's goals would be met, but not without the help of an assistant coach whom he later would call one of his best friends.

Two

If I didn't come to play for Coach Boyle, I wouldn't be where I am now. He's one of the top high school basketball coaches in the country, and for me to play for him, it's an honor.
—Derrick Gordon

Winston Smith was stuck.
Quite frankly, the 14-year-old did not need yet another hardship to smear the first year of his high school career. He already had been struggling to keep up in class. Taking tests were more of a chore than they should be, and trying to keep up with the thick, small-print books every student was assigned to read simply was near impossible. He was getting by, though. Barely.
The most difficult part of the year was the realization that he would have to become acclimated with a new culture at a new school in a whole other demographic. Winston was ready to pack his belongings and move away from Summit, New Jersey, an affluent suburb located 20 miles outside Manhattan, to live with his mother in Irvington.
Fresh off the crack epidemic from the 1980s, Irvington was recognized as one of the most dangerous cities in the country. High crime rates, murder, gangs, and the lingering remnants of a time when a heavy drug influence reached its peak in Essex County were reasons to never cross through those town lines. However, it was a breath of fresh air to Winston, who finally was under a roof with his mother instead of his abusive, alcoholic father.
Since his permanent address was legally changed, Winston was no longer eligible to attend Summit High School. Right away, the family began to research several schools outside of Irvington that catered to

special-needs students. Winston had a learning disability that caused him to be two reading levels below his grade and required more time to take tests, so his new school would have to be receptive in a way others would not. St. Anthony, located in Jersey City, seemed to be a fantastic fit.

But after further investigating the curriculums and reputations of schools throughout the surrounding area, Winston's family discovered that St. Patrick High School offered the best program for students like Winston. So in the fall of 1993, Winston found a new home at the three-storied Catholic school in Elizabeth known for its rich history of religious education.

At the time, a man living in Livingston named Rae Miller had begun dating Winston's sister, Denise. At age 15, Rae had packed up his life and fled from his native Jamaica to finish high school and attend college in the United States.

Naturally, he fit in nicely. Rae made friends, did well in the classroom, and even competed in football and track. Playing wide receiver proved to be an enjoyable pastime, a pleasant surprise even to the scrawny teenager who had never picked up a football before.

"I was just okay," Rae would say years later with a sheepish laugh. "I just learned the game of football when I was 15. When I came to the U.S. I really didn't know what the whole thing was about."

Track, though, was a different story. Rae competed with the best of them in the Sunshine State and eventually earned a scholarship to run the 100-meter dash exclusively at Florida Memorial College. Track never translated into a career, but it still did wonders for a young man trying to fend off the obstacles of experiencing culture shock. It enabled him to fit in.

Just as Rae was about to graduate Florida Memorial in 1991, his parents joined him in the States but moved all the way up north to Union, New Jersey, a stone's throw from Elizabeth. Oddly enough, Rae was right behind them in packing his bags for the Garden State, certainly a less enthralling destination than the always-sunny place Rae called his home for over seven years.

"It was something I really didn't want to do," Rae said. "I wanted no part of it. I had no interest in being in a place that wasn't always warm."

Still, a job offer as an auditor for Kemper Insurance in Summit was too good to pass up at the time, so he gave in. To fill in his free time, Rae had the urge to work with kids. He always had this innate ability to connect with adolescents, perhaps because he was so educated on how to deal with major life issues such as moving, making new friends, or understanding what it's like to worry about fitting in. Moving from Jamaica to Florida will surely do that to anybody in that position. Rae eventually landed at St. Patrick and decided to help coach the basketball team just in time for the 1992–93 season.

A year into his time at the high school, conveniently located just several miles away from Livingston, he began dating Denise and took a liking to Winston. Rae enjoyed Winston's company so much that he found himself helping his future brother-in-law with homework and accompanying Winston during his first trips on a school bus. More than anything, Rae offered his undivided companionship. It was something Winston had been looking for.

"Winston needed a lot of assistance because he just couldn't make anything happen for himself," Rae said. "Winston and Denise came from a fractured home; they weren't able to be young kids. They weren't able to be in a normal family setting."

It was a situation that hit Rae like a ton of bricks. How could he not care for this family? Rae remembers a promise he made to his father right before hopping on that life-changing flight to Florida.

"I told him that I was going to help someone," Rae recalls. "I wanted to help someone because I thought about all the people that ever helped me. I wanted to give back."

It was a promise that also altered the history of high school basketball forever.

Rae loved the idea of volunteering his time for the good of the kids at St. Patrick. He just did not understand the activity he was supposed to be teaching. *What the hell is a box-out? You can't just pick up the ball and run with it? Why not?*

Things were going so well in Rae's life. He loved his job; his relationship with Denise was blossoming, and Winston was getting good grades and was flourishing on the basketball court. Still, he was wholly and utterly lost when it came to digesting the game of basketball.

"I didn't understand any of it, but I was always talking with the kids, and I was very good with the kids," he said. That was enough to stick around.

In 1993, Rae switched jobs and migrated to AIG, another profitable insurance corporation, which enabled him to make a steady income and even acquire a brand new, company-issued car.

One day Kevin Boyle's car broke down, and he was in desperate need of a means of transportation. Right away, Rae offered Boyle his new car. After that, one thing led to another and an unbreakable bond formed despite Rae's first impression of the Celtics' head coach.

"I thought to myself, 'This guy is crazy. This guy is going to blow a gasket,'" Rae said. "But I got engulfed in all of it. I loved his passion, and I loved working with the kids. I was so involved with Winston, too, and he was really coming along. It's amazing how I came to be involved with all of it."

Rae began serving as the liaison between coaches and parents, making sure all lines of communication were open. That role started unintentionally, as he spoke to college coaches and advisors on behalf of Winston by the time his senior year rolled around, and he committed to play ball at the University of Massachusetts in 1996. It was a hefty duty that Rae still embraced 18 years later, when the St. Patrick basketball team found itself on the verge of making history at the 2010 City of Palms Classic.

♣

When the plane touched the ground safely at Orlando International Airport on a mid-December day, people poured out of the gate ready to soak in the warm weather. Some travelers presumably hopped on a flight to the Sunshine State simply to escape the cold and get some distance from the office.

For the players of St. Patrick, however, this was far from a vacation. Boyle and his team were about to embark on high school basketball's biggest tournament, one that was broadcast on ESPNU for millions of eyes to see. This was a business trip.

It was the record-setting tenth time since 1992 the Celtics came to compete in the City of Palms Classic, a showcase that developed into a hurdle they had yet to overcome. Boyle's teams entered zero for nine when it came to capturing the championship trophy and had lost in the final game in 1994, 1996, 1997, 2002, and 2008. Runner-up prizes were never deemed an accomplishment. Not to Boyle, at least.

This time, the trend had to be reversed. If Boyle were to coach this team to a top ranking in the country that year, recording three wins in three games was a near necessity. In actuality, high school basketball is very similar to college football since one loss can cost a team the national title, and two or more losses will bump a team off the national spotlight.

Some players welcome that kind of stress, the kind that turns the stomach and causes pressure to crack the comfort levels of the mind. One of those players was Derrick Gordon.

Two years earlier, in the same tournament as a sophomore, Derrick had the game of his life by pouring in 27 points against John Wall—the No. 1 overall selection by the Washington Wizards in the 2009 NBA draft—and Word of God (North Carolina) in a 77–69 win at Bishop Verot High School. As a senior, he was ready for another chance to turn heads.

"It's probably the gym," Derrick chuckled. "I really like playing there for some reason. I don't want to say it's the crowd, but the crowd really gets me going. It feeds my confidence."

Derrick got off to a hot start in St. Patrick's first game of the 2010 tournament against Whitney Young, a basketball powerhouse based in Chicago. After Whitney Young scored the game's first six points, the Celtics rode a 17–4 run to build a comfortable lead by the conclusion of the opening quarter.

Whitney Young was playing its third game in as many nights, and St. Patrick took advantage of its opponent's exhaustion as the game wore on. Strong second- and third-quarter play put the game clearly out of reach by the fourth quarter.

Derrick was the star of the night, draining six three-pointers en route to scoring a career-high 37. With the final three minutes yet to unravel and the crowd buzzing over the offensive explosion by this little school from New Jersey, Derrick exited the court to a cascade of applause.

Mr. Florida had struck again.

As he clasped a towel and finished accepting high-fives from teammates at the end of the bench, Dick Vitale exclaimed on-air that Derrick Gordon would surely be a "diaper dandy" throughout his freshman year in college.

"To be honest, I wasn't expecting to score that many points," Derrick admitted. "My confidence just kept getting bigger with all the threes I hit. Coach always told me he wants me to have that confidence when I'm shooting."

It was his hot hand that enabled the Celtics to earn a convincing 91–68 win and a date with the winner of Mater Dei (California) and Christ School (North Carolina) in the semifinal round two nights later.

"It always comes back to hard work," Derrick said two weeks later when reminiscing about that night. "For (Vitale) to say that, for someone like him to call me a 'diaper dandy,' it's great. It's an honor. I just have to remain focused because then more good things are going to happen."

Derrick's lean frame mirrored his meek personality. He was a polite, well-mannered kid from Plainfield, New Jersey, who carried himself differently from many of his overly playful teammates, who never let an easy joke pass. Derrick's demeanor was always focused and driven.

He was liked by the rest of the guys, mostly because he commanded respect for how he handled his business. The scrawny 15-year-old who matched John Wall shot for shot and competed for a starting spot two years ago was now the seasoned veteran everybody looked up to.

Unlike many of his other high-profile classmates who engaged in a long, dragged-out recruiting process, Derrick committed to Western Kentucky before the start of his junior season. Many felt the choice was questionable with his two best years ahead of him, but he signed, nonetheless, simply because he felt comfortable with the coaches, who showed relentless interest and faith while courting him.

With a successful junior season in the rearview mirror and his senior year off to a rousing start, Derrick began to hear snickers from the public regarding his college choice.

"I still have people coming up to me saying I should pick a higher school and stuff," he said.

Watching a star athlete go through the recruiting frenzy seems enviable from an outsider's perspective. Who would not want countless college coaches begging for a chance to show off their campus, pay for a free education, and provide all the wonderful things college sports entail?

Truth be told, it often becomes a burden on the shoulders of 16- and 17-year-olds. It takes maturity and confidence to make what could be the most important decision of one's life in the midst of feeling in the middle of a tug-of-war match the high stakes of high school basketball often present. Still, Derrick never wavered.

"I know I made the right decision," he said. "I know I don't have to worry about a bunch of college coaches calling me now. So now, I can just focus on winning this national championship."

Just knowing he made the right decision to attend college was great, simply because his twin brother, Darryl, did not have that chance.

Darryl always loved basketball as much as his brother. As kids they would play until dark every night in the narrow driveway with hopes of one day playing together in high school or college. They were the best of friends, a bond that every young boy without a brother so desperately covets.

Darryl ended up playing on the junior varsity team as a freshman at Plainfield High School but did not have the potential or drive Derrick always seemed to possess. After all, Boyle often jokes about how he could've had Derrick arrested for stalking him during his freshman year, always pressing to know if he'd be able to practice with the varsity team or watch the upperclassmen practice.

Darryl's lack of height—he stood ten inches shorter than his six-foot-three brother—and eroding dream of tasting success at the next level made the alternative of hanging on the streets seem more attractive.

Getting caught up in the scene on the West End of town lured Darryl into a world of violence and drugs. He stopped going to school by sophomore year. It did not matter if Derrick tried coaxing his brother into returning to the safer pastures of the school hallways lined with lockers. Darryl made his choice.

One night in May of 2009, a fight broke out that led to Darryl pulling out a gun and firing several shots at a man. He was arrested and charged with attempted murder. The victim did not die from the gunshot wounds, but a big part of Derrick did the day his brother was sentenced to five years, one month, and six days in prison.

"It tears (Derrick) up," Sandra Gordon, their mother, would say.

Thinking of his brother sitting in a tiny, one-man cell inside the Albert C. Wagner Youth Correctional Facility in Bordentown, New Jersey—an hour away from Plainfield—consumed Derrick every moment of the day. It even prompted him to get a tattoo that read, *MBK*, short for "My Brother's Keeper." He also decided to change his number from 32 to 5 in college to honor the number Darryl used to wear on his red and white Plainfield jersey.

While the pain at home affected Derrick mentally, he tried to keep those dark thoughts away from the basketball court. Derrick started as a sophomore for a Tournament of Champions-winning team, averaged just over 12 points per game as a junior, and morphed into one of the most feared players in New Jersey as a senior. Don't ask him to explain it in detail. He just loved a challenge.

"It's one of the reasons why I came to St. Pat's," Derrick said. "I love the spotlight. Playing all these big games, you're forced to take it to another level. I want to show reporters and all the people that I belong. I want to prove I'm one of the best in my class."

Mater Dei, known for producing Heisman Trophy winners John Huarte and Matt Leinart among other football stars, registered an upset victory over Christ School in the other quarterfinal. It turn, the Monarchs would get their chance to upend the team that quickly became the talk of the town.

Derrick's self-assurance caused him to look one step ahead, knowing that if St. Patrick won the semifinal it could mean a meeting with Winter Park in the championship. After all, the opportunity to shut down Duke-bound point guard Austin Rivers, the son of Boston Celtics coach Doc Rivers, on defense would mean a whole lot more than any 30-point outing on offense.

"For me to match up against Austin Rivers, it's big," Derrick said. "He's considered to be one of the top players in our class."

The following night's result meant Derrick would not get his wish, though, since Milton (Georgia) pulled off a 63–62 upset of the local Florida team. Nevertheless, his first task was to help orchestrate a strong defensive showing against Mater Dei's top guns, Xavier Johnson and Shaqquan Aaron.

Mater Dei kept pace with the Celtics in the early going but blinked in the second quarter as Michael Kidd-Gilchrist broke out and created a slight separation on the scoreboard. Coming off a pedestrian 13-point, eight-rebound performance against Whitney Young in the quarterfinal, Mike helped his less energetic team to a 32–22 lead at the half.

"We got tired, to be honest. We played in a real hot gym, and we needed a couple of timeouts, and coach didn't give it to us," Derrick told the *New York Post*.

The Monarchs, supported by superb showings from Johnson and Aaron, tied the game, 33–33, midway through the third, but Mike and Derrick flipped the switch. The two worked together to puncture Milton's resistance and assembled a scintillating 28–8 run that spilled into the fourth.

Mike finished with a game-high 34 points and 13 rebounds, while Derrick added to his success down South by scoring 17 on seven of 12 shooting as St. Patrick held on for a 71–61 win. Boyle was going back to the final.

"We feed off each other," Derrick said of his chemistry with his star sidekick. "We used to always talk about playing together at the same college. That's how much we enjoy playing with each other. Man, we just get each other going."

Mike and Derrick, as it turned out, knew they would eventually play college ball just over 150 miles apart. But for now, the dynamic duo needed just one more evening of magic on the court together for St. Patrick to end nearly two decades of disappointment at the City of Palms Classic.

Recent history suggested the Celtics were in a good spot, since two of the previous three tournament winners hailed from New Jersey. St. Benedict's Prep took the trophy in 2007, and Paterson Catholic, which closed its doors at the conclusion of the 2009–10 school year due to a mountain of financial issues, won in 2009.

Boyle had as good a chance as ever to add his program to the list. His star small forward was looking like a true All-American, his other senior leader was playing the best basketball of his young career, and even freshman center Dakari Johnson was making strong contributions down low.

Oddly enough, one of the biggest question marks entering the season was about another senior: point guard Jarrel Lane. He had never started a game before in high school, and was all of five foot ten and 155 pounds soaking wet. Jarrel was caught behind Kyrie Irving in the depth chart for his entire varsity tenure, causing many to wonder how he would react to in-game situations—especially the highly magnified ones in which St. Patrick so often found itself.

The Rahway native could have opted to transfer to another high school in the area, but he made the wise decision to stay on the St. Patrick bench for games and play his heart out in practice while guarding Kyrie one-on-one.

"Being at St. Pat's has helped me become the best player I can be," Jarrel said, "and there's no way I'd have this kind of experience somewhere else. I learned how to be patient and poised. Even guarding Kyrie in practice had me thinking that since I was used to playing against him, everything else this year should come easy."

It was a sterling education that paid dividends as Boyle turned a desperate gaze toward Jarrel when practice started in the fall.

"It's been fun. Kevin Boyle is a great coach, but everybody knows that," Jarrel said. "That's why I've learned so much and become a better player in my four years here."

His raw talent, high basketball IQ and ability to protect the ball on offense earned him a hoops scholarship to University of Maryland-Baltimore County. Despite other offers from Towson and Iona, he committed to the school in August, right before classes at St. Patrick resumed. From that point, he turned his attention to being the best facilitator he could be.

"I wasn't nervous about the team," Jarrel said. "Everyone was motivated. Everyone had the same mind-set."

Naturally, that mind-set was created by Boyle: win or else.

Sure enough, just three games into the young season, the Celtics replayed that motto in their heads before taking the court in the City of Palms championship game.

Milton, a big Georgia high school in northeast Fulton County that exceeded 2,600 students, was still excited—and shocked, perhaps—that it had taken down Rivers and Winter Park in the semifinal. Milton was new to the national basketball scene, clinching its first-ever state championship in 2009–10. Taking down the top player in the country was big. Knocking off the second-best player in the country and his nationally ranked team would be even bigger.

Shannon Scott, a highly regarded point guard committed to Ohio State, was Milton's best player and naturally became the focal point of Boyle's complex plan to earn this coveted victory. But unlike the other squads St. Patrick bounced in the tournament, Milton was equipped with several scoring options to complement its most dangerous threat in power forward Julian Royal and shooting guard Dai-Jon Parker.

A Georgia Tech signee, Royal stood six foot eight, but carried just 200 pounds with him. His frame was comparable to the Celtics' wiry power forward, Austin Colbert, but his scoring ability was much more developed. Royal's 20-point outing against Winter Park certainly proved that. Meanwhile, Parker made a name for himself as a defensive whiz bound for Vanderbilt—and bound to give Mike and Derrick fits.

Milton traded punches with St. Patrick in the opening four minutes, during which the referees called nine combined fouls. Jarrel was sent to the bench with two fouls and Boyle inserted Dakari to gain a size advantage over the opposition. The Bronx native quickly made an impact by grabbing several rebounds and tipping in a missed shot that allowed the Celtics to enter the second quarter tied, 15–15.

Both teams played inspired defense in the second, but Mike broke through in the final three minutes and anchored a miniature 8–3 run that gave his team a slim 33–28 lead at the half. Boyle's halftime speech seemingly sparked St. Patrick to open the game up in the early stages of the third quarter.

Dakari scored his seventh and eighth points of the game with a layup, which put St. Patrick up, 39–30, and the advantage eventually ballooned to 45–32 with four minutes to go. It appeared Milton was in big trouble, and the Celtics were about to run away with the City of Palms Classic. They were a team that fed off transition offense, usually signifying quick spurts of baskets and usually burying the other team for good.

Only, this run did not put Milton to bed.

Several defensive lapses by the Celtics and timely shots from Scott and Royal got the Eagles back within striking distance. Just like that, the cushion was gone, and Milton trailed by just three entering the fourth.

Getting caught in a grudge match was uncharted territory for Boyle's current team. St. Patrick won comfortably by 32, 24 and 10 points in its previous three games, so the entire country was about to witness how the boys in white and green would react in meaningful crunch-time minutes.

Tied at 55 with 5:30 remaining in the contest, Milton continued to penetrate the front-line defense and get to the free-throw line. The seconds continued to melt off the Nevins Gymnasium scoreboard. Royal handed the Eagles their first lead in three quarters, 59–58, by drilling a pair of free throws with 4:01 left. Boyle was growing louder, as he was heard screaming encouragement over the television microphones on press row.

"The colorful Kevin Boyle," one announcer quipped as the other chuckled.

This was no time to sit and calmly watch his team's fate unstitch on this late December night. A major jump in the *USA Today* rankings was at stake. Hell, the group's national championship prospects were on the line.

The eighth lead change of the final four minutes came when Scott hit two shots from the charity stripe and Milton went ahead, 67–66 with 10 seconds left. St. Patrick had drawn up a play that seemed rather simple, even to a basketball novice: keep the ball in the best player's hands. In other words, the Celtics opted to live or die with Michael Kidd-Gilchrist in the driver's seat.

Milton chose to foul with 5.3 seconds left because St. Patrick was not yet in the bonus. The Celtics had enough time to toss in a pass, throw up a shot and possibly get one last-ditch tip-in if the initial attempt went awry.

Jarrel, who had not taken a shot in his limited time due to foul trouble, stepped outside the line near half-court and accepted the ball from the referee. He smacked it once and threw it in to Chris Martin.

Four seconds.

Two Milton defenders collapsed and, for the first time all quarter, the Eagles swayed from the 1–3–1 zone formation that shut down St. Patrick. Mike was not open.

Three seconds.

Jarrel took three steps just outside the arc and watched with horror. His team might not even get a shot off.

Two seconds.

Chris handed the ball back to Jarrel, who extended his left arm and let it fly. Boyle tracked the entire trajectory until the crowd exploded.

Swoosh.

St. Patrick's players celebrated their improbable 69–67 triumph in the City of Palms Classic championship game by mobbing Jarrel and tackling him into the front row of seats along the right baseline.

"It was kind of a broken play because initially it was supposed to go to Mike," Jarrel said. "Even though it was a broken play, Coach Boyle told us to be mindful of looking for the guy who makes the inbound pass because teams forget about that guy a lot."

Jarrel emerged from the pile and stood on the court in front of dozens of joyous fans. He threw his hands in the air and let out a bellowing scream. He emptied the tank of emotions.

"It was just one of those shots," he said two weeks later. "I knew it when I let it go."

Jarrel's last-second highlight was the first buzzer-beater to clinch a championship win at the City of Palms Classic since 1989, when Flint Hill (Oakton, Virginia) edged Lincoln (Brooklyn, New York).

"I was excited, not just for the shot, but for the team," Jarrel said. "St. Pat's has been in this tournament so many times without a championship, and it was great to pull out a tough game like that."

Mike, who finished with 25 points and 12 rebounds against Milton, was awarded the tournament's Most Valuable Player and, along with Derrick, was named to the All-Tournament team.

"Mike is such a great player. He's so versatile," Jarrel said. "It makes it a lot easier to find teammates on offense when the defense is keying on Mike the whole time."

Who knew? The most feared scorer in New Jersey, and maybe the entire United States, could not get open. In turn, it allowed Jarrel, an unheralded backup for three years as a high school player, to capture the moment, to hit the biggest shot of his young life.

"I don't know what the future will bring," he said, "but I probably have to put that one on top of the list."

After witnessing that miracle shot fall through the white twine, the consensus was there was something special about this team.

Three

*Coach Boyle just has this special ability to
motivate guys to play hard for him.*
—Shaheen Holloway

Kevin Boyle and the Celtics returned to New Jersey with an unblemished 4–0 record and a heightened level of confidence. They recorded wins over three nationally ranked teams and, most important, found a way to captivate millions of ESPNU viewers by edging a Top-10 squad in storybook fashion. Even Boyle was pleased with the trip.

An improbable championship win at the City of Palms would be negated, however, if Boyle's crew couldn't tame the rest of the competition back in their home state. The first assignment was facing the defending Tournament of Champions winner.

Trenton Catholic became the first Mercer County team to not only reach the Tournament of Champions title game, but to win it, too. Led by Delaware-bound junior Khalid Lewis and a strong supporting cast, the Iron Mikes won 22 of their final 23 games en route to their first time finishing as kings of the Garden State in 2010.

Before handling Camden Catholic, 53–39, to punctuate a dream season, they squeezed past St. Anthony in a triple-overtime affair in the Non-Public B championship. Very few, if any, predicted this likable and overlooked team to get the best of Hall of Fame coach Bob Hurley in a chess match that ended 57–56 in favor of Trenton Catholic. After all, it seemed every year that game was the dinner table reserved for St. Patrick, St. Anthony, or Paterson Catholic.

Not this time. St. Patrick was banned from the state playoffs,

Paterson Catholic—in the program's final game—ran out of gas, and Hurley was left stunned.

On March 23, the final night of the high school basketball campaign, jubilant players danced around the court once the buzzer sounded at the IZOD Center, but one player couldn't help fighting back tears of happiness. Maybe it was relief. Either way, Frantz Massanet deserved the moment.

The Iron Mikes senior shooting guard was directly affected by the tragic earthquake that struck Haiti on January 12. His two parents were born in the ravaged country and still had family members living or visiting there at the time of the disaster.

"At first when it happened, I was in a rush to get ready for school. I didn't see anything," Massanet said that night outside the New Jersey Nets locker room. "Then in school people were asking me if I was okay. I had no clue why people kept saying that, but then a teacher pulled me in a room and told me what happened."

He soon learned that two of his aunts had passed away and several of his other family members were affected by the earthquake that registered a 7.0 on the moment magnitude scale, which is used by seismologists to measure the size of the quake in terms of energy released.

The Haitian government reported between 217,000 and 230,000 victims that had been identified as dead; 300,000 were injured, and one million were homeless, according to news reports.

"It's a plus, kind of, because people were worrying about where their family members were, and a lot of mine were able to get in touch with me on Facebook," Massanet said. "That helped me begin to get in the right state of mind again."

It was a wonderful moment for Massanet and the Trenton Catholic community, one they will never forget. In turn, the Iron Mikes' win was the conclusion of a season Boyle could not wait to toss away into the cobwebs of his memory.

Everybody figured St. Patrick's game against Trenton Catholic this year was a forum of revenge, in a twisted way. Not to Boyle. This was just the fifth game of a new season, a brand new opportunity for his thriving team to get better.

The Celtics surrendered the first two buckets of the contest but then turned it up a notch. They got off to a hot start in front of a packed crowd at Rider University and never looked back.

Michael Kidd-Gilchrist and company's suffocating interior defense forced the opposition to shoot five for 24 in the first two quarters, enabling St. Patrick to enter the locker room at halftime with a 40–17 lead. Boyle had spent hours during practice pleading with the boys to play relentlessly on defense. It was working.

Barely hanging on thanks to an eight to two run to open the third quarter, the Iron Mikes closed within 17. But another spurt from the Celtics put the game out of reach by the fourth. Four players reached double figures in the 72–57 romp, including Mike, who finished with a game-high 17 points to go along with eight rebounds and four assists.

A booming statement was made, but the coaching staff still felt the output was far from sterling. Several nights later, after practice at Public School 28, Rae Miller, one of Boyle's most trusted advisors and an assistant coach who had the ins and outs of basketball down to a science after the last 18 years studying under Boyle, approached Jarrel Lane in the hallway.

"I need your fucking (starting) team to stop losing games in practice (against the second unit)," Rae urged while digging his index finger into the point guard's chest. "That's how you lose on the court in a real game. I'm sticking that on you. It's your job now."

Funny how a single clutch three-pointer can attract more responsibility. Jarrel was not a superstar, nor did he force statisticians to use much ink in the scorebook. But that night, the St. Patrick Celtics became his team.

For Jarrel, to think a former player named Shaheen Holloway carried the same weight on his shoulders nearly two decades ago made the daunting task even more surreal.

♣

Bounce, bounce, clank. Chris Clemons, about to finish up his junior season at St. Patrick in the spring of 1992, watched his little cousin retrieve a missed shot.

Bounce, bounce, swish. The basketball instantly jumped off the concrete and into the hands of Shaheen Holloway, who released a high, arching attempt that kissed a chain net on its way down to the concrete again. It became the summer soundtrack of the two relatives in a park located in Orange, New Jersey—a completely different setting than Shaheen's five-bedroom home in South Jamaica, Queens.

Holloway had just spent his eighth-grade season embarrassing his peers on the court, which was no little feat considering he was several notches below six feet tall. He was going to be a pure point guard, wherever he went to school. The question was, would it be Bishop Loughlin or Forrest Hills?

Clemons, meanwhile, developed a whacky idea that seemed simpler in his mind than it truly was. *What if Shaheen didn't go to high school in New York, and he played ball with me during my senior year? Wouldn't it be great if I were able to play with my little cousin on the same team?*

He threw it out there, a long shot that would likely miss. Bounce, bounce, clank.

"At least come see it," Clemons begged.

"I was nervous," Holloway recalled. "I never did the whole shirt-and-tie thing, and I never went to Catholic school before. But I had my family, and I had my friends."

The supposed future prize of Bishop Loughlin or Forrest Hills reluctantly visited St. Patrick High School in Elizabeth, a place in close proximity to his aunt, who resided in Hillside.

"There were a lot of drug problems (in Queens)," prominent trainer Sandy Pyonin said. "He had to come to New Jersey, or else he'd never make it. They weren't his problems, but he wanted to be special and clean-cut. The first time I saw him play was in a summer league game in September of his freshman year. He had 37."

Holloway's aunt already was pulled on the side of Clemons, saying she'd be more than happy to have her little Shaheen live with her while he attended school in the Garden State.

Before ironing out the details, Holloway first wanted to see the school and watch the basketball team practice.

"At the time they had Clemons and (Charles) Lott, but didn't have any good guards," Holloway said. "When I saw the school and saw their team on my visit, I noticed it. I said, 'That could be me.'"

A vision was born. In actuality, Holloway quickly learned another vision was well on its way toward becoming a reality when he shook hands with Kevin Boyle. "(Boyle) seemed like a cool guy, and he sounded like a good person," Shaheen said. "You could tell right away, though, that he had a passion for the game. You could tell he had this vision of what he wanted the program to be."

Holloway agreed to become a Celtic. His older cousin's idea actually panned out, a shot-in-the-dark suggestion that would do more for Boyle's program than the young coach could've ever dreamed.

"It was a combination of things," Holloway said of choosing St. Patrick. "I wanted to play for coach Boyle and coach (Chris) Chavannes, and another thing is that I needed a fresh start. I needed to get out of the city."

On his side, he had his cousin, his aunt, and a couple new friends. He also had Boyle, who, according to Holloway, made him "feel at home more than anybody."

"He helped me get on this journey I'm still on right now."

Holloway's freshman season, the 1992–93 academic year, saw the Celtics kick off a run of Union County dominance that reached all the way to the 2010–11 season. Backed by a strong senior core consisting of Lott and Clemons, as well as the team's freshman point guard, they won the conference and county titles. "This was back when winning (the county) was bigger than winning the state championship," Holloway would say. "At least for us, it was."

They drew from tough experiences such as playing in the City of Palms Classic in Florida, a nationally known tournament in which they lost two of three games. "Yeah, we lost, but the experience was unbelievable," Holloway remembered. "The talent there was so good."

It was on to the state playoffs. This was unfamiliar territory for Boyle, armed with a dream and a wizard of a point guard. Holloway and Boyle's first run together eventually ended with a state-playoff loss to then-powerhouse Marist. The rivalry between St. Anthony and Marist didn't come too close to mirroring that of St. Anthony and St. Patrick in 2011 because "both teams were from Hudson County, so it didn't get quite the publicity," according to Boyle.

Nevertheless, Holloway's output garnered plenty of press, as the freshman sensation netted a season-high 35 points. It opened eyes everywhere.

So, who the hell was Shaheen Holloway, and who the hell was Kevin Boyle, these two no-names taking the high school basketball landscape throughout New Jersey by storm?

After the loss to Marist, Holloway said, "from there, that's when the real journey began." Not just on the court, either. Shaheen was a small but talented basketball player with loads of potential. In school, on the other hand, he was simply a menace.

"He came in here as a foulmouthed, undereducated kid," St. Patrick's animated, story-telling extraordinaire principal Joe Picaro said. "I was always on his back about behaving. He had such poor habits. But by the end of the year we had him doing things properly. He then went back to Queens for the summer, and he'd come back with all those habits again. Round two."

Still, Picaro's bane was Boyle's right-hand man on the court. Picaro dreaded Shaheen's so-called round two; Boyle couldn't wait to see Shaheen's round two unravel.

"We really got breaks with kids like Shaheen," Boyle said. "He moved out of the city and elevated his play to beat anybody."

Shaheen played on teams during his sophomore, junior, and senior years that competed against a national schedule.

St. Patrick was ranked No. 18 in New Jersey, while one opponent, Simon Gratz of Philadelphia, was No. 1 in the nation thanks to a North Carolina-bound forward named Rasheed Wallace.

"The place was mobbed," Boyle said. "It's like we were finally on the scene, on the map. Shaheen had a real good game. Late in the game one of our kids broke a 2–3 zone and threw down a tomahawk dunk. After that a Gratz player took the ball and punted it. We were up 44–42 with six minutes to go, and they ended up going on a big run, and we lost by ten."

Still, it was a new, valuable lesson for the growing program, which had played five of the best 15 teams in the country that season. "We were starting to get established, and we were trying to get respect," Boyle said. "We were playing everybody."

It was clear Boyle and his point guard were changing the culture, bringing St. Patrick back to its glory days from the 1930s, '40s and '60s.

"I don't want to take credit for any of it. Coach Boyle did this," Holloway said. "This was his program, and Chris Chavannes, too. It was a tremendous run we had. In a way, I think coach Boyle tried to emulate Bob Hurley, and once he reached the level, I was so happy. Coach Boyle is the only coach who would drop whatever he's doing to go and play with you or shoot around with you. It's one of the many reasons why I appreciate him."

As a sophomore, Holloway and the Celtics won the Union County championship by defeating state juggernaut Elizabeth for the second straight year. "I didn't know the history behind Elizabeth (High School), really. But when we were getting onto the bus to go back, it was crazy. People were fighting. People were threatening us. It was crazy."

The Celtics then faced Hurley's St. Anthony team, still the class of the state, at the Jersey City Armory in the state playoffs. The Friars hadn't lost there in decades—that is, until Holloway and Boyle pulled another rabbit from their hats and sent Hurley packing for the spring and summer. "Who knew," Holloway reflected, "this little school in Elizabeth became what it was becoming just because of a coach who was so fiery compared to anybody else."

It didn't matter that St. Patrick later fell to Paterson Catholic in the North Non-Public B finals, thanks to a game-winning shot at the buzzer by Tim Thomas, who would eventually go on to enjoy an extended NBA career. The Celtics were onto something. The competition level had been altered, winning was expected, and the school had a brand-new All-American in Shaheen Holloway.

That wasn't the only new title the 15-year-old Holloway was given that year as a sophomore in high school. In fact, it only made his success even more impressive, considering "dad" was the other.

Holloway's daughter, Shatanik, was born on September 22 of his sophomore year. As Shaheen realized he had to mature and be there for his daughter, while juggling basketball and school, he surrounded himself with the right people.

"The whole St. Pat's family really helped him," Boyle said. "He was close with Dorothy Picaro, and they talked every day. He also had a great relationship with Chris Chavannes, and was able to get the right amounts of discipline and attention here."

Dorothy Picaro was the school secretary, the popular faculty member whom everybody adored. "Shaheen called her mom," Joe Picaro recalled of his wife and Holloway's tight-knit bond. "When the team went to Vegas (for a tournament), I got a shirt for the whole team to sign for the house, and Shaheen wrote, "To Mom." My wife was very professional about her job, though. One time Shaheen came up to her and hugged her, and she said he couldn't touch her. But she loved him so much."

Holloway spent many of his lunches speaking with Dorothy, asking for advice or just shooting the breeze.

"She was the best," he said. "She was truly one of the best people I've ever met in my life. She was very sweet to me. She helped me with a lot of things—just life. And I used to get in trouble a lot, so I was in the principal's office all the time. She was just truly a wonderful, wonderful human being. There was just a lot of support from her. Mrs. Picaro helped me out with talking to me. I had to grow up very quickly and a lot quicker than the average 15- or 16-year-old has to."

Boyle, with two little kids of his own at the time, offered his help, too. "He's a great person, and he's the type who would give you the shirt off his back," Holloway said. "My sister was shot while living in Brooklyn, and Coach Boyle came to my house to be with me and lend a helping hand. No one else did that."

The two also developed a unique understanding, a code they both honored. "The way to react to him was taking him aside and say, 'You're disrespecting me by not going hard. And the second time, I'll call you out in front of everyone.' He understood that and respected it. He liked that I called him out alone," Boyle said.

Despite the stress that weighed on him, Holloway turned into a role model for the students at St. Patrick. Joe Picaro couldn't believe his eyes.

"He didn't go back (to Queens) the next summer, and he blossomed educationally and as a person," Picaro remembered. "One time at school the next year, some freshmen were fooling around in the hallway, and he turned to them and said, 'Hey, we don't do that stuff around here.' Then on the court, Shaheen would be diving for loose balls, taking charges, and hustling all the time. Meanwhile, this kid was an All-American. He didn't have to do all that stuff.

"But Kevin wouldn't allow it to be any other way. I would observe practice time to time and if I thought the kids were disgruntled or weren't having any fun, I would've said how we need to change this. But all I saw was a team dedicated to winning. They had a mature approach."

Another example of Holloway growing as a young man, one of Picaro's favorite Holloway tales, involved Shaheen approaching his principal after school toward the end of the year and expressing how upset he was that "he didn't make it."

"I thought it was some basketball award or something," a puzzled Picaro said.

"No," Holloway painfully retorted, "Mr. Picaro, I'm so upset because I didn't make honor roll."

Holloway was so used to success on the hardwood that he felt it was the perfect challenge to step up his game in the classroom, too. It was the type of progress Joe and Dorothy Picaro had hoped for their teacher's pet. When it came to basketball, the two always marveled at Holloway's abilities, knowing he was generating recognition for the school.

"What changed this program around was Shaheen Holloway," Joe Picaro said. "He worked so hard, and he was a superstar. So then, we had Kevin Boyle and Shaheen Holloway. They were two peas in a pod when it came to determination and hard work. After that, it was nothing but hard work around here. College coaches would always say that Kevin's practices were harder than their own."

In Holloway's junior year, St. Patrick's season ended with a loss to St. Anthony in the state playoffs. Named an All-American for the second time in row, though, Holloway was establishing himself as one of the best guards to ever play in New Jersey. The college letters poured in and so did the chronic praise for the Garden State's best player, who was a transplant from Queens trying to become the first person in his family to go to college.

"In his world, he could've succumbed to surrounding himself with the wrong people or chose a path that wouldn't be good for him," Boyle said. "But he became a player who could be one of seven to ten guys to be considered the best guard over New Jersey's history over four years. Maybe Dajuan Wagner (Camden) had one year better or Kyrie (Irving) had two years of being better, but (Shaheen) was a second-team All-American as a sophomore, a three-time Parade All-American, and he didn't have the supporting cast we've had in recent years."

"The first time I saw him, he pulled off this spin move on (Lincoln High School's Stephon) Marbury, and the place went nuts. That was his signature move," high school sports broadcaster Mike Quick recalled.

"If Kevin is the CEO, then Shaheen is the junior CEO because he brought visibility to that program."

The contest Quick referred to was a game in which Lincoln, the Coney Island juggernaut which produced Marbury, Marbury's half brother Jamel Thomas, Marbury's cousin Sebastian Telfair, and Lance Stephenson, led by four at the half. Holloway spearheaded a ferocious comeback after being down by as many as 15, only to lose, 79–70.

Marbury poured in 30 points and played a wonderful point guard, dishing out several flashy entry passes to Thomas, who led the Big East in scoring while at Providence before being shut out on NBA draft night in 1999—a gut-wrenching tale told in Ian O'Connor's account of Telfair's high-school life entitled *The Jump*.

Despite that loss, the Celtics were on the national radar. They were not only playing with the best in the state, but the best in the country. It was due, in large part, to Holloway's rising stardom.

"He was just electrifying," Boyle said.

One game late in Shaheen's time at St. Patrick, the Celtics were facing Providence High School from Charlotte, North Carolina—a strong program riding the talents of future NBAer Antawn Jamison. In that contest, Holloway recorded 13 steals.

"They had this cocky guard who was constantly talking, and you literally saw Shaheen just deflate him," Boyle said. "It was like watching Shaheen stick a pin in him. It was the most incredible 12 seconds of basketball I've ever seen."

Holloway stripped the ball from the overzealous opponent, made a layup while getting fouled and then converted the ensuing free throw. The same sequence of events occurred on the next inbounds attempt. Then Holloway picked a steal for a third time and hit a layup. The poor defender just refrained from making contact that time.

Eight points in what Boyle said "might have actually been ten seconds; maybe less."

That remarkable spurt proved to be a microcosm of Holloway's time at St. Patrick. One moment, the Celtics were beginning to awake from a three-decade slumber; the next, they were among the best high school programs in the nation. All it took was one break, one player to execute what Boyle had preached.

"Growing up in Queens with my brother and my sister, I wanted that type of pressure. I was always so used to playing with older guys and better competition. St. Patrick just did a great job of helping me stay humble. It was great because I had my family in New York and my family in New Jersey. And I became the first one in my family to go to college."

Holloway accepted a scholarship offer to play at Seton Hall University, a stone's throw away from that court where Chris Clemons begged his little cousin to attend high school with him. After his senior year, during which he averaged 22.5 points, nine assists, and five steals per game, Holloway signed a national letter of intent to play for the Pirates and coach George Blaney.

"I think one of the biggest reasons why I chose Seton Hall over all the other colleges was because it was local, so I'd be around everyone in my support system. I was different from a lot of kids, who always wanted to go to the big school with the big name," Holloway admitted. "I wanted a smaller place so I could pace myself. Coach Boyle wanted to turn things around at St. Pat's, and he did it. I wanted to do the same thing at Seton Hall."

Seton Hall's basketball team had reached the peak of college basketball in 1989, when it lost to Michigan, 80–79, in overtime of the NCAA Tournament championship game. By 1996, the Pirates had atrophied to being an average Big East program that always took a backseat to the likes of Ray Allen's UConn Huskies and Kerry Kittles's Villanova Wildcats.

That changed by the time Holloway was a senior in 2000, when Seton Hall took March Madness by surprise and reached the Sweet 16. That year he was named the Big East Most Improved Player.

"He had an outstanding career at Seton Hall, and midseason through his freshman year he was in contention for Player of the Year," Boyle said. "Tommy Amaker came in his sophomore year (to take over for Blaney), and he had a different style. It took Shaheen time to adjust, but again, he ended up having a great college career. He's five foot eight at best and came a long way to be the player he was."

Over his four-year stay at Seton Hall, Holloway became the Pirates' all-time assist leader with 681, scored 1,588 points, recorded 231 steals and hit 185 three-pointers in 116 games. He earned All-League status three times and All-Metropolitan accolades in each of his four seasons.

After college, Holloway played professionally in England for the

Chester Jets and London Towers as well as a season in Ulm, Germany, and Istanbul, Turkey. Back in the States, he played for the Brooklyn Kings of the USBL and teams from Newark, Las Vegas, and Chicago of the ABA. He was invited to three preseason NBA camps with the New York Knicks, New Jersey Nets, and Golden State Warriors, but he stopped pursuing his professional playing career to become a coach and obtain full custody of his then-eleven-year-old daughter, Shatanik, in 2005.

Holloway used a stint as an assistant at Bloomfield Tech and a three-year tenure serving in the same role at Iona to join Kevin Williard—the former Iona head coach—as an assistant at his alma mater, Seton Hall, in March 2010.

"It means everything. It was always one of my dreams to be a coach," Holloway said. "Helping out with the kids, it's a challenge, but it was a challenge for me to move to New Jersey and play for coach Boyle, so I'm a guy who loves a good challenge. That's why coach Boyle and I got along so well. That's why he doesn't care about having the best record. He just wants to beat the best competition. That's why all those kids come back to his camps every year."

Boyle is reminded of his first superstar player whenever he looks up at the green banner that reads "Holloway 10" on the wall of St. Patrick's gym. Holloway, meanwhile, always looks back to all that Boyle taught him, and he plans on using that as far as basketball will take him.

"I learned a lot from every coach I've played for. (Boyle) gave me the green light whenever I played, but also taught me how to be a team player," Holloway said. "I had to learn to be a point guard and not just a scorer. Coach Boyle just has this special ability to motivate guys to play hard for him. It takes a special type to coach to win with or without talent. He should be in the Hall of Fame."

♣

Shaheen Holloway sat courtside near Rutgers coach Mike Rice, St. Joe's coach Phil Martelli and Kentucky assistant Orlando Antigua—there to watch John Calipari's most prized recruit, Michael Kidd-Gilchrist, at the SFIC Basketball Festival at Kean University in early January 2011.

Across the way on the sideline was Boyle, becoming increasingly agitated over his team's slim lead over rival St. Benedict's Prep in a game St. Patrick desperately wanted.

The two rivals seem to butt heads every season, knowing the winner could walk away with the coveted label as the top powerhouse in not only the surrounding Union and Essex Counties, but also all of New Jersey. In the 2009–10 edition of this highly magnified blood war, the Gray Bees rallied for a thrilling 65–64 win in the final seconds, sending thousands of roaring onlookers into a state of hysteria.

St. Benedict's Texas-bound point guard, Myck Kabongo, a native of Toronto who was listed as one of the best juniors in the country and later spent his senior year at Findlay Prep in Nevada, drove the lane trailing by one and converted a running jumper with five seconds remaining to clinch the win. This one hurt the Celtics. After all, the shocking finish left them broken on the hardwood of the Dunn Center, located in their own city of Elizabeth.

It also translated into a slap in the face of Kyrie Irving, who openly heard whispers of Kabongo being the Garden State's most decorated floor general. From a team standpoint, everything about this loss irked Boyle and his troops.

Sitting in the locker room with a 42–33 lead over St. Benedict's this time, St. Patrick's players waited for the worst from Boyle because a nine-point lead certainly did not represent how dominant the team could be. Not this year. Not ever.

"It's a nine-point game, and we have 42 points. We should have 60," barked Boyle, whose team looked nothing like the one that ran past Cranford, 90–41, for its sixth straight win three days prior. "We didn't rotate on defense, and they have guys hitting threes from everywhere!"

The Celtics did, in fact, fail to stop the opposition from draining long jumpers. It did not matter that the undersized Gray Bees failed to capitalize in the paint. Playing in his second game with the team upon transferring from a school in Toronto a week prior, point guard Tyler Ennis was able to funnel the ball to North Carolina State-bound forward Tyler Harris, another import from Long Island power Half Hollow Hills West, for several costly three-pointers.

St. Benedict's blazing six-for-11 output from beyond the arc cancelled out four threes off the hot hand of St. Patrick senior Chris Martin, an athletic five-foot-eleven sharpshooter from St. John's College High

School of Washington, DC who was making an immediate impact in his first year with the team. In addition, an 18–5 margin in bench points also helped rookie head coach Roshown McLeod, a former NBA player, and the underdog Gray Bees remain afloat.

"We're the best team in the country," Boyle snapped, his voice getting noticeably louder. "Now, it's time to show it. The defense has to spread the floor more. We're up nine. It should be 20."

Boyle and his coaches gathered briefly to discuss their approach to adapting to Ennis, whom they had little to no scouting reports on.

"I'm going to make a decision here," Boyle sternly said. "With the point guard, we're going to double him. Once he gives it up, we sprint back to man-to-man. Got it?"

Another sentence of Xs and Os was interrupted with a warning that time on the clock in between halves was running out.

Boyle glared at his team and left the boys with one last thought that sparked a fire, and ultimately an incentive to bust open the basement door and dash upstairs to the court like a stampede.

"Last year, this team beat us!" Boyle shouted. "Someone comes into your home and pisses all over the fucking floor, and you don't come here wanting to knock them out? Let's put an end to this!"

He kicked the blue locker beside him and stormed away.

Boyle's way of effectively penetrating the minds of each player wearing a green and white uniform was always an exact science. Scold, overly compliment, and motivate. Lather, rinse, and repeat.

Austin Colbert scored the first bucket of the third quarter by collecting a quick pass from a driving Jarrel Lane and throwing down a two-handed dunk. St. Patrick eventually swelled its lead to 50–37 minutes later, but another roadblock forced the team to take its foot off the gas pedal. Mike was called for his fourth foul with 3:15 left in the quarter, sending him to the bench with only one foul left before being disqualified.

Mike's foul trouble prompted Boyle to call upon junior Tyrone O'Garro, a soft-spoken six-foot-seven junior forward who had not gotten much playing time, to check in. Nehemias Morillo converted two free throws, and St. Benedict's crawled within 51–44. The last thing Boyle wanted was another close game that would go down to the wire. In basketball, a team will eventually get burned by playing with fire too often. The Celtics needed to resuscitate their swagger before their in-state rival grasped the momentum in its entirety.

On the next possession, Jarrel wasted some time by slowing down and holding the ball near midcourt. This was the perfect situation for them to execute Boyle's latest go-to play, which called for both Chris and Derrick to cut from under the basket and find a way to get open beyond the arc for a jump shot.

Jarrel found Chris on the right corner and St. Patrick was back in business. Chris drilled his fifth three-pointer of the contest, prompting Boyle to pump his fist. That dagger put his squad up, 54–45, with one more quarter to play.

Harris opened the fourth with a running jumper and a layup off a turnover, bringing the Gray Bees' deficit back to single digits and forcing Boyle to insert Mike back into the game with four fouls. Risky, yes, but the unit that had been on the floor during the end of the third and beginning of the fourth simply was not clicking.

Despite several defensive lapses and two costly turnovers, Tyrone remained in the game. Mike handled the ball and attacked the basket as if he had not committed any infractions all afternoon, making Boyle nervous.

"Easy, easy," Boyle cautioned from the sideline whenever his superstar caught a pass.

Mike was not letting last season's result present itself again. Not this year, when everything was supposed to be different. He weaved through double-teams and drove to the basket with authority every possession. Scouts marveled at his "motor" and his uncanny tendency to play every sequence like it was the final minute of a state championship game. This was just another example. Four fouls, be damned.

He drew fouls on consecutive possessions, hitting both free throws after the first and one of two in his second trip to the line to gain a 59–49 lead with 5:11 remaining. Another ill-advised foul called on Tyrone kept St. Benedict's from flatlining, as that gaffe translated into a pair of layups by Harris and Ennis in a 35-second span to cut the deficit to six.

Tyrone looked frazzled on the court, but Boyle still did not look down toward the bench for reinforcements. Austin and Dakari Johnson also had four fouls. Plus, Tyrone's superior athleticism matched up better against McLeod's gritty team.

Boyle's faith in Tyrone was rewarded soon thereafter as he nailed a long three-pointer from the right side to reclaim a nine-point lead. The outpouring of approval, mixed with an evident sigh of relief, from Tyrone was a direct symbol of St. Patrick's 73–65 victory. It sure was not pretty, but the team got the job done when it counted.

Tyrone, oddly enough, was the lone player on the team who was honored after the game with a wooden plaque for his outstanding academic achievement. His day went from bad to great in a matter of minutes. He would sign for that any day.

In a contest that ended with 49 combined fouls, Mike scored 25 points, pulled down 14 rebounds and went 12 for 14 from the line. Each team committed 15 turnovers, and the two were separated by just two points in the paint, in favor of St. Patrick. The difference was a strong first quarter and keeping the Gray Bees from capitalizing on a prolonged run throughout the remainder of the contest.

Boyle was very diplomatic in his post-game interviews with reporters, recognizing St. Benedict's as an elite program, which had been immediately elevated upon Ennis's surprise arrival.

"In their first eight games they really didn't have anyone to handle the ball," Boyle said. "We kind of mailed it in during the second; Ennis did a very good job. Every play ran through him, and it's funny how a point guard can change everything. I think he'll help that team, without question."

Harris paced the Gray Bees with 25 points and ten rebounds and was a major factor in facilitating St. Benedict's chronic comeback attempts.

"We didn't do as good a job as we should have with him," Boyle said.

The majority of Boyle's assessment of his team's seventh win in as many games was spent on Chris, who scored 22 points in 31 minutes.

"He came away with 20 points per game in one of the best Catholic leagues in the country (in DC)," Boyle said. "He's a hell of a shooter, but his handle has to get better."

"But I think Ray Allen has to work on his game, too," he quipped, referring to the Boston Celtics star who is known as one of the deadliest long-range shooters in history. "For high school, I'm not afraid to have two small guards on the floor at the same time because of (Martin's) ability to shoot. It's a beautiful thing to have on the court."

Chris had yet to commit to a college, even though more and more Division I programs had been inquiring about his services. Boyle claimed he would be best suited for an Atlantic-10 school and "some Big East schools in certain situations."

Boyle took a different tone as he addressed the Celtics in the locker room downstairs. Rather than reminding his bevy of collegiate recruits of how special they were, he opted to acknowledge the importance of his role players—especially Tyrone.

"I like all of you guys. I really do," Boyle stated, scanning the entire room. "If I didn't like you, you wouldn't be on the team. I'm going to put all of you in key games. I want you to respond, and, all of a sudden, you'll be in tougher games. Jarrel did it last year. You all have to accept who you are. Nobody here should care about stats. I sure as hell don't. People want to see you make plays. Some of you guys, you have to keep working."

As he looked at Tyrone, point guards Hakim Saintil and Trevis Wyche and fellow sophomore Jason Boswell, Boyle said, "For some of you guys, maybe that time will be next year."

Mike and Derrick, along with the rest of the regulars, stared back.

"You can't get what you want if we don't achieve what we want as a team. Does that make sense?"

Every player nodded.

"Mike, you'll probably be an All-American and whatnot even if you score eight points a game, because of where you are in life. Player of the Year? You won't get it unless we win."

Mike agreed.

"Individual things can't be accomplished if we don't do it together," Boyle continued. "You're all in a good spot right now. We've got uno (Mike), dos (Derrick), tres (Chris) scoring. We don't need many points from other guys.

"Austin, you took a jumper today that I really liked and another that I didn't, but I didn't say peep. Dakari, man, we need to see more energy. You're carrying around 265 pounds, and in Florida you looked like a top-five player in the country. But today, people are going to walk away wondering, 'Why didn't the big guy get in more?' That's what people are saying right now. You need to play so hard that people, instead, will walk away saying, 'He's going to be a 20 and 10 player if he keeps working.'"

Dakari slouched on the wooden bench and agreed. Never before had he been challenged by a coach. Welcome to life with Boyle.

"Tomorrow we're going to have a good practice, and Monday we have Plainfield. We're going to refocus," Boyle promised.

Every player broke the quiet moment and livened up as Boyle congratulated them on another good win.

"There are only 100 seats in that gym," Boyle said, walking away with a furtive grin on his face. "Maybe we can sell 'em for 100 bucks each."

Tyrone was the first of many to break into laughter.

Four

He's a straight-faced tough guy. You can see he's tight when he's coaching. But off the court, he goes out of his way to help kids. ... People ask me where I went to high school and sometimes I get a face that says, 'Oh, yeah, you played real basketball.'
—Paris Bennett

The Celtics of St. Patrick had been followed around by Blowback Productions cameras and a never-ending line of reporters in 2010–11, but things used to be very different in the early days of Boyle's reign. There were hardly ever newspapermen at games, and any time high school results made the sports section it seemed every last drop of ink was used on Bob Hurley and St. Anthony.

"It was so different for us then because it was so hard to be noticed for doing something good," Celtics assistant coach Rae Miller said. "St. Anthony was always the marquee game, even when Shaheen Holloway and Winston (Smith) were seniors. We worked to play St. Anthony (in the state playoffs) ever year. It didn't always happen."

St. Patrick was denied the chance to play Hurley's Friars in both the 1992–93 and 1995–96 seasons because of losses to Paterson Catholic in the postseason. This was a time when Hurley's legacy truly began building steam. He had just gotten past the era of coaching both his sons, Bobby and Danny, and had finished No. 1 in the nation as recently as 1989.

"They were always so good, even back then," Rae said. "They were dominating the state in all facets of the game. That's why it was always our goal to play them and eventually, somehow, get to that level on a consistent basis."

Thanks to players such as Charles Lott, Chris Clemons, and Winston Smith, the Celtics thrust themselves back onto the radar in New Jersey by 1992. Soon thereafter, Holloway became Boyle's first big-time player, an All-American who attracted attention from across the country and helped St. Patrick win the county championship in 1993, 1994, and 1996 after suffering through a 26-year drought.

Holloway's teams cracked the national rankings, an accomplishment that came a lot sooner than even Boyle had predicted, and turned the school into a perennial contender due to the influx of talent that thirsted for a chance to play for the state's young, up-and-coming coach.

"Without question," Boyle said, "back when Shaheen was here, there was a lot of energy, and it helped attract other kids."

One of those kids turned out to be the second coming of Holloway in a sense that he brought St. Patrick to yet another level. Al Harrington was a little-known ninth-grader who spent one year at Roselle High School, where he wasn't talented enough to start for the freshman squad. He came to St. Pat's and started on the varsity as a sophomore, when Holloway was a senior, and averaged six points per game.

"He was a humble kid that came from a good family. They were church-goers," Joe Picaro said. "He put up 1,000 shots every morning and 1,000 more every afternoon. You could just see his determination and dedication. He was the lead in the school play and turned around the gospel choir, making it okay for guys to be in it.

"We had the tallest choir ever. We had six-foot-ten Herve (Lamizana), six-foot-ten Sam (Dalembert), and six-foot-eight Al, and a kid named Jermaine Clark, who was six-five. Half the basketball team joined choir once Al did. It used to be that the choir had 50 kids in it with five or six boys. After the services, I'd say to the kids, 'That was great, wasn't it? We need more guys.' So after Al joined, it turned into a 50–50 ratio with 150 kids. He was an excellent role model, a great basketball player and student in school."

By his junior year in 1997, he was a First-Team All-State star who was the linchpin when it came to clinching a fourth Union County title in five years.

"He was the baby-faced assassin," high school sports guru and television personality Mike Quick said. "I remember I spoke at their banquet, and it was Al's sophomore year. I talked about this kid who couldn't even shave yet, but I knew he was going to get bigger and stronger. He had this innocent way about him. The first time I saw him, I heard he wanted to bypass college and go straight to the NBA. Man, he was good, but I didn't think he could go to the NBA then. So I guess he exceeded his expectations because those expectations weren't as high when he first came in. He wasn't a Mike Gilchrist, where expectations were there from the beginning."

According to both Rae Miller and Boyle, Harrington's junior year presented one of the toughest coaching assignments. To complement Harrington, the Celtics were armed with a guard from Brooklyn named Corey White and two big men, Clark and Jerome Holman, who would eventually join the And 1 Tour.

Harrington was a noble, unassuming kid despite his growing stature in the basketball world—not just as a highly coveted recruit, but as a potential NBA prospect. The others, however, were hard-headed teenagers from New York who had their own way of responding to situations on and off the court.

"That was a group that was a little bit off. They were just very different," Rae said. "We had to try to mold them into a great group of kids. These guys just had a different street mentality. It was a big challenge."

The next year, a six-foot-ten Haitian Canadian center named Samuel Dalembert showed up.

"We had to find a way to learn to build a team with big guys," Rae recalled. "We had to learn how to manage all of them, too. Kevin was used to winning with a lot of guards and small players. We had to find a way to get the most out of this group."

Rae maintained his belief that the 1998 team was a cornerstone in the Celtics' rise. "That taught us how to beat people," he said. "That was definitely the era that formulated what happened the next decade."

By Harrington's senior year, he became the best player in the country, according to *Parade*, Gatorade and *USA Today*. The only outlet that didn't recognize him in that way was McDonald's. He was learning from Boyle and legendary coach Sandy Pyonin, who ran the NJ Roadrunners AAU program and helped condition hundreds of Division I players and 32 NBAers over 35 years out of a tiny gym in Union.

Harrington rode his bike every day from Roselle to the Young Men's and Young Women's Hebrew Association in Union, where Pyonin had developed a reputation as the world's most prominent basketball trainer.

"He had a 98 percent focus," Pyonin said. "He had the burning desire to be great. He listened to everything I told him, and he's just a great kid. He wasn't the most aggressive, but when you come down here to play for me, you have to be competitive. He would shoot 2,000 shots a day."

Meanwhile, Harrington, the six-foot-eight, 220-pound small forward, established himself as the next poster boy of the Celtics with potential to become Boyle's first-ever NBA alumnus. Holloway never cracked an NBA roster despite a terrific career at Seton Hall University.

"Back when he was at Sandy's gym, he couldn't make a layup, but he had a beautiful touch," Boyle's childhood friend, Mike Brown, said. "So I wondered who Kevin was going to keep on his team; Al or this kid from Shabazz (High School)? I said, 'Take that kid (Al) because of that touch.' All of sudden he was playing with Shaheen and grew from six foot five to six foot eight real quick.

"In a county game, Shaheen dished off to Al for a hard dunk, one of those dunks where he's hanging on the rim and his legs go outward. You saw right then and there that he was going to be great."

"We finally got there with Al's teams," Rae said. "That's the definitive point when we made a big move in that direction. We finally understood what it takes to get consistently good. St. Anthony was always there. They were the top of the mountain."

In the 1997–98 season, Harrington developed plenty of respect as a senior leader, and the hype that surrounded him mirrored that of Holloway two years prior.

"I said Al needs to be selfish," Brown said. "Look at all the NBA's big-time scorers like Kevin Durant, Kobe Bryant, and so on. He needed to be selfish a little more. He could get his shot off against anybody. He just knew how to position himself."

Managing a hotshot superstar was something Boyle had grown accustomed to, so when the media bug bit the team throughout certain matchups, it became a normalcy, not a scary proposition that was out of the ordinary.

On December 31 of that year, Harrington scored 29 points and grabbed 21 rebounds to lead St. Patrick, ranked sixth by *USA Today* at the time, to a 56–47 win over Dunbar, the Baltimore area's No. 1 team, in the Slam Dunk to the Beach Tournament in Lewes, Delaware.

Four days later, Harrington was at it again. This time, he scored 23 points and pulled down 13 rebounds as the Celtics edged New York City power Christ the King, 60–56. With the score knotted at 53 with 2:09 remaining in the fourth quarter, Harrington reverted back to his clutch ways, and Clark came through with a driving layup and three-point play to hand St. Patrick a lead it wouldn't relinquish.

"We were a little tired," Boyle told the *New York Daily News* that day. "Al was like a B-minus or a C-plus, but he did step it up in the last six."

Harrington told the *Daily News*: "Early on, my shots were rimming out. But I felt comfortable. As a team, we weren't hitting any shots. But then our pressure worked, and we started getting every rebound. This puts us in a good situation now. They played very well, but we came through."

Moving past another nationally known program such as Christ the King and all-world guard Omar Cook certainly put the Celtics on pace to cruise through the rest of the year and possibly clinch the first state title with Boyle at the helm.

A 63–59 loss to Hargrave Military Academy (Chatham, Virginia) one week later brought St. Patrick back down to earth, showing it wasn't invincible, even with Harrington leading the way. The major Division I recruit finished with 28 points and seven rebounds, but fellow high-level prospect Korleone Young and his squad got the best of Harrington and Boyle.

"My individual stuff doesn't count because he won the game," Harrington said in the report before commenting on his rivalry with Young as being the top player in the class of 1998. "I did want to outplay him. Maybe people won't say that he's number-one so fast."

Later that month, St. Patrick scored a much-needed, confidence-building, 11-point victory over Seton Hall Prep in the fourth annual Coalition to House the Homeless tournament at the Dunn Center in Elizabeth. Harrington netted 22 points—including ten of his team's 13 points in a key third-quarter run—and was aided by Clark's 15 and Walter Price's 12.

By this time, Harrington was entertaining a multitude of Division I scholarship offers, namely from Seton Hall, Georgia Tech, and St. John's. However, there was a lot of buzz that he would forgo his college eligibility and jump straight to the NBA.

"I heard he's coming, that it's 99 percent that he's coming," said one NBA scout, who requested anonymity, in multiple news reports. "Those are the conversations I've had, and that's my gut feeling, too. I am a fan."

The 1998 NBA draft was slated with potential All-Stars, including Kansas's Paul Pierce, Arizona's Mike Bibby, North Carolina duo Antawn Jamison and Vince Carter, an unconventional athletic big man from Germany named Dirk Nowitzki, and probable No. 1 overall pick Michael Olowakandi, a center from Pacific. Multiple media outlets projected Harrington would be a low first-round pick if he chose to enter, but Harrington remained silent on his impending plans. He and his family even stopped talking to the media as the state playoffs neared.

In the weeks leading up to his decision, which he ultimately would reveal in a news conference at the high school, Picaro claimed Harrington kept a level head and didn't take advantage of his celebrity status. "There was no fanfare with him here," Picaro remembered.

Harrington and company reached their goal by blowing past opponents in the county and state playoffs and entered the Tournament of Champions final with a 26-3 record. Sure enough, Boyle and the Celtics upended Brandin Knight—the younger brother of former Stanford guard Brevin Knight—and Seton Hall Prep by a score of 62-49 to clinch the Garden State's highest championship honor.

In just one decade, Boyle became a man of his word. He told Picaro and Athletic Director Red Migliore he would bring the program to the top. He sure did.

Harrington, who posted 22 points and 11 rebounds per game as a senior, finished his three-year high school career at St. Patrick with 1,278 points and per-game averages of 21.9 points and 10.7 rebounds.

"After Al's last week of basketball, and he comes back and I said, 'Wow, Al, you had some exciting week,'" Picaro said in a tongue-in-cheek kind of way.

Harrington on a Monday attended the Gatorade dinner, where he was honored for his achievement as the best high school player in the country.

The next day he was named Player of the Year at a news conference at the Meadowlands at noon.

On Wednesday he won the Tournament of Champions.

Thursday consisted of Harrington missing school to appear on *The Rosie O'Donnell Show* to sing an entertaining rendition of "Anything you can do, I can do better …" with the colorful host.

Then, on Friday, he competed in the McDonald's All-American Game.

"So he looks at me with a big smile and said, 'Oh, Mr. Picaro, it was wonderful.'"

"I looked at him and said, 'Well, welcome back to reality. You have detention.'"

Enjoying the perks of being a nationally known star apparently tipped the scales in favor of skipping the next level and continuing a growing trend of jumping from high school to the NBA. Getting advice from one of the most prominent players to have reaped the benefits of such a move, Minnesota Timberwolves superstar forward Kevin Garnett, also helped.

"This has been a lifelong dream of mine," Harrington, Boyle's second McDonald's All-American, said during a news conference. Picaro supported Harrington in choosing to pursue his dream, even if that meant casting aside a college education. A picture of Harrington and Picaro with their arms around each other still sits in the principal's office desk.

"He was a guy who was very hungry. He worked his butt off," Picaro said. "After three years of working with coach Boyle, he was in the NBA right away. When he first came to St. Pat's, he wasn't very skilled. I'd be blown away if someone had told me then he would be named the best player in the country and go to the NBA. But that kid was just a sponge. That's how he became number one."

The 1998 NBA draft was held at General Motors Place in Vancouver, British Columbia. The home of the putrid one-year-old Vancouver Grizzlies, the arena was filled with college stars—and a handful of high schoolers such as Harrington, Korleone Young, and Rashard

Lewis—with hopes of beginning the long journey toward greatness on the sport's biggest stage.

The Los Angeles Clippers chose Olowakandi first overall; the Grizzlies made Bibby the second pick, and the Denver Nuggets opted for Kansas center Raef LaFrentz third. Harrington had heard the highest he could've gone was No. 5 to the Golden State Warriors, so when the Toronto Raptors made Jamison their selection at No. 4, he wasn't surprised. In addition, it'd be a long shot for the new franchise to take high-school kids in consecutive years, since the Raptors rolled the dice on an 18-year-old named Tracy McGrady at No. 9 in 1997.

The Warriors wound up with Carter; the Dallas Mavericks went with burly Michigan forward Robert "Tractor" Traylor at No. 6; the Kings were elated to end up with flashy point guard Jason Williams of Florida at seven; and the Philadelphia 76ers chose St. Louis freshman Larry Hughes at eight. The names kept flying off the board, and soon Harrington fell out of the lottery. Multiple small forwards were taken instead of Harrington at the halfway mark of the first round as Matt Harpring, Pat Garrity, Roshown McLeod, and Ricky Davis rounded out the top 21 selections.

Picaro said three NBA teams in the top 20 told Harrington they would select him but never did. At No. 24, the San Antonio Spurs plucked St. John's guard Felipe Lopez, who had been a major recruit out of Rice High School in New York.

The Indiana Pacers were up next and were hoping to add depth to a roster that came within one game of upending Michael Jordan's Chicago Bulls in the Eastern Conference finals. Reggie Miller, Rik Smits, Chris Mullen, and Mark Jackson formed a strong core, but all had more than nine years of mileage to their names. Coach Larry Bird coveted a youthful athlete who would translate into a contributor in two or three years down the line. Harrington fit the mold.

NBA commissioner David Stern approached the podium on the stage of General Motors Place and announced to the world that St. Patrick High School now had an alumnus in the NBA. "With the 25th pick in the 1998 NBA draft, the Indiana Pacers select Al Harrington."

"When Al was getting drafted, my heart was pounding a little bit," Picaro remembered. "I was relieved when he was selected. I told him afterwards, 'Al, this is a good lesson for you. Three teams said they were going to take you and then didn't.'"

Harrington stood in the corner of the green room and cried upon hearing his name. "The higher the expectation, the less nervous you are," Picaro said. "I try to stay even-tempered about it, but, of course, we're very proud."

No one was more proud than Boyle, the coach who finally had one of his boys in the NBA.

♣

Unlike the previous game, against St. Benedict's Prep, Boyle was somewhat pleased with his team's 20–7 second-quarter run and 37–20 cushion at halftime against Plainfield at Rahway High School.

Austin Colbert did not see much action in the second half of St. Patrick's win over the Gray Bees, mostly due to a lack of toughness and foul trouble. This night, however, things started to look up for the six-foot-nine sophomore.

"You did two positive things," Boyle said. "I thought you hedged well, and you went after rebounds. That's the best I've seen you do that this year."

Austin took kindly to his coach's approval and used his new attitude to sweep away any negative thoughts that began to poison his confidence. Freshman center Dakari Johnson, on the other hand, was a different story.

"Dakari, we need you," Boyle continued. "Again, in Florida you were a beast. I need you to get some boards. You're energy level is just not there. You're not ready to play."

Rae added to Boyle's verdict.

"Every rebound, you're going up with one hand," he said extending his right arm. "Maybe you got away with that in past years. I know you're only 15, but you're playing a grown man's sport now."

Boyle and his coaches dismissed the team's halftime gathering and sent the players outside the classroom and into the gym for the third quarter. Before the clock started, Dakari was pacing back and forth in front of the bench, stewing in the harsh lecture he absorbed several minutes ago. Michael Kidd-Gilchrist ran up to him and offered words of encouragement.

"C'mon, man," he said pounding his teammate's chest. "We need you."

"I've been pleased with Dakari's ups and downs," said Dakari's mother, Makini Campbell, an English teacher at St. Patrick. "It's the downs that you're able to learn from. After the City of Palms, he kind of hit a wall. It just had to do with the routine. His deficiencies in his social life, it having been the first time he had practiced or played at that magnitude. Everyone was patient that he'd learn from this experience. I think he was focused and spoke about what he was feeling. Kevin is very open with parents, too. That's what sets him apart. Sometimes parents complain, and it falls on deaf ears and vice versa. Kevin always communicates with the parents of his players."

Boyle also taught his seniors to communicate with the underclassmen, creating a revolving door of team leaders.

Mike's brief message got through to Dakari, who played the entire third quarter and recorded six points and five rebounds. He was the main catalyst in helping his team build a 56–28 advantage by the start of the final eight minutes.

Dakari was pulled from the game just 49 seconds into the fourth and was welcomed by several applauding teammates anxious to give their mammoth freshman center high fives for his hard work. It was a breakthrough everyone on the team was waiting for.

With 5:39 remaining in the contest, Austin grabbed an offensive rebound and converted the put-back while getting fouled. He pumped his fist and looked over at Boyle, loudly approving of his sophomore's increase in intensity.

The two young big men found their fire. Finally.

Austin hit the ensuing free throw and St. Patrick led, 61–33. The Celtics ran set half-court plays for the rest of the game and eventually walked away with a 68–38 victory. Chris Martin led them with 14 points; Derrick Gordon chipped in 13, and Mike 12. The most notable output in the balanced scoring effort was Dakari's.

"Guys, it's all about concentration," Boyle said as the team was undressing in the classroom. "We're controlling the ball, catching the ball with our feet planted, and, most importantly, with our eyes.

"There's a picture of Pete Maravich, who averaged 44 points a game in college, where his body is lying on the ground, but he's following his shot with his eyes the entire way. His chest is about to hit the ground and he's still watching. That's concentration and focus."

Several players did not really understand the message Boyle was trying to convey. They were too busy marveling at Pistol Pete's scoring average. Mike, in particular, was enamored.

"Forty-four? Damn," he said, shaking his head with a smile.

"Yeah, and he would have had about 55 a game if they played with a three-point line, too," Boyle offered.

Boyle carried himself as a basketball encyclopedia, always up for an in-depth discussion involving old-time players. Ask him about any player in college or the NBA. Challenge him to a statistics trivia match. Chances are you would lose.

Instead of continuing to show off his vast basketball history knowledge, he switched gears by handing out some constructive criticism to each and every player.

"Tyrone," he said glaring at his junior forward, who was making major strides and playing himself into the rotation, "you're playing some good basketball now, but I still think you need to slow down."

Boyle then walked toward Dakari, still untying his size 18 Jordan sneakers in the second row of desks.

"Maybe I'm pushing a little too hard here, but I still want to see (the scores being) 21–7, 24–8, 22–10 at the end of the first quarter," he said. "I want to see that consistently. The defense is getting a little better, but I'm a little upset that you guys aren't talking as much as you should be.

"Dakari, switch! Austin, I got 'em! Switch back, Jarrel," Boyle yelled, waving his hands in front of the chalkboard.

"We've got to start talking to each other. If it's a big game, it could be the difference. It could be the difference between just number one in the state and number one in the country."

St. Patrick's eighth win of the season was now a thing of the past, as coaches began discussing the importance of the team's next game, against Winter Park in Florida later in the week. Derrick did not get the chance to guard Austin Rivers in the City of Palms Classic like he had hoped, but he knew the time had finally arrived. It was just another plane ride away.

"Winter Park hasn't lost too many games in Florida over the last few years," Boyle said. "You have to be ready if you're called upon."

After cautioning his team that Winter Park's home gym was capable of holding about 500 more fans than Bishop Verot High School, he gave the boys the week's schedule leading up to Friday's game.

"We travel Thursday," Boyle said. "We'll get there around midnight and we'll get to the hotel at around two. Then it's 10:30 practice, lunch at three, and game time at seven. Then we'll be up late celebrating, hopefully."

A flight down to Winter Park was just the beginning of one of the most important weekends of the season for the Celtics. Their game against the top player in the country was slated for 7:00 p.m. on Friday. On Saturday, they would enjoy a team trip to Disney World and then head to Springfield, Massachusetts, on Sunday morning for their game on Monday against Bishop Gorman (Nevada) at the 2011 Spalding Hoop Hall Classic at Blake Arena on the campus of Springfield College.

Much like the City of Palms, the Hoop Hall Classic showcased some of the best teams in the nation. St. Patrick fell to Findlay Prep by one point in the event there last season, so this once again would be a business trip.

"Bishop Gorman is a good team, and this is a dangerous trap game," said Boyle, who could not help but look ahead. "Last year we ran out of gas at this time."

He did not have to sternly command that it would not happen again. Everybody in the room already knew.

The consensus feeling amongst the team was that if St. Patrick was going to handle Winter Park, Dakari would need to play the way he did the last time he stepped into a Florida gym. There was no exact theory as to why the freshman played so well in the City of Palms and then steadily declined once he landed back home. Through so much experience handling first-year players on this high level, though, Boyle had his thoughts.

"It's his first time playing against this level of competition," Boyle said. "He's carrying around 265 pounds, and we returned to school, so he's getting up at 5:30 in the morning and not getting home until seven thirty or eight at night. He's probably just tired. Maybe he hit the rookie wall."

Perhaps challenging Dakari's effort and calling him out in front of the entire team at halftime of the Plainfield game ignited an inner fire. At least Boyle thought so.

"He was a little upset after the first half, and I think he responded," Boyle said. "Now, he gets a chance to play on ESPN2, and I think it'll reenergize him even more. We'll see."

The Celtics were encouraged by Austin's renaissance in their last win. Now, they just needed the sophomore to continue his stronger play while hoping Dakari would follow suit. As much as the game against Winter Park was about Dakari and Austin staying on course, the media had other ideas.

This was about Kidd-Gilchrist and Rivers, the two who seemed to be the superstars in the running for National Player of the Year honors.

Like Mike, Rivers entered averaging well over 20 points per game for his 15–4 team. At this point in the campaign it was too early to decide on a clear front-runner, so this game served as a major measuring stick for each big-time recruit and NBA prospect, at least for those who believe regular season head-to-head matchups hold any water in the voting process.

"You have the two best players in the country, I think, clearly," Boyle said to reporters after the win over St. Benedict's Prep. "Mike's job is to carry your team to a Tournament of Champions and a top-three national ranking. And it's hard for them not to give it to him if he wins (against Winter Park), if the season means anything."

Rivers walked onto the court after both teams concluded their final huddles before tip-off. The television announcers quickly made it a priority to point out the inscription written on the side of the Duke-bound point guard's sneakers that read, "M.o.a.M."

Man on a Mission.

Winter Park, the defending Class 6A state champion, was still listed among the Top 25 teams in the country in the *USA Today* poll despite four losses. More than anything, high school basketball analysts subscribed to the theory that Winter Park would always have the best player on the court at all times, giving the team a significant advantage over whichever opponent it faced.

St. Patrick would be the best team the Orange County school played thus far, simply because it was up for debate whether Rivers was truly the most gifted scorer on the premises. As the *Orlando Sentinel* reported on the morning of this contest, the Wildcats defeated preseason No. 1 ranked Duncanville, of Texas, at the City of Palms Classic two years ago and fell to No. 1 Findlay Prep at the same venue in 2010.

"But never before has Winter Park played such a high-profile game in front of its home fans," Buddy Collings wrote in that morning's *Sentinel*.

The sold-out crowd of about 2,000 was treated to a media blitz for days. All the hype and excitement, however, was deflated within minutes.

Consecutive layups by Dakari and Chris punctuated a hot start by the Celtics and handed them a 17–8 lead with just under two minutes to go in the first quarter. Derrick converted another fast-break layup in the final seconds, and St. Patrick did exactly what Boyle urged the team to do: deliver a knockout punch as early as possible.

A 23–8 deficit at the start of the second prompted Winter Park coach David Bailey to call for a switch on man-to-man defense. Rivers was now on Mike, but that just opened the floor up for Dakari to dominate the paint. The Wildcats' tallest player was seldom-used junior forward Michael Merlano, at six foot nine, but their roster consisted of just two other players over six foot four.

Dakari appeared larger than life, and his energy was evident. He was sprinting back on defense, working to gain position down in the post and talking on defense. Everything Boyle and the assistant coaches begged for was on display.

"He might be 15, but he plays like he's in his twenties," one announcer gushed about Dakari.

Several days prior to that, Boyle pressed the issue with Johnson behind closed doors. He questioned his desire and squashed his elementary school and AAU ego. That embarrassing, murky dialogue was left up north, miles and miles away from this hot gymnasium that saw St. Patrick running away with another healthy lead on another highly regarded team.

As Dakari made his presence felt on the court, Chris was heating up. He drilled two straight shots from behind the arc to swell the Celtics' advantage to 38–18 with 2:59 left until halftime. Chris had

15 points and was an unblemished six for six from the floor. Things were clicking.

With St. Patrick up 43–24, the teams departed for the locker rooms. Rivers was held to just 13 points, while a balanced attack—led by Chris's 15, Derrick's 11, and Mike's nine—was paving the way for this game to finish as a boring blowout.

"I just told them (at halftime), obviously they have a tremendous scorer in Austin Rivers, and they're playing at home, which means a couple big shots here, a couple big shots there, the momentum is completely back in their favor," Boyle said. "You expect teams like that to make another run because the ball is in (Rivers's) hands so much throughout the game. He's so crafty, so obviously we were expecting them to answer back."

Boyle was right. This one was far from a sealed victory, simply because everybody knew Rivers was capable of putting his team on his back—no matter what the numbers on the scoreboard read.

Rivers drilled three three-pointers en route to 14 points in the third, and Winter Park ultimately cut its deficit to 52–45 with two minutes left in the period. St. Patrick entered the fourth with some momentum after Mike pounced on a loose ball and assisted on a big three-pointer from Jarrel to make the score 57–47.

Winter Park stayed close the rest of the way but was not able to conquer the Celtics' overbearing height advantage and energy. Rivers finished with 38 points on 12-of-26 shooting, while Mike scored 21 and grabbed nine rebounds. The Player of the Year debate was not settled, but St. Patrick's ability to overcome a tough opponent outside its home state certainly was, once again.

Rivers became just the fourth player to score 38-plus points against the Celtics in a game Boyle's team won. NBA players Antawn Jamison, O. J. Mayo, and Lance Stephenson were the others.

"Rivers got his 35 or whatever, but you know what? We thought we actually did a nice job defensively," Boyle said. "We're proud of that. We're proud we can go play these types of teams, with the O. J. Mayo's, and play our game. We're very proud of that. So, we're always up for that challenge."

On to the next.

FIVE

Anybody that gets close to Bob Hurley has to be one outstanding coach.
—Sandy Pyonin

The bell had rung several minutes previously, and Samuel Dalembert was in front of his locker, one flight of stairs and across the hallway from where his next class already began, talking with anyone in sight.

He stuck out like a sore thumb, all six foot ten of him, and felt it was more important to make sure everybody was having a good day and his peers were in good spirits. Dalembert would quickly pop his head in the school nurse's office to see if she got over her cold. He'd then migrate to catch some of his friends strolling into their lunch period and conjure up a lighthearted discussion about their after-school plans. It's just how he was wired.

"Sam was so sociable, so friendly, that he was always late for class," St. Patrick Principal Joe Picaro said. "He'd start these conversations with people and continue those conversations well after the bell rang for class. It wasn't his fault. It was just the type of person he was; just a fantastic kid."

Dalembert always put the well-being of others in front of his, mostly because it was his hope to develop relationships with as many kids as possible for the sake of making his move to New Jersey from Montreal a lot less daunting. Born in Port-au-Prince, Haiti, in 1981, Dalembert moved to Montreal when he was 14 years old to attend high school at Lucien-Page. After suffering a season-ending broken toe at the start of his sophomore year, he felt his chances of playing college ball in the United States were dramatically sliced.

With knowledge of family members in New Jersey, Dalembert

opted to make his move to another country sooner than expected. After weeks of deliberation, he was finally enrolled at St. Patrick, quickly making his reputation known among the couple hundred students as a friendly giant with a heavy accent—the mayor of the hallways.

One day he had just concluded one of his infamous chitchat sessions and paced to Picaro's office to obtain a late slip. Dalembert's behavior secretly brought joy to St. Patrick's principal, simply because he so desperately craved an atmosphere in which every pupil in his building got along. In the same breath, though, he rolled his eyes every time the basketball team's star center ducked his head in the doorway and kindly requested a hall pass while sincerely apologizing.

"That day, I told him how it's gotten to the point where if he was late one more time, he'd be suspended, and I'd have to ask his aunt, whom he was living with at the time, to come in for a conference," Picaro remembered.

Sure enough, the very next day, Dalembert approached Picaro with a wide smile, unaware of how much trouble awaited him.

"His aunt came in, and he was never late again," said Picaro, whose policy with in-school suspension stated that the punishment was lifted once the student's guardian showed up. "Once he was embarrassed like that, he was never late. Again, it never had to do with him being a wise guy or anything like that. He was just so bright and so sociable."

Dalembert was also transforming into one of the most dominant big men in the country, one Kevin Boyle was counting on to ease the burden of losing Al Harrington to graduation. The Celtics were coming off their first-ever Tournament of Champions victory in 1998 but were returning very few dependable, experienced players.

After sitting out the mandatory period upon transferring to St. Patrick, Dalembert averaged seven points and seven rebounds since his first game in a green and white uniform on February 1. He was the perfect complement to Harrington and Jermaine Clark, mostly because it's not every day a mobile player standing at Dalembert's height becomes an addition to a high school basketball team midway through a season. It didn't matter that he was a borderline star, a tough kid to scout due to how maddeningly raw his skill-set was as a junior.

"He was limited offensively, that's for sure, but he made the most of what he had," said Mike Quick, who covered Dalembert as the host of *High School Weekly* on MSG Network. "Kevin did a great job with him. When Kevin brought him in, Sam bought into what Kevin was preaching. But you never walked out of the gym saying, 'Oh my God, Samuel Dalembert.' He's a hard guy to explain."

Puzzling, maybe, but there was no doubt Dalembert had the personality and God-given stature to develop into a force in New Jersey.

"When we were selecting the Tri-State All-Star Team we were saying, 'Do we take him? Do we not take him?' He was so hard to define because there were a lot of guys wondering if he'd play in college," Quick added. "He was never a sure thing. He'd give glimpses of brilliance, though. He drifted at times. Maybe that was his personality."

Ready or not, though, Dalembert held the keys to unlocking another championship run for Boyle and the Celtics in 1998–99. If his scintillating summer blowing away scouts at the Nike Camp in Indianapolis was any indication, a repeat was in the cards.

In September of his senior year, Dalembert gave a verbal commitment to Seton Hall University coach Tommy Amaker and left other offers from Villanova, Kentucky, and Rutgers on the table.

"It's where he felt most comfortable," Boyle told Dick Weiss of the *New York Daily News*. "He knows a lot of their players, Charles Manga and Shaheen Holloway, and he really liked Tommy."

If anything, the Pirates were thrilled to welcome a shot-blocking artist with a legitimate post presence to a team that already had worked feverishly to get a junior point guard from Rice High School named Andre Barrett to commit in the near future.

That same month, Boyle received a phone call from a well-known out-of-state AAU coach, who said he had 13 kids, ranging in height from six foot nine to seven foot three, with interest in playing for a big-time high school. Obviously, St. Patrick was a hopeful destination for many.

"I told him I can't take them, though," Boyle said. "I said, 'Sorry,' and then I hung up."

Soon thereafter Boyle was coaching his own AAU team, and his mother-in-law called him to relay a message from Boyle's wife, Kelly: she was on her way to the airport.

"I thought, 'what the hell is she doing at an airport?'"

"She went to go pick up Herve Lamizana," Kelly's mother replied in a don't-shoot-the-messenger tone.

"I said, 'Who the hell is Herve Lamizana?'"

"He came, and he was about six foot five, not six foot nine, didn't speak any English and was wearing a suit that probably cost no more than 20 bucks," Boyle remembered of the stranger who was sitting in the family living room. "My mother-in-law made him eggs and then Brendan (Boyle's son, who was three at the time) attacked him with a Wiffle ball bat. That made Herve smile."

Boyle called the AAU coach to see why he had sent one of his players against his wishes. He never picked up.

"What was I going to do? So he lived with Sam and his aunt, and I went to Joe Picaro and told him the situation," Boyle recalled. "He was furious, but he had good grades from his school in Africa."

Herve's first practice took Boyle by surprise, as he looked every bit of a raw player who had only taken up the game one year prior. "He was shooting the ball from his chest. I thought, 'Oh, boy,'" Boyle grumbled, rolling his eyes. "But then he stood under the basket and pulled off a windmill dunk."

Lamizana was born in Abidjan, Ivory Coast, a country in West Africa, and had been in the United States for only two years, putting him in a similar position as his senior teammate Samuel Dalembert. Still, his frame supplied him with a tremendous advantage over smaller opponents, yet opened the window for him to possibly play the small forward, power forward, and center positions in college if he hit one more growth spurt.

He was cut from the same cloth as Dalembert: an unrefined, athletic big man with the ability to block shots and use high energy to pique the interest of multiple Division I coaches.

The lowest point of the 1998–99 season came in late January, when the Celtics wilted in the fourth quarter of a 62–47 loss to Seton Hall Prep—the team they had defeated twice in the previous year—in the fifth annual Coalition to House the Homeless Classic at the Dunn Center.

Seton Hall Prep trailed 44–39 entering the fourth, but clamped down defensively and held top-ranked St. Patrick scoreless in the opening six minutes, twenty-seven seconds of the final quarter. Seton

Hall-bound forward Marcus Toney-El netted twenty-five points and helped shut down Dalembert.

"I told the kids, 'Remember this game,'" Boyle had told the *New York Times*. "Remember this game; remember the feeling. They wanted the game more than you did. They turned it up a lot, and we didn't respond."

The bitter taste of defeat kept the best team in New Jersey hungry. The Celtics enjoyed another 20-win season and did enough to win another Union County championship and a Non-Public B title. Lamizana finished the campaign having averaged seven points and eight rebounds, proving he was good enough to be the next in line of St. Patrick All-State candidates.

Dalembert went on to play two years at Seton Hall before foregoing his junior and senior seasons to enter the 2001 NBA draft. As a freshman he averaged six points, six rebounds and 3.6 blocks—good for seventh in the nation—en route to being named to the Big East All-Rookie Team. The next year he posted 8.3 points on 56.5 percent shooting, 5.7 rebounds and 2.1 blocks. It was evident an NBA team would benefit from a coachable kid who had not yet reached his ceiling and possessed a knack for altering shot attempts in the paint.

The 2001 NBA draft was held in the theater at Madison Square Garden, and the event was known as the one in which the Washington Wizards gambled the ultimate gamble by selecting a high school center, Kwame Brown, first overall. It marked the first time a high schooler was No. 1, but this also became the night Boyle had alumnus No. 2 reach the NBA.

With the 26th overall pick of the first round, the Philadelphia 76ers chose Dalembert ahead of a French point guard named Tony Parker and Arizona sophomore Gilbert Arenas.

Boyle quickly garnered the sterling status of a coach who sent players to high Division I programs and, in some cases, to the NBA.

St. Patrick wasn't just a school trying to get back on the map in terms of high school hoops. No, the small school in Elizabeth was turning into a superstar factory with the expectation to win a trophy year after year.

In 1999–2000, Lamizana served as the linchpin for a team that was transitioning back to running a guard-oriented offense upon the arrival of a speedy freshman point guard named Mike Nardi. The senior captain, who had grown to six foot ten, saw his game take off after verbally committing to the Rutgers Scarlet Knights in October.

Lamizana was widely considered as the best player in the Garden State, alongside Camden's Dajuan Wagner, John F. Kennedy's James Lattimore, Mendham's Jeff Schiffner, and Linden's Jamaal Tate. Also regarded as a Top-30 player in the nation, it seemed Rutgers nabbed itself a steal recruit.

Thanks to the kid who had been playing organized ball for just four measly years, the Celtics captured a third straight state title and fifth straight Union County championship in 2000.

If the public hadn't noticed beforehand, they finally got the hint this time around: St. Patrick was making a case to be dubbed the next big dynasty in New Jersey at the dawn of a new millennium.

♣

In January of 2011, the St. Patrick basketball team left the warm weather in Florida and arrived at Bradley International Airport in Hartford, Connecticut, where there was nearly two feet of snow on the ground that complemented an unwavering chill in the air. Just two days after disposing of Winter Park on national television, the mission of escaping the toughest weekend of the season was just half over. Two climates, two challenges.

A 30-minute bus ride north on Interstate 91 brought Kevin Boyle and his team to the birthplace of basketball, Springfield, Massachusetts. Next on their agenda was the high-profile Spalding Hoop Hall Classic at Blake Arena on the campus of Springfield College, just over one mile away from the Naismith Memorial Basketball Hall of Fame.

Akin to the City of Palms Classic, this tournament featured the best programs in the nation, such as St. Anthony of Jersey City, Oak Hill Academy (Virginia), Mount Vernon (New York), Milton (Georgia), St. Thomas More (Connecticut) and Findlay Prep (Nevada).

St. Patrick was slated to face Bishop Gorman, another powerhouse from Nevada, on Monday afternoon, meaning the team could squeeze in one full practice and one pregame shootaround.

On Sunday afternoon, the Celtics used the auxiliary gym down the hall from the main arena, where Findlay Prep was cruising past St. Andrew's of Rhode Island. Austin Colbert began his rebounding drills seconds after placing his bags down on the row of chairs that lined the back wall.

The sophomore walked out of bounds in back of the basket, where Dakari Johnson and Michael Kidd-Gilchrist were warming up with point-blank jump shots. He hurled a basketball at the white wall, leaped and grabbed it before landing on his feet, elbows and hands parallel to the hardwood. Assistant coach Rae Miller shook his head, walked over, and took Austin by surprise as he swatted the ball right out of his hands on his second repetition.

"With authority," Rae urged while stuffing the ball back into Austin's stomach.

Austin had come such a long way the last few games when it came to showing more aggressiveness. His past phase of sluggish play generated a constant vigil among the coaches: if their six-foot-nine power forward failed to exert full strength on one play—practice, or not—one of them would notice.

Austin collected himself, with Rae standing with his arms folded next to the wall. He lobbed the ball at the wall again and ferociously snatched it before landing.

"That's what I want to see," Rae exclaimed.

On the other side of the court, Chris Martin and Derrick Gordon wasted no time launching three-pointers. At one point Chris drilled five in a row, and Derrick hit seven. Junior point guard Da'shawn Suber, slowly gaining more minutes in situations where Jarrel Lane needed a breather, was prancing up and down the sideline, working on his dribbling. The ball bounced off the floor every second, in and out, crossover, in and out, crossover. It was the picture of another one of Boyle's underclassmen working feverishly to gain the coach's trust.

The active warm-up session was halted as Boyle called his team into a huddle near midcourt. He sympathized with each player's inevitable fatigue from playing several games the previous week and the rigorous travel schedule.

"But we need to have a good workout today," he said. "Let's get it going!"

Sprinting toward the baseline under the basket, the players formed three lines for a full-court drill that called for three players to run a synchronized sprint to the other end while yelling each other's first name before firing a chest pass. The Celtics took this tedious part of practice very seriously, knowing assertive, forward passes while running up the floor led to so many fast-break points.

Upon examining more than 15 minutes of the drill many coaches call "the weave," Boyle instructed the starting unit to set up a half-court set against the second team for a lengthy, game-speed scrimmage.

The practice was ultimately called about 45 minutes later because the players had to get back to the hotel in time for study hall. One of the glamorous events at the Hoop Hall Classic was the annual skills competition, which allowed the most talented prospects in the country to participate in a dunk contest, a three-point shooting challenge, and a half-court skills showcase.

Derrick and Chris would have loved to show off their touches in the three-point shooting contest, while Mike could not help but wear a devious smile on his face when asked if he would enjoy competing in the dunk gala.

But school came first, Boyle reminded them. Midterm exams were scheduled for Tuesday morning, just hours after the conclusion of the team's game against Bishop Gorman nearly 200 miles away from the school.

As Boyle ended practice with some encouraging thoughts, word had spread that the New York Jets defeated the heavily favored New England Patriots in the second round of the AFC playoffs and punched their ticket for the league championship game in Pittsburgh.

Assistant coach Rich Biddulph caused boisterous laughter and cheers as he exclaimed, "I guess this is the year for teams featured on HBO, baby!"

Waking up in a spacious Hilton hotel room with a bevy of new teammates several hundred miles up the East Coast far from his roots in Washington, DC, reminded Chris Martin just how much his life had changed over the last few months.

After spending three school years terrorizing opponents in one of the most respected Catholic school leagues in the country at St. John's College High School and traveling to the metropolitan area in the summer to visit family from his mother's side, he made the biggest decision of his life.

"I was always thinking about coming up here," he said one day after practice. "I think about my family up here a lot, and I would always visit in the spring and summer. I was just very fortunate to end up at a great place like St. Pat's."

When Chris made it known he was opting to pack his bags for life up North, his AAU coach, Nate Britt of the DC Assault, began recommending high schools in the area. He was told about St. Anthony and several other prominent basketball institutions, but St. Patrick piqued the most interest. Chris also had already been acquaintances with Mike, Derrick, and DaQuan Grant, so that certainly sweetened the deal.

"Those three really welcomed me with open arms here," Chris said. "Then I found out for myself that there are a lot of good guys on this team."

Adjusting to life in New Jersey was not too difficult, but the ways people dressed and the types of music they listened to were the first cultural differences that struck Chris.

"And sometimes you can hear it in the way I talk," he added in his typical soft-spoken manner with a hint of southern drawl.

Chris fit in well with Boyle's systems from the start, jumping into the starting lineup and quickly establishing himself as the Celtics' third-leading scorer behind Mike and Derrick.

"Once I started playing real well, the younger guys started looking up to me," he said.

Up to that point in the season, Chris remained a player in one of the most fascinating situations on a high-profile team. He was the new kid in town, who blended in with his peers. He transformed into a senior leader despite playing just a handful of games in the program. He also was the only senior on the roster who had not yet committed to a college.

While Jarrel Lane was headed to UMBC, Derrick to Western Kentucky, and Mike to Kentucky, Chris chose to keep his options open with hopes his new environment would breed more attention from collegiate scouts. It was working, as more and more Atlantic-10 and Big East schools came to watch him in action.

The Hoop Hall Classic would surely serve as another platform for college coaches to get a glimpse at the sharpshooter. At this stage of Chris's senior campaign, every game was a tryout. With no set destination in his near future and many of his teammates enjoying the security of knowing they would move on from St. Patrick to obtain a higher education and a golden opportunity to play basketball at the next level, the situation could have eaten away at Chris. Instead, he was taking it in stride, actually relishing the fact that patience is something that usually pays off in the end.

Chris and his team as a whole were in a similar position. Ranked second in most national polls, the Celtics could do nothing but continue on their path of taking care of business and hopefully reaping the benefits of current top dog Oak Hill Academy losing a game. That wish came true the night before St. Patrick arrived at Springfield, as the Warriors fell to Milton on Saturday evening. With a victory over Bishop Gorman, the Celtics could thrust themselves into the driver's seat.

Boyle spoke to his team for nearly 15 minutes before taking the court downstairs inside Blake Arena, going over offensive sets—most of which were created to give Chris plenty of open looks from beyond the arc. He then left his team with an inspiring thought: "Last year we lost number one here. Let's not let it happen again."

He was referring to the team's 71–70 heartbreaking loss to then-defending champion Findlay Prep at the Hoop Hall Classic a year ago, nearly to the day. Trailing by two, Kyrie Irving drove to the basket and was fouled with one second remaining. He hit the first free throw but missed the second. Though Mike grabbed an offensive rebound, his last-ditch put-back was blocked, and the game was over.

Boyle was displeased with contact made on Mike, telling *The Republican*, "I guess the refs chose to pass. In my opinion he should have been at the line, but I'm not the ref."

The questionable call squashed a chance for the second-ranked Celtics to unseat the Pilots from their top spot. Typical of Boyle, the sting never exited his body. One year later, he stressed several times that an unfortunate turn of events would not occur again.

Derrick opened the game with consecutive layups, prompting the ESPN play-by-play announcers to gush about his potential for the following season at Western Kentucky. Yes, this was the kid who lit up the City of Palms Classic and continued to blossom as a senior. Bishop Gorman's Roscoe Allen, a six-foot-nine junior who was regarded as one of the best shooting big men in the nation, drilled a three-pointer shortly thereafter to put his team on the board. Boyle spent several minutes in the locker room devising a plan to limit the open looks Allen would get. That lofty defensive assignment belonged to Mike, who later drilled a jumper while getting fouled and converted the ensuing free throw for a 9–5 lead midway through the first.

Bishop Gorman used its immense size advantage to keep the game tight, 16–15, at the end of the opening quarter. Every player on the floor was over six foot five, testing the Celtics in a way their other opponents had not. Boyle recognized this mismatch and called upon Dakari to enter the game, with hopes he could quell the height difference, at least in the paint. Several fans in the first couple rows began snickering about the freshman's six-foot-ten frame.

"He's only 15?"

"I read he's supposed to grow to seven foot two."

"He might be bigger than Shaq one day!"

While Dakari generated a lot of chatter amongst those in attendance, the clear fan favorite was Mike. Dozens of people walked into the arena decked out in Kentucky gear and scrambled for their cameras to get a quick shot of the Wildcats' future superstar.

More flashes came from the stands as Mike scored six straight points to give St. Patrick a 30–22 lead with just under two minutes to go in the second. Bishop Gorman was in trouble, not just because of its inability to stymie the National Player of the Year candidate in the open floor, but because Shabazz Muhammad—another high-profile recruit who would eventually be named the top rising senior in the country by several recruiting outlets—was chained to the bench with three fouls and just five points.

Tyrone O'Garro, who had played especially well of late and was certainly adding to his case to get more minutes, entered the game and quickly hit a layup off a feed from Derrick. After outscoring Bishop Gorman 18–12 in the second, the Celtics entered halftime with a 34–26 advantage. Mike led all scorers with 14, while Derrick had eight, and Chris had seven. Considering a very flawed first half by the opposition, Boyle felt the score should not have been as close. But in the wake of an exhausting week, he strolled into the locker room feeling content.

"I know you're playing hard, but we don't want to get beat and then get called for a foul at half-court," Boyle said. "We only went to the foul line six times. We're not getting enough offensive rebounds, those types of things. Traveling is just an excuse because nobody cares. The *USA Today*, nobody cares. People aren't saying, 'Oh, he's sick,' or 'Oh, they're tired, so they should be number one.' You guys have to step up."

Assistant coach Frank Peralta jumped in to offer his tidbits of advice and observations.

"Guys, Muhammad has three fouls too," Frank said. "I don't believe he'll come back nearly as aggressive. Let's go. You guys are playing well. I think you guys can do better in the lanes. That's the only thing."

"Okay, let's go, guys," Boyle snapped. "We're up eight. It's our ball when we come out, right?"

"Yes," Frank said.

"Okay, we have to finish it out," Boyle continued. "A lot of you look really tired, but you have to suck it up. C'mon."

Players stood up clapping and began to funnel out. As Dakari walked with his head down near the doorway, Boyle grabbed his shirt and asked about his energy level. Dakari nodded as if to say he was fine, which prompted the wheels in Boyle's head to turn again. Could he count on his freshman project to play more meaningful minutes with little gas in the tank? It was evident Boyle was trying to put more trust in Dakari, ultimately adding to an already deep rotation.

If nothing else, more time from Dakari would make the next 16 minutes of game-time easier to swallow. Two more quarters, and St. Patrick would officially become the top team in the nation. Two more quarters, and Boyle and his group could finally return home.

The story of St. Patrick's first-half success was defense. It held Bishop Gorman to 28.6 percent shooting and did exactly what Boyle asked: contain Muhammad and Allen.

For most of the third, the teams traded baskets until the three-minute mark, when the Celtics collectively found another burst of energy and widened the gap. Mike recorded a pair of three-point plays in a span of two minutes, and Chris followed up with another rainbow jumper from behind the arc in the far left corner seconds before the buzzer sounded to give St. Patrick a 55–41 lead entering the fourth.

Chris punctured the frontline defense once again, hitting his fourth three-pointer in the opening minute of the final quarter. He held up his shooting hand after watching the ball fall through the white twine and heard Boyle scream, "There you go, Chris!"

It was an image that played like a broken record throughout the season, one that seemed to give every basketball fan in New Jersey a reason to believe the Celtics had too many weapons for any opponent to handle.

Two possessions later, Chris ran along the right side of the basket and accepted a quick pass from Derrick in the paint. Chris took two dribbles and hurled his body toward the rim.

After that, things went black.

He was lying motionless on his back under the basket upon being tackled to the ground by a defender trailing behind him. Meanwhile, Mike and Derrick were being separated from a cluster of Bishop Gorman players as two referees whistled frantically. Boyle ran to one of the referees, angrily pleading for an intentional foul. Several minutes went by. Chris was still down.

A handful of Springfield College trainers, event employees, and St. Patrick trainer Karen Magliacano crowded around him as he slowly lifted and bent his knees. Did he just get the wind knocked out of him? Was there blood? Did he sustain an ankle or wrist injury? Was it his shoulder? Or worse, did he smack his head on the hardwood?

Onlookers could not gauge how badly Chris was shaken up. St. Patrick personnel did, however, and it revealed an ugly truth. The team's best shooter had blood dripping from his nose and looked dazed. He could not respond to simple questions coherently and failed to remember where he was or how he got there.

Chris was slowly brought to his feet and escorted to the last seat on the end of the bench. As Karen and coach Frank continued their attempts at conversation, Chris grimaced while laboring to widen his eyes after each lethargic blink. Showing many symptoms of a possible concussion, he was taken out of the gym and downstairs.

On the court, Hakim Saintil had entered the game to shoot Chris's free throws and misfired on both. St. Patrick still led, 60–44, with just over six minutes to go. Bishop Gorman did not get much closer as the time ticked away, and Mike sealed the 79–63 victory with a thunderous one-handed dunk in the waning seconds.

The crowd created an enduring applause that serenaded the Celtics off the floor, knowing there was a new top team in the nation. Needless to say, though, what should have been a celebration in the locker room was actually a period of worry for Chris.

Boyle, already aware of his third-leading scorer's status, collected himself to address the team strictly about the game and the upcoming week.

"I told you guys before this was a trap game," Boyle said. "From one to 15, I'd say only two of you looked fresh and awake. I'm (tired) myself, so it's good we were able to gut it out."

"We just have to make sure to be ready for this week," Boyle cautioned. "Linden is going to give us a good game. They're scrappy. Back when we had Corey (Fisher) and all them, they picked us off at Elizabeth. We could've been number one then, too. Linden is going to look to do the same thing this time."

More than 30 media members began to clog the narrow hallway that led to St. Patrick's locker room, hoping to find out what truly occurred when Chris was fouled. Assistant coaches were still coming through the door, and they stopped when they saw Boyle was wrapping up his speech by reminding his team how important midterm exams were over the next couple of days back home.

"It's important to take care of that. We have to do well on tests," Boyle said. "Mr. Picaro will be very upset. We have mandatory study hall, and I'm sure you'll handle more studying there than you would at your houses."

Jarrel collected his black knapsack and began to look through each locker.

"Yo, where did Chris put his stuff?"

Jason Boswell and Tyrone jumped in to help Jarrel find the two bags Chris had left behind. Meanwhile, Boyle walked out into the sea of notebooks, recorders, video cameras, and lights.

"I thought we didn't have great energy early on," Boyle opened. "We came out a little flat and tired. Mike had a tough first quarter defensively, but in the second he played well enough and turned it up. In the third, we were able to create some separation."

"Last year we lost it here," Boyle continued. "But this year we hope to regain it. It's exciting. We love the challenge of being here, and people kind of circle their calendars for us. Now it gives them more incentive."

Chris had yet to be treated at the local hospital in Springfield, so Boyle was very general with his statement.

"He's been a great fit for us because he stretches the defense," Boyle said. "He's been averaging about 24, 25 points against the best teams we've played. He's been great so far."

Some reporters continued to poke at Boyle for information on Chris.

"He has a possible concussion," he offered, squinting toward the light beaming off the three video cameras tilted toward his face.

Jarrel tried to cast aside the negatives and remind everybody a new No. 1 had taken over the nation.

"This was a great win for us," Jarrel said. "This put us at number one in the country after a tough weekend."

Derrick, fresh off a 24-point outing, showed more emotion when talking with reporters.

"That's one of our brothers," he said. "For him to have a concussion, I don't know, I'm just praying for him. I just want him to be okay."

Meanwhile, Mike, who had just scored 27 points, passed on giving interviews. According to the *New York Post*, Mike's mother, Cindy Richardson, said he was too distraught to speak.

Nobody knew if Chris truly was fine. Gathering his bags and getting ready to inhale a chicken and mashed potatoes dinner provided for the team, coach Frank just shook his head when the word concussion exited his lips. He then gave the most chilling quote of all behind the closed locker-room door.

"Let's hope that's all it is."

Six

I wanted to be with a guy who is as great as any high school or college coach in the country. Coach Boyle taught me how to manage kids. He taught me how to get each individual kid to run through a wall for you.
—Grant Billmeier

By the time Al Harrington was a senior at St. Patrick, attendance numbers at every one of his basketball games would rival that of the pathetic hometown New Jersey Nets. No matter the opponent, no matter the traffic one had to sit through, no matter the increase in ticket prices for high school events, thousands of fans who took great pleasure in watching future stars made their way to catch a glimpse of the National Player of the Year in their own backyard.

The Celtics saw a major spike in attendance whenever they played at the Thomas Dunn Sports Center, an indoor sports complex that became part of an eight-building establishment on the grounds of Elizabeth High School. With more than 5,200 students at the time, Elizabeth was named the largest high school in the country in terms of population. That overwhelming statistic attracted a plethora of spectators by default, and the arena certainly possessed more appeal than any other venue Kevin Boyle and his team graced.

A gigantic gymnasium such as the Dunn Center might have seemed like Madison Square Garden to any small child whose days of adopting the game of basketball were still in their infancy, but that spectacle wasn't exactly why a seventh-grader named Mike Nardi pleaded with his mother to take him to 600 Pearl Street on many winter nights during the 1998 season.

Nardi fell in love with the way St. Patrick's basketball team conducted its business on the court. He admired Boyle's run-and-gun philosophy, which ultimately resulted in many open-court slam dunks from Harrington. It was a point guard's dream team. The Jordan brand uniforms and sneakers added a nice touch, too.

Even as a young teen, Nardi knew he was destined to live prosperous high school and college careers. He had his head on straight, not something every teen could brag about, and always knew the value of a good education. Thanks to the strict parenting by his mother Sheila, Nardi was a disciplined adolescent, evidently wise beyond his years. That astuteness birthed a well-thought-out plan, one that took Nardi and his mother on a tour of some of the most reputable high schools in the state when it came to academics and basketball.

By the time his eighth-grade year rolled around and Harrington had graduated from St. Patrick before entering the 1998 NBA draft, Nardi understood his talent on the court far exceeded that of his peers. He was going to be a big-time player for a big-time program. He toyed with the idea of attending Seton Hall Prep, knowing its coach, Bob Farrell, had the glowing status as one of the best hoops teachers anywhere. St. Benedict's Prep was a legitimate option as well, but a strong academic reputation, his dream of playing for Boyle's guard-oriented offense and wearing those green and yellow Jordan uniforms outweighed it all in the end.

"Basically, I was going for a school with a good reputation academically and with basketball," Nardi said of choosing St. Patrick. "It was like visiting a college. I wanted to meet Coach Boyle and talk with him. I remember watching games when they had Al at the Dunn Center, and I just fell in love with the way the team played. I wanted to find out if I could fit in somehow."

Nardi did more than just blend in with the rising basketball program. He played some junior varsity games at the beginning of his freshman year but then saw increased minutes on the varsity level.

"We had a guy fail off the team for a semester because of bad grades, so it opened up a spot. I remember my first start and everything."

His first start, ironically, was against Seton Hall Prep in the Homeless Classic at the Dunn Center in Elizabeth, midway through his freshman year. It was rare for a player to blossom in Boyle's system so quickly. The slender, six-foot speedster, however, was making a name for himself around the Garden State in a hurry. One year later, Boyle even dismissed the unconventional way of turning to a sophomore to lead a team with state-championship hopes and let Nardi know he was his floor general.

"My sophomore year, it was more of a tough-love thing," Nardi said. "He told me that I had to step up, and that he wanted this team to be mine. He told me that he wanted to get on me in front of people in games so they would see how well I handled it. He was making me a leader before I even knew it."

It was one of those psychological tactics Boyle so often used to teach one of his players a lesson, not just about basketball, but about life in general. Even without basketball, one has to be a leader to make it in the real world.

"(Boyle) is the ultimate competitor," Nardi said. "He was also a guard, so it was like we were the same type of player. Maybe he saw a little of himself in me. I was a little quicker and athletic, but we had the same mind-set."

Every day in school, Nardi would spend his lunch period eating with Boyle so the two had a chance to go over certain plays together. Principal Joe Picaro teased Boyle by saying, "It's you and your son."

Nardi and Boyle's personalities were, in fact, scarily similar. Losing was just not an option to the ultimate Boyle guy, the point guard who would dish out the ultimate assist the autumn before his sophomore year began.

Grant Billmeier truly enjoyed his freshman year at the Pennington School, a coeducational prep and boarding school that sat on 54 acres in the small town of Pennington, New Jersey, several miles outside of Trenton. The six-foot-ten Billmeier used his mammoth stature to open the eyes of scouts around the country even as a 14-year-old, but he wanted something more. If basketball was truly going to serve as an easy track to college, displaying his talents on a bigger stage seemed like a logical avenue.

"Pennington is a really great school, but I wanted to be a part of something bigger than myself," Billmeier said. "I wanted to be with a guy who is as great as any high school or college coach in the country."

That meant finding a way to play for Boyle.

Billmeier lived in Pennington, an hour drive from Elizabeth, and realistically wasn't ready to make that type of commute every morning and evening. While Billmeier was torn between his wish and the burden of reality, Nardi and his mother were in the process of moving from their small apartment in Avenel—a community in Woodbridge—to a more accommodating three-bedroom house in Linden, a town next to Elizabeth. Nardi and Billmeier had developed a relationship dating back to their sixth-grade year via travel basketball, so the two reconnected after their freshman campaigns.

"We've been playing with each other since sixth grade, and I was jealous of him," Billmeier recalled. "He was always preparing to compete for a Tournament of Champions title, always on television, always in the newspaper, and I wanted to be a part of everything that St. Pat's is all about."

Nardi understood where his friend was coming from, knowing what it was like to dream about the big things. So, he worked up the courage to ask Sheila if his friend could live with them during the week and throughout the basketball season if Billmeier decided to transfer.

"(My mother) knew the Billmeiers and had no problem lending a helping hand to someone who was trying to do something good for himself," said Nardi, who gladly helped Billmeier unpack his belongings in one of the two bedrooms on the second floor.

"Playing St. Anthony and playing in front of 5,000 people a lot was an opportunity I wanted to be a part of," Billmeier admitted. "You feel special when you play for St. Pat's. You have the Jordan brand and all that, all the best gear; you're all over the newspapers, and on television a lot. It's big-time. My parents did a lot of background work. They found out what the school was all about and saw that its academics were as good as any, too."

It didn't take long for Nardi to see just how determined his new roommate actually was when it came to succeeding. Billmeier and his father tried contacting Boyle on the phone several times right before making the transfer official but couldn't get a hold of him.

"So I just decided to roll on my own," Billmeier said. "I later told (Boyle) that I have a place to live, so you don't have to worry about anything with me, and I'm coming."

Billmeier had come too far at that point. His love for basketball ran too deep for a roadblock to alter his chance at competing at the highest level.

"I just love basketball and always have," he said. "Even at 10 years old, when I'd walk into the house with blood on my knees from playing, everybody knew I loved the game. It's in my heart."

Nardi shared a similar sentiment, the embryo of a brotherhood that flourished once the move was settled, and Billmeier was enrolled at St. Patrick High School in the fall of 2001.

"It was a great feeling, but finally meeting a kid who loved basketball as much as I do was the best part," Billmeier said. "We had the same dreams. It was like we were brought together as kids and then in high school to make each other better."

The two realized they were joined for a reason and ran with it. When Boyle would dismiss his players from practice in the early evening, normally many would go home and delay the drags of homework by relishing in another session of video games. Meanwhile, Nardi and Billmeier hopped on their bicycles and headed for a small gymnasium on Green Street in Linden.

"We'd sneak into gyms all the time," Billmeier said. "He's small, so he'd climb through the window and turn on the lights. We knew the owner. He'd probably kill us if he ever found out. But we'd go there every day after practice and put up 500 more shots, and he'd help me work on my post game. While everybody else was going home after practice, we would ride our bikes to the gym to do it all over again."

It was an admirable, albeit comically unlawful, way of inching their way toward success. While Billmeier sunk into this routine that validated his decision to leave Pennington, his friends back home didn't always show support.

"Definitely, many people wanted me to stay," Billmeier said. "We won the prep state championship my freshman year. And when you make a move like that, going from a gorgeous prep school like Pennington to Elizabeth, people are going to question you and your decision."

It didn't matter. Life was too good at that point, for both Nardi and Billmeier. Despite a sophomore season that ended with a loss to St. Anthony in the state playoffs, they continued to flourish as two of the best high school players in the state and country. The tutelage of Boyle was rubbing off on Billmeier, too, as he developed into one of the few centers in the area who was good for at least ten points and ten rebounds per game.

"(Boyle is) just so intense," Billmeier said. "I never played for someone like him. He was intense every second of every day. You can't take a play off, or else he'll call you out. So if you didn't want to get yelled at in practice you had to bring it every day. He prepared me for college, because in a college practice, if you take one play off you'll find yourself on the second or third team."

Due to his consistent knack for churning out points and rebounds against high-level programs, loads of colleges inquired about Billmeier's interest in their respective schools. Recruiting is always the endgame when it comes to the business side of high school basketball, and Billmeier was starting to realize that once Boyle began counseling the kid he called "G-Banger" through the dialogue.

"He would talk about it with me," Billmeier said. "He made it a point to advise me about going to a school where I'd eventually play and going to a school that should fit my style and all that stuff. But he never said, 'You should go here.' He would suggest some schools that were good with big guys. That definitely helped me."

Picaro also aided Billmeier's quest to land an education at a top-notch college.

"They were both very good students. Mike was always on the First Honor Roll, and Grant eventually made it, too," he said. "But when Grant first came here his father asked if he should be put in the special needs program. They worked it out with guidance, but I wouldn't let it. I guess he cried the blues to his dad, and I relented, begrudgingly. I called Grant into the office and said, 'Grant, if you can't do something on the basketball court, what do you do?'"

"'I work harder, Mr. Picaro.'"

"I said, 'Okay, well, we're going to do the same thing in the classroom.' He needed a little encouragement. He made Second Honor Roll right after that."

Billmeier repaid Picaro in a way that still makes Picaro smile with appreciation.

"When he was a student here he would always come up to me and say how I shouldn't be shoveling my own snow," said Picaro, who still keeps a picture of Nardi and Billmeier posing with his wife in their caps and gowns in his house. "Whenever it snowed, he would come over to shovel the cars out of the driveway."

While Billmeier was planning official visits to Pittsburgh, Rutgers, and Michigan, Nardi had already benefited from growing into a Boyle Guy, the kid who conditioned himself to play four quarters of in-your-face basketball and would run through a wall for the good of the team. In the midst of seeing more and more letters from Division I colleges in the mail, he also took kindly to absorbing any kind of advice from celebrated alumnus Shaheen Holloway, who had just finished his sterling career at Seton Hall University and was trying to stick with any team overseas.

"Shaheen always tried to be around as much as he could, even when he was playing overseas and whatnot," Nardi said. "He always came, always wanted to lend a helping hand. He'd always talk to us and try to help. He knew what it meant to represent St. Patrick. The name on that jersey meant more than anything to him and still does. If it weren't for him, St. Patrick wouldn't be what it is today."

For most of his junior season in 2002, Nardi was sidelined with a broken ankle, but he came back in time for the county tournament and the state playoffs, where the Celtics eventually lost to nationally ranked St. Anthony in the North Non-Public B grand stage. Future Division I players Donald Copeland (Seton Hall), Elijah Ingrim (St. John's, New Mexico) and Terrence Roberts (Syracuse) were just too much to handle. "Their senior experience made them too good," Nardi would say.

That loss caused Nardi to burn. He wanted to win it all in his senior year. "It wasn't just me. It was the entire team," he said. "That summer we worked our butts off. I remember working out all the time. We had this core group of guys who wanted it so bad."

Nardi, Billmeier, Robert Hines and Jai'sen Patterson formed the core of a team nobody could bang around with, one that assistant coach Rae Miller recalled as the toughest the program had probably ever seen.

"We had kids then who were less refined," Miller said, "because they were all bruisers and tough guys. We had to find a way to manage them, too. It was a challenge to do that."

Motivation was never an issue, though. Early-morning workouts consisted of runs to and from the Goethals Bridge, the gateway to Staten Island from the port of Elizabeth, before the homeroom bell rang at school, certainly providing enough concrete evidence of the team's passion.

A jagged zeal for revenge and one last chance to win a state championship also masked how tough an assignment the 2002–03 team proved to be for Boyle. Rae also conceded the staff had many trying days of managing high-profile teens, mostly due to the return of Derrick Caracter, a problem child who began his high school career at St. Patrick as a freshman but opted to attend Scotch Plains the following year.

Caracter arrived at St. Patrick as a 13-year-old trapped in a burly, six-foot-eight, 260-pound frame. The *Star-Ledger* had published a lengthy profile of Caracter the summer before he entered eighth grade. The seed of overwhelming hype was planted, something many thought would turn disastrous for a kid who still carried around a stuffed orangutan named Ollie.

"It was a challenge trying to bring Derrick along because he wasn't a kid that was ready to be coached hard," Rae admitted. "We kind of had to spoon-feed him."

After a magnified decision process that involved a player some claimed was every bit as destined for greatness as LeBron James, Caracter chose St. Patrick for high school. He wore out his welcome rather quickly, failing to adhere to the strict academic and behavioral policies drawn up by Picaro. Chronic tardiness and misbehavior resulted in a yearlong suspension, one that triggered Caracter's exodus from the blanket of Picaro and arrival at his hometown high school, Scotch Plains-Fanwood.

Scotch Plains coach Dan Doherty grew to despise Caracter's immaturity, telling the *New York Times* he remembered his troubled center saying, "I don't understand why I have to be here in math class. I don't need this. I'm just going to go to the NBA."

By the conclusion of his sophomore year, he left Scotch Plains-Fanwood and returned to St. Patrick as a junior in time for Nardi and Billmeier's senior year.

"That was a really good team, though," Rae said. "It was one of the toughest. Everybody knew that once we showed up, you wouldn't mess with us."

This intriguing bunch, which consisted of two hungry leaders, a bevy of apt role players and a headache, started the campaign ranked among the top five in the *USA Today* national poll but lost an early season game to Oak Hill on a neutral court in Texas and then fell to Rice in the City of Palms Classic, dropping the Celtics to 12.

Nardi didn't let his commitment to Villanova alter his desire to win on the team for which he currently played. Billmeier, who had signed with Seton Hall, also embraced his role as cocaptain, anchoring a front line that dominated the paint on a nightly basis. Even Caracter was contributing a great deal, upon finding some peace with Boyle's teachings and Picaro's regulations.

Eventually, the long road ended with the Celtics clinching the Tournament of Champions title by thumping Camden Catholic, 61–38, at the Continental Airlines Arena. Nardi and Billmeier handed the trophy to Picaro's wife, Dorothy, who was battling cancer. It was a moment both Nardi, named the High School Player of the Year by the *Star-Ledger*, and Billmeier called the greatest moment of their young lives.

"Not just winning the game, but all the stuff that went into it," Billmeier said. "I remember coach making us run early in the morning from school all the way to the Goethals Bridge and then back. I remember coach picking me and Mike up at six thirty in the morning for school. We lost in my sophomore and junior years, so it was all that hard work that paid off."

The latest trophy added to the already-crowded case in the corridor near St. Patrick's small school gymnasium was the product of determination and a twist of fate.

"It's just ironic how things worked out," Billmeier said. "There would be no way I'd be able to take the train from Pennington to Elizabeth every day because that's over an hour. Realistically, I wouldn't have been able to go if Mike hadn't moved to that new house."

Nardi was named to the Big East All-Rookie Team as a freshman at Villanova and was the only player to start all 35 games. He averaged 11.8 points as a senior and was a member of the heralded four-guard lineup that also consisted of Allan Ray and NBA mainstays Randy Foye and Kyle Lowry. That team entered the NCAA Tournament as a No.

1 seed and reached the Elite Eight, where the Wildcats fell to eventual champion Florida.

In achieving his goal of playing at a big college also known for sterling academics, Nardi credited Boyle for his success.

"Honestly, that's the guy who made me the player I am today," Nardi said. "He taught me how to work out. He taught me how to be overly dedicated to something, no matter what the job was. If I called him late at night and asked him to shoot around with me and help out with my jumper, he'd say he'd be there in 15 minutes. That's a guy with a wife and three kids, too. He's just the most dedicated, passionate person I've ever met."

Meanwhile, Billmeier thrived at Seton Hall and made his mark as a hard-working big man who cracked the regular rotation during his four-year tenure on the Pirates. In the middle of his sophomore campaign in December 2004, Dorothy Picaro's battle with cancer took a turn for the worse.

"When my wife died, Grant was the last visitor she ever had," Joe Picaro said. "He came from the campus of Seton Hall to the hospital because he really wanted to give her a picture he had in his room of him and Mike handing the Tournament of Champions trophy to her while she was battling cancer.

"She was in an induced coma, and she died hours after he left. I tried to change the subject because I didn't want everyone to cry, and eventually asked him to be a pallbearer. He said, 'I'll be there, Mr. Picaro.' But then I said, 'But wait, you might have a game or practice.' He said, 'I'll be there.'"

Shortly after the funeral, Billmeier played in a televised game. At one point the announcer said, "Even though he's having a good game, Grant Billmeier is playing with a heavy heart because his high school's secretary passed away."

The camera zoomed in on one of the center's sneakers with the words "Mrs. Picaro" written in marker on the side.

"I then get a call from one of my old graduates who lives in Texas to offer his condolences," Joe Picaro said. "I learned this game was nationally televised, because he saw the sneakers. It was just a great tribute to someone who loved St. Patrick basketball and who loved Grant so much."

Billmeier's four-year tenure at Seton Hall included two NCAA tournament appearances. His freshman year concluded with a loss to Mike Krzyzewski's Duke Blue Devils in the second round, but not before upsetting Arizona, which boasted NBAers Andre Iguodala and Channing Frye.

After a down sophomore season, Billmeier and the Pirates were picked to finish 15 out of 16 in the Big East, only to make the Big East Tournament and then fall in the Big Dance to Wichita State, which then defeated No. 2 Tennessee.

"We started out kind of rough, but that's when we had Donald Copeland (of St. Anthony High School). We didn't necessarily have the best talent, but we had guys who came from winning programs and who knew how to close games out and finish strong."

It was Billmeier's way of saying that Bob Hurley, in Copeland's case, and Boyle were to thank for such accomplishment long after they departed high school.

♣

Sitting at his office desk tucked away in the basement of the school upon returning from St. Patrick's strenuous weekend, Kevin Boyle leaned back on his chair and tried to jog his memory regarding the depth of each of his previous teams.

For the first time this year, he was about to find out just how deep his current team was. Just several days after it became official that the Celtics sat atop the current *USA Today* national rankings, Boyle and his team were stuck in an odd place, one that would certainly define their mental toughness.

Chris Martin, who had been so spectacular so quickly in his new surroundings, was sidelined indefinitely with a concussion and was ordered to stay home from school that week while all his teammates underwent their midterm exams and practiced every day in preparation for upcoming games against Elizabeth, Linden, and Union. Chris stayed in Plainfield and sat in bed while watching one movie after another in between reruns of *Martin* and *The Jamie Foxx Show*.

It took nearly two months for the players to learn each other's tendencies and gel well enough to rattle off a victory every time they stepped on the court. Now, the chemistry was altered, leaving Boyle wondering what outcomes would develop without St. Patrick's best shooter.

The Celtics did just fine in their first game without Chris, cruising past Elizabeth, 60–31, thanks to a lockdown defensive effort that held the opposition to three points combined in the second and third quarters. All nine players scored. Michael Kidd-Gilchrist finished with a team-high 17 points, and Derrick Gordon added 13.

Defense remained the one aspect of St. Patrick's identity that never wavered, and that was evident in its 64–40 triumph over Linden the next day. The Celtics held the Tigers, who had knocked them off two years ago at the Dunn Center in Elizabeth, to just 13 for 45 from the floor and capitalized on Mike's near triple-double.

"They defend you all over the court, they don't make anything easy, you don't get an easy shot," Linden coach Phil Colicchio told the *Star-Ledger*. "They showed why they are so good by the way they defended."

Mike ended up with 19 points, 11 rebounds, and eight assists, but his stellar performance in the first half enabled his team to enter the locker room with a commanding 32–21 advantage that only swelled as the game went on.

It appeared life without Chris was not so daunting, after all.

Two wins in two days left the Celtics feeling more confident about their abilities to hold off in-state foes without Chris. But Boyle woke up the next day with the stomach flu and did not make it past his bed before vomiting. It was a brief virus that passed within 24 hours, as he was able to show up to his next game against Union at Plainfield High School.

"One of the pipes froze in my house, too," Boyle halfheartedly laughed, shaking his head after admitting he still was not at full-strength. "I'm just a mess right now."

After a brief exchange with assistant coach Rae Miller about the bug that came over several of his players, he walked into the classroom down the hall from the gymnasium doors and approached the chalkboard. He knew this pregame speech would be loaded with sympathy for the team, as it would be without starting point guard Jarrel Lane, who did not go to school due to a similar illness. He waited for a pale Da'shawn Suber, Jarrel's backup, to finish keeling over the garbage can in the corner from fear of throwing up.

"The *USA Today*, they could give a shit if you're all sick," Boyle said.

"A lot of us have come down with some virus, but we have to grind this one out. There are no excuses if we lose."

Da'shawn listened with his head down on the desk.

"This is the reason why this team is built the way it is," Rae offered, trying to encourage his players. "We're able to sustain injuries. You're good enough to kick anybody's ass. You're probably going to be tested tonight, so we have to look sharp."

"This is a good opportunity for Union," Boyle cautioned. "It's easy for us to come out flat. We're playing in a small gym with a small crowd. Union is a good team; they beat Linden, and I saw them play in the summer. They're definitely good enough to keep it close, hold the ball, and eat a lot of the clock."

Union entered the night with a pedestrian 6–5 record but had lost by just two against Plainfield and four against Seton Hall Prep. Boyle was right. With a win over Linden and several close games in their back pocket, Union was a sneaky club that had potential to make things interesting if the Celtics did not come out firing.

"If you're not sweating in warm-ups, you're not ready to play," Boyle said. "At the start of the game, at the start of the second half, you should be sweating. Most upsets happen when the other team comes out strong and finds a way to go up 14–4 or something. If we get rebounds, run in transition, and find a way to get to the line, that won't happen."

Boyle proved to be prophetic after St. Patrick scored 19 unanswered points to open the game. A new-look starting lineup consisting of Derrick, Da'shawn, Mike, Austin Colbert, and sophomore guard Trevis Wyche pressured Union into missing its first ten attempts before opposing guard Nana Ansah hit a three-pointer with 15 seconds left to cut the deficit to 19–3.

It was ironic, however, that the best quarter of the season was followed by arguably the worst. Union executed a 12–2 run that spanned over four minutes to crawl within 21–12. Mike converted a three-point play upon getting fouled after a layup and then hit a jumper, but another defensive lapse left Chris Foreman wide open for another shot beyond the arc.

Boyle called timeout. With a vein protruding from the side of his neck, Boyle sternly scolded Jason Boswell and Derrick for not communicating on the floor. The brief reminder of talking to each other before switching men on defense did not resonate with the unit on the floor, as Foreman beat Trevis and hit a backdoor layup to make the score 26–17 with 2:21 remaining before the half.

The frustration reached new heights for a seething Boyle when sophomore guard Hakim Saintil, a transfer from St. Anthony in Jersey City, got tied up with his counterpart near the sideline. Both players wrestled for a loose ball, and after the whistle blew, neither relented. The scrum resulted in Hakim shoving the Union player. A double-technical foul was called, and Hakim was immediately taken out of the game.

"Unbelievable," Rae yelled in Hakim's ear as he sat on the first seat on the bench with a stoic look on his face. "Unbelievable!"

The Celtics brought a 29–19 lead with them down the hall and into the near classroom during halftime. They also carried the weight of knowing a potential blowout turned into a close game thanks to eight minutes of shoddy defensive efforts and mental gaffes.

"You're both going for the ball, and the result is a routine jump-ball call. It's completely ridiculous," Boyle said to Hakim with disappointment dripping off every word. "Nobody is punching you or pushing you. It's basketball, for Christ's sake! We talked about this yesterday. You're being too aggressive, and you're fouling way too much."

"And, Austin, you look soft as shit," Boyle continued. "You come out and it's like …"

Boyle's irritation left him unable to finish the sentence.

"If there's any guy who should be pissed off at me, it's him," Boyle said pointing at Austin's backup, Tyrone O'Garro. "He should be thinking about why I should play him more. Tyrone has a right to think, 'Look at my numbers compared to his when I play. Meanwhile, he's going to be at Duke or UCLA, and I'll be playing at Columbia or something.'"

The team was too tightly woven to have certain egos seriously poison its chemistry. The starters respected the reserves and vice versa. After all, friends would not use their status on the depth chart as ill motivation against another friend. Still, Boyle got through to the players with a harsh, yet truthful, comparison.

"You have to think of it like if you're working for me in an office while the economy is bad, and one of you has to go," Boyle said. "But today it's back to the old shit, Austin."

"Derrick, you have to start making shots and looking more confident in your shot," Boyle scolded. "All of you look tired and disinterested. The only guy who's playing hard every day in practice is the best player in the country. Mike's trying to get all of you guys going."

Mike had his head in his hands, noticeably itching for the speech to conclude so the second half could arrive.

"Hakim, the shot you took was not a bad shot," Boyle said. "But if I'm you, I'm looking for the better scorer. I'm thinking, 'Where are the post players?'"

Boyle understood that his younger players were learning on the job. Such was life without Jarrel. Da'shawn, Trevis, and Hakim had been sparingly used throughout the year up to this point, and the trio—all of whom Boyle had privately recognized as the backcourt of the future—found themselves thrown into the fire on the best high school basketball team in the country. What better way to learn, Boyle thought. After all, Shaheen Holloway, Nardi, and Kyrie Irving were in similar positions at one time.

In the third, Mike scored 12 of his game-high 32 points and helped the Celtics pull away with a 20-point lead. Boyle emptied his bench in the fourth, allowing Trevis to handle the point and command enough minutes to accumulate a career-high 11 points.

Moments after the team recorded its thirteenth win in as many games, 66–45, over Union, Boyle took a more passive tone when addressing his players.

"Guys, I'm trying to get you ready for college," Boyle claimed, shrugging his shoulders. "That's why I'm coming down on you all so hard. I see potential in all you guys. For the most part, I thought you did a great job.

"There's not a bad guy on this team. Not one of you is a jerk—there's no criminals, no bad guys. Ten out of 15 of you are in the National Honor Society, for Christ's sake. You're all great people. But, Hakim, we're just repeating ourselves. You have to calm down. Now you're an example in front of the whole team because you can't control your emotions. At halftime in Winter Park, that was the third or fourth time we talked about this. We talked about it yesterday, too. So, you come out the next day and pull that? You're better than that. I know you are."

Hakim unlaced his sneakers slowly while looking at the ground, but he was listening intently.

"A lot of you guys were in an unfamiliar position tonight," Boyle said. "But you have to figure it out. You have to figure out what plays we're running and when—whether it's Kentucky or 1-4-X.

"You're at a stage where he was," Boyle said, making an example of Derrick. "He was low in the pecking order a couple years ago, but as he got older he started to get credit in the house.

"Trevis, you had a good game. That's two in a row for you. You have to know, though, when we're running Power, the ball always goes to the wing. You didn't recognize that in some instances, but you did a nice job."

Trevis might have been a practice player in previous weeks, but this time he felt honored to be recognized in a postgame gathering. He shook his head forward several times and looked over at Da'shawn, whom Boyle walked toward in the second row of desks.

"Sube, you're a good player, but you have to guard people," Boyle said. "You got beat off the dribble four or five times, and it caused us to collapse."

Austin waited for his reassurance. It was a common ground for which the players could always count on their coach.

"I know it's hard to calm down sometimes, but you're all going to get your chance," Boyle said. "To keep minutes you have to produce numbers. This is a business. Austin, maybe your length is more important, but on the other side Tyrone is putting up more productive stats. You need a fire in your belly for Ty to wait another year. I know it's there. I want to see it."

The verdict was in. Boyle learned a lot about players he rarely saw in game situations, but, more importantly, he was pleased to escape with another win despite the ailment that kept Jarrel from suiting up.

"Jarrel is so important because he's an excellent on-ball defender," Boyle said, heading outside, where another fresh coat of snow covered the black pavement of the parking lot. "He knows every set inside and backwards, and that says a lot, since this team runs more sets than most. Tonight we had some guys in different spots, so we just were not cohesive. But Gilchrist was phenomenal. He's working hard for an undefeated season, and that attitude was no different tonight."

Mike, playing like a man possessed, knew his expectations grew on this night. Like many times before, he had to be great.

"I had to be," he said. "Jarrel was out, and Chris was out, so I had to take over. I'm trying to get that championship, and I've got to do what I've got to do in order to get that. It's all about confidence in basketball."

So far, that confidence had taken the team a long way.

SEVEN

I firmly believe the best thing that ever happened to Corey Fisher was getting out of New York and staying with Kevin Boyle. He wouldn't have ended up at Villanova.
—Mike Quick

The alarm clock was buzzing on the nightstand, and Corey Fisher rubbed his eyes after grimacing when he noticed it was time to get up at 4:45 in the morning. The hardheaded freshman in high school hated every bit of it, yet he had no choice but to avoid the snooze button and trudge down the multiple flights of stairs of his building inside the Castle Hill Houses, catch the first of three buses, and make sure he had enough change jingling in his dress-pants pocket to pay for a cab ride.

Fisher was from Castle Hill, an area of the Bronx just minutes away from Yankee Stadium that spreads over two square miles, which had become a lot quieter and safer than it used to be. The cracked asphalt along the crooked sidewalks leading up to the fourteen-building apartment complex distinctly mirrored how this place had been.

Back in the 1970s and 1980s, it wasn't unusual for the 43rd Precinct to call in 50 murders and more than 2,000 burglaries throughout any given year. Over the two decades leading up to Corey's childhood, though, the broken area had cleaned up substantially.

Still, it had its rough spots. Corey was once jumped by two people and required eight stitches on his face. For his mother, Keisha, enough was enough. Her son couldn't have the Bronx as his only image of life. She wanted more for him—the namesake of his great uncle, Guy Fisher, who had fallen into the traps of bad decisions at a young age.

Guy Fisher was a central figure in the drug trade that defined the corrupt times in Harlem. In 1977, he purchased the Apollo Theater and became the first black man to own and operate the world-renowned establishment that hosted the likes of the Jackson 5, Luther Vandross, Marvin Gaye, Aretha Franklin, and Stevie Wonder, among other legendary performers. Guy also was a member of The Council, an African-American crime organization that had a stranglehold on the heroin influx in the city from 1972 to 1983.

One year after making the Apollo Theater his own, fellow racketeer LeRoy "Nicky" Barnes—portrayed by Cuba Gooding Jr. in the hit film starring Denzel Washington, *American Gangster*—was tried and put behind bars for life by Rudolph Giuliani, a prosecutor who eventually became the mayor of New York City. Nearly a year after his conviction, Barnes opted to be a government informant in the pending investigations of Fisher and his organization.

In 1984, Guy was convicted of continuing criminal conspiracy, drug trafficking, and murder, and was sentenced to life in prison without eligibility for parole. He is currently serving a life sentence at the United States Penitentiary Allenwood in Pennsylvania.

Corey, meanwhile, did not meet his great uncle until he was in seventh grade. Since then, Guy had transformed his life behind bars, writing several books of essays and earning a PhD in sociology. He took it upon himself to educate his family on the paths of life: down the good road or down the bad road.

Keisha and Corey's father could not make their marriage work but chose to play influential roles in their son's world. They both agreed to help Corey choose the good road. Part of that choice was enrolling Corey, a talented basketball player, at St. Patrick High School in New Jersey.

He didn't have the grades to get into St. Raymond's High School in the Bronx—"the place I really wanted to go," he would say. Nevertheless, his ultimate destination wasn't exactly a stark contrast to his native city; Elizabeth was widely regarded as one of the most dangerous places in the country. Still, it was far from the South Bronx. That was a good thing for Fisher, and everybody knew it.

So every morning that alarm clock would go off, well before the sun rose, and Corey began his obstacle course of a trip to his new school. Fisher said he knew he had to be at Penn Station no later than 5:15

a.m. He then would take two trains, a bus, and a short cab ride to 221 Court Street to be on time for homeroom.

Principal Joe Picaro desperately wanted Fisher, who was traveling about two hours every morning and evening, to find success in the classroom. He also made it loud and clear if Corey's grades weren't up to par, he couldn't play on the basketball team, which was looking to repeat as Tournament of Champions winners in 2004.

"I wouldn't want people to think we're a bandit school. I remember telling Kevin, don't you ever embarrass St. Patrick or embarrass us. I wanted him to win the right way. I always made sure we understood we are a high school that just so happens to have a good basketball team. And if you don't work, you don't play," Picaro firmly said.

"They were set to play the best team in Pennsylvania, and I suspended three players for bad grades. The team lost by one point. That's just an example of how we've never lost sight of who we are. During the school day, nobody cares about basketball. We always have made sure to treat the players like every other kid in school."

At the beginning of his freshman year, Fisher came to the St. Patrick guidance counselor and said he couldn't read especially well. It was a disguised request to be placed in the special-education program.

"So I picked out a long paragraph of a book to read, and he read it beautifully," Picaro said. "I said, 'This kid can do it.' His freshman year, he got in trouble a lot. Sophomore year, it was the same thing."

Fisher, who was part of the Celtics basketball team in 2004 that failed to win any championships—county, state or Tournament of Champions title—for just the third time since 1995, was evidently struggling to find peace. His routine was anything but normal for a kid, and he was a ticking time bomb on the court. As Mike Quick put it, "It was like you were waiting for the time when Corey Fisher just walked off the court and out of the gym."

A product of an AAU team called the Juice All-Stars, for which Sebastian Telfair once played and Lincoln Coach Dwayne "Tiny" Morton ran, Fisher went by the nickname "Slow Motion" back home. Coincidentally, his progress of developing into a levelheaded player Boyle could count on seemed to be moving in slow motion.

Corey was acting up in school, and his grades were in shambles.

"He was a big pain in the butt," Athletic Director Red Migliore said.

Chris Chavannes was the high school's disciplinarian at that time and eventually told Fisher he was on the brink of being expelled.

"So we were all sitting in the office with his mother and said, 'We're asking you to withdraw Corey from St. Patrick.' Corey interrupted," Picaro said. "He said, 'I don't want to leave.'"

Picaro and Chavannes were stunned.

"He said, 'I like it here,'" Picaro remembered. "We just said how he was always in trouble, he was almost failing three classes, and he just said how much he likes it here. We gave him another chance, and from that moment on, everything changed. He completely turned around."

Corey was suspended for the first 12 games of his sophomore season, one in which the Celtics won the Union County tournament for the second time in three years and the state title for the third time in the decade, but lost in the Tournament of Champions title game to Seton Hall Prep, 63–60.

During that year, he was turning the corner, turning into the person his mother, father, and great-uncle had wanted him to be. Despite the heartbreaking loss to the Pirates on the biggest of stages, Kevin Boyle and the Celtics were back to their winning ways. Fisher's renaissance continued into his junior year, when he was put into the special-needs program and saw his grades vastly improving.

"He just didn't believe in himself academically at the time," Picaro said. "That junior year he was finally able to relax and get educated."

The 2005–06 season was an education in itself for the players of St. Patrick, too. First, the team had to regroup upon learning Derrick Caracter was leaving the school once again to attend Notre Dame Prep in Massachusetts.

The Celtics, who would play nine out-of-state opponents, opened the year with wins over Saints John Neumann and Maria Goretti Catholic High School (Philadelphia) and Glenn High School (Kernersville, North Carolina), but were picked off by Brentwood Academy (Tennessee), 63–56. They rattled off six consecutive victories over a span of three weeks but once again were stunned.

Christian Brothers Academy, an in-state foe, and Rice High School of New York City posted back-to-back one-point, upset triumphs over St. Patrick. Boyle and company rebounded by constructing a ten-game winning streak before suffering their final setback of the season, a 60–55 loss to Episcopal Academy (Newton Square, Pennsylvania) on February 11.

Fisher and his sidekick, a fellow All-State candidate named Jeff Robinson, helped the Celtics notch a 65–52 win over Plainfield in the Union County championship and then cruised past Newark Academy in the first round of the NJSIAA state playoffs. Those wins afforded the Celtics a chance to face rival St. Anthony in the North Non-Public B finals.

In that contest, Boyle further established himself as a fellow resident on the paramount of high school basketball coaching when he thwarted Bob Hurley and the Friars, 41–32, at St. Peter's College. One could argue that moment became Fisher and Robinson's induction into St. Patrick lore. They took down the rival and became everlasting heroes.

St. Patrick easily handled Wildwood Catholic, 83–57, to capture the overall Non-Public B crown for the second straight year. Once the Tournament of Champions came about, the Celtics ran past Haddonfield by 24 points and punched their ticket for the final against Linden.

Thanks to a 17-point performance by Fisher, St. Patrick squeezed past the Tigers, 61–54, and won its second Tournament of Champions crown in four years and third overall under the direction of Boyle. Mike Nardi and Grant Billmeier were no longer the last Celtic legends to unlock the keys to a title; Fisher and Robinson had earned that legacy.

In that contest, Fisher received a ton of support as senior Yves Mbala—a six-foot-seven forward who ended up at LaSalle—earned the MVP award by scoring 15 points and grabbing 11 rebounds, while Ruben Guillendeaux chipped in 14.

The storybook ending enabled the Celtics to finish the season No. 11 in *USA Today*. Fisher, who averaged 14.9 points and 4.2 assists, was named the New Jersey Player of the Year by the *Star-Ledger*.

"Corey was his own player," teammate Paris Bennett said. "So many guys could play like Allen Iverson or something, but Corey Fisher was Corey Fisher. He was athletic, he was kind of on the stronger side, and he knew how to use his body."

He also knew how to win, not just against the odds of being raised in a rough neighborhood but on the hardwood. The following year proved that even more.

Fisher began his last year of high school completely different than the way he began his first.

"I didn't like him the first time I saw him. You could tell he could play, but of any kid under Kevin Boyle, Corey matured the most over four years," Mike Quick said. "His senior year, I think he realized, 'I've got to do other things.'

"I challenged him when I put him on the first team of the Tri-State All-Star Team as a junior, saying, 'If you act next year like you do, you won't be on this team. I can promise you that.' I never saw a kid grow up as fast as he did. He was a great player who matured more than any other kid."

That maturation enabled Boyle to count on his senior All-American candidate to act as a leader during practice and games. Fisher desperately wanted a repeat Tournament of Champions title run because he wanted to go out on a good note, perhaps triggering those in the St. Patrick community to remember him as arguably the greatest player to ever step onto the court in a Celtics uniform.

Sure, Al Harrington and Samuel Dalembert were in the NBA and nobody could ever touch the legacy Shaheen Holloway had left, but it was feasible to label Fisher as one of the best, in terms of offensive abilities.

His spike of production at school also enabled him to follow in Nardi's footsteps, earning a scholarship at Villanova for the fall of 2007. Comforted by the thought of attending college, Fisher focused on willing his team to another historical campaign as a senior.

The Celtics kicked off the year with six straight wins—two against out-of-state opponents—before falling to DeMatha (Hyattsville, Maryland), 57–49, on December 30, 2006. After that, Fisher and company rolled through their schedule with ease, including a showdown with No. 1 St. Benedict's Prep, a game in which Robinson drilled four three-pointers and netted 21 points en route to a 66–60 victory. They went on to defeat five additional non-New Jersey teams, including

Huntington Prep of West Virginia. In that matchup with future NBA player O. J. Mayo, St. Patrick stole a 78–76 thriller in overtime thanks to a 37-point outburst from Fisher.

"His senior year, he did things that were as great as anything I've ever seen from any player ever," Quick recalled.

At that point, the Celtics were just a handful of wins away from finishing as the top basketball team in the nation in 2007. It was a milestone that Boyle promised to Red Migliore and Picaro two decades earlier and that would bolster his reputation.

Coming off the victory over Mayo and Huntington Prep that put St. Patrick atop the national poll, Boyle and his crew had to face Linden in the Union County tournament final two days later.

Linden garnered the reputation as a tough, well-coached team that always amped up its play whenever St. Patrick was the opponent. The Tigers possessed a strong core in junior point guard Desmond Wade and seniors Muhammad Wilkerson, Darrell Lampley, and Jerry Jones, but that group didn't exactly appear on the same level as Fisher, Robinson, point guard Dexter Strickland, fellow sophomore Paris Bennett, and big man Quintrell Thomas.

Perhaps that's why the 63–51 thrashing that Linden posted against St. Patrick was so puzzling to the public. How could the top team in the nation be upset in the Union County tournament, a playoff bracket the Celtics used as a proverbial layup line for the state playoffs?

Fisher's dream, however, wasn't derailed completely. St. Patrick licked its wounds and rebounded with a 91–35 win over Morristown-Beard and another blowout victory against St. Mary of the Assumption. It was déjà vu all over again, as Hurley and the St. Anthony Friars were waiting in the wings to duke it out for the North Non-Public B state crown on March 7 at Rutgers University.

As it turned out, Boyle got the best of Hurley for the second straight year as the Celtics walked away with a convincing 62–46 triumph. Corey's impact on the history of St. Patrick's basketball program was summed up nicely by none other than Hurley himself. The Hall of Fame coach finished shaking the hands of each of Boyle's boys, approached Fisher and offered one thought: "I'm so glad you're graduating."

The Celtics rode that momentum through the rest of the state playoffs and Tournament of Champions, ultimately finishing the

2006–07 season dancing in the middle of the Continental Airlines Arena court after thumping Bloomfield Tech, 85–61, for the program's second straight TOC crown and fourth overall under Boyle's watch.

Fisher, who averaged 22.3 points, 6.1 rebounds, and eight assists that year, had done his job. Meanwhile, Jeff Robinson—a Memphis commit—was named the Gatorade Player of the Year. The two formed a duo no other team could match, at least in New Jersey.

Though the loss to Linden extinguished the hopes of ending up No. 1 in the country, St. Patrick finished No. 2. That incredible accomplishment wouldn't have been possible without registering wins over St. Anthony, St. Benedict's Prep, and Seton Hall Prep, the three other Garden State juggernauts who combined to post an 83–3 record. All three losses were to Boyle. The large gap between St. Patrick and the other big-time programs in arguably the nation's most talented state was enough for *USA Today* to hand Boyle its annual National Coach of the Year award.

In two decades, Boyle went from being the unlucky individual strapped with the unpleasant task of managing misfits on a losing team of a distressed program to holding the first-rate distinction of the best coach in America.

Corey Fisher went on to Villanova and enjoyed a four-year career as a stellar scorer for head coach Jay Wright. Fisher made an immediate impact as a freshman and helped the Wildcats reach the Sweet 16 of the NCAA Tournament. He grew into his role as a sophomore, when he sparked a trip to the Final Four. In his junior year, he became the 52nd Villanova player to reach the 1,000-point mark.

In November of 2010, Fisher was selected to be featured on the cover of *Sports Illustrated*, along with BYU's Jimmer Fredette and Kansas State's Jacob Pullen. The cover, which portrayed the three superstars as animated superheroes, evidently raised more awareness of Fisher's abilities, since he finished in the final ten candidates for the Bob Cousy Award as a senior.

Below a cartoon of Fisher crossing his arms while wearing a dark blue Villanova jersey, the caption read: "Can a Streetball Legend Become a Champion?"

It was a valid question, because even before Fisher became one of the most popular players in college basketball, he was a so-called celebrity on the playgrounds of New York City, especially on the hallowed grounds of Rucker Park.

The historic park was named after a Harlem teacher and playground director for the New York City Parks Department, Holcombe L. Rucker, who started a basketball tournament in 1950. The original court used for that inaugural tournament was on Seventh Avenue between 128th and 129th Streets.

Now, it is located at 155th Street and Frederick Douglas Boulevard in Harlem, across the street from the former Polo Grounds site. Back in the 1960s and 1970s, Wilt Chamberlain, Kareem Abdul-Jabbar, and Julius Erving would play the best kids to never make it to the NBA. Eventually, players such as Kenny Anderson, Rafer "Skip to my Lou" Alston, Stephon Marbury, Sebastian Telfair, and many others followed. Ask anybody in the basketball world about Rucker Park. An unrivaled history never left the place.

Legend has it that in 1978, James "Fly" Williams, a Brooklyn product, scored 100 points in a single game. The former Austin Peay State University standout was a first-round pick of the Denver Nuggets in the 1974 ABA draft. He then was sold to the Spirits of St. Louis, a team for which Bob Costas announced games. After the NBA/ABA merger, Williams ended up without a team but was selected in the ninth round of the 1976 NBA draft by the Philadelphia 76ers.

Corey Fisher, meanwhile, trumped that mind-boggling performance in an organized summer league game at Watson Gleason Playground in the Bronx the summer going into his senior year of college.

He scored 105 of his team's 138 points and hit 23 of 28 from behind the arc in a 138–130 win over GymRatsNYC. It was just a little sample of what Fisher was capable of, a majestic example of how special was the kid who left the city for a better life and truly blossomed under the guidance of Boyle.

"I firmly believe the best thing that ever happened to Corey was getting out of New York and staying with Kevin Boyle," Quick said. "He wouldn't have ended up at Villanova."

♣

The calendar changed from January to February in the middle of a spurt during which St. Patrick built off of its big win over Union on January 25, 2011. Still without Chris Martin due to a concussion, the Celtics recorded victories over Newark Tech, Cranford, and Newark Tech again—by scores of 78–50, 84–29, and 79–55, respectively—to run their record to an unblemished 16–0.

February 3 brought Boyle and company to Plainfield High School to take on the Cardinals for the second time that season. Plainfield presented an ample test, considering its depth of talent, which included point guard Sekou Harris, Justin Sears, and Jahmal Lane—all Division I prospects.

The packed house was there to watch their Cardinals take on the No. 1 program in the country, which consisted of several Plainfield residents. Taylor Plummer and Derrick Gordon were originally from the Union County city, and Michael Kidd-Gilchrist and Chris had stayed with the Plummers on occasion.

Clinging to a 35–25 advantage at the half, Boyle was a tad irritated about his team's inability to own the offensive glass and limit its turnovers.

"First of all, you're not rebounding like Michael Gilchrist can," Boyle said. "Also, we have to start using common sense. If we split the guards on offense and the little guy ends up guarding Mike somehow, we have to notice that. How do we not find him?"

Mike bowed his head in disappointment, not just about his mistakes but because this marked the first game in which he hadn't cracked the starting lineup.

Two days prior to tip-off, New Jersey was hit with a dangerous ice storm that ravaged the northern part of the state. Mike had slept over at the Plummers' house, but he and Taylor felt their ride to make practice wasn't safe. "It's just a policy we have, outside of a medical issue or a funeral," Boyle said of his rule about drawing up his starting lineup if a player misses practice.

"Guys, this game is far from over. We're only up 10," Boyle sternly said. "I think they're going to come out with a triangle-and-two on Mike. Let's see if they actually do it."

"Mike and Derrick, on these plays don't be afraid to curl a little bit to the corner when we're running Detroit," Boyle blurted, feverishly scribbling on the marker board. "We'll find some shots that way. You can still run Power 2, Utah, or Detroit, but you have to pay attention."

The Celtics came out in the third firing on all cylinders and eventually paved the way for a 77–56 victory.

"Believe me, we played a good game," Boyle said to his players afterward. "We just have to keep our composure and concentrate. Your defense creates the offense. I've had some new ideas with what we're going to do in the near future. I didn't want to show them tonight unless we absolutely needed to against a triangle-and-two."

As Mrs. Plummer strolled into the locker room with a tray of cupcakes decorated with green icing and green sprinkles, Boyle spoke about the possibility of Chris visiting his doctor and getting clearance to practice.

"Ideally, we'd like to have him back for the St. Thomas More game on the 13th," he said. "He's seeing the doctor tomorrow and also may need a custom-made mask, so that could take some time."

While Chris was still healing, Derrick took it upon himself to make up for his teammate's absence. The Western Kentucky-bound shooting guard posted 26 points—16 in the first half—and drilled five three-pointers.

"It was really important," Gordon said when asked about building an early lead. "This was an away game in a hostile environment. Before the game we said we needed to come out and throw the first punch."

"After the first couple I knew I was in the zone. That's probably my best performance this year outside the City of Palms game. I didn't know how good I'd feel before the game. I just wanted to go out there and show the town how much better I've gotten, because I still have people telling me how I shouldn't have gone to St. Pat's. People thought I'd never play here, so I should just stay at Plainfield. I showed them."

He once again showed the ability to forget any off-the-court disturbances, too. Several nights earlier the ice storm meant the scheduled trip to see his brother at a correctional facility in Bordentown had to be put on hold. In addition, he walked out of practice onto the sidewalk of Court Street to find the passenger's side window of his car smashed in.

When the police arrived, one of the cops asked about the team and how its season was coming along. The officer finished writing up the police report, and as he handed it to Derrick, he cracked a smile and said: "I guess Boyle's still got it."

(Photo courtesy of Grant Billmeier)

(Photo courtesy of Dean Kowalski)

(Photo courtesy of Adrienne Accardi)

(Photo courtesy of Dean Kowalski)

(Photo courtesy of Dean Kowalski)

(Photo courtesy of Adrienne Accardi)

(Photo courtesy of Adrienne Accardi)

(Photo courtesy of Adrienne Accardi)

(Photo courtesy of Adrienne Accardi)

(Photo courtesy of Adrienne Accardi)

(Photo courtesy of Adrienne Accardi)

(Photo courtesy of Adrienne Accardi)

(Photo courtesy of Adrienne Accardi)

(Photo courtesy of Adrienne Accardi)

(Photo courtesy of Adrienne Accardi)

(Photo courtesy of Adrienne Accardi)

(Photo courtesy of Adrienne Accardi)

(Photo courtesy of Adrienne Accardi)

(Photo courtesy of Adrienne Accardi)

(Photo courtesy of Dean Kowalski)

Eight

The position I'm in both academically and athletically is 100 percent attributed to Kevin Boyle and St. Patrick High School. I wouldn't trade anything about my experience with him for anything.
—Dean Kowalski

Like so many times before, Michael Kidd-Gilchrist was there for his St. Patrick teammates when they needed their All-American the most.

With the Celtics up just five points with six minutes to go in a game against Linden, the Kentucky-bound small forward connected on a much-needed three-pointer to create some separation and ultimately squash the opponent's hope of pulling off an upset of the top-ranked team in America.

After the game Boyle spoke about Linden's improvement from the last time the Celtics faced their Union County rival. Playing a team several times during the regular season affords the chance to make adjustments, and that's exactly what the Tigers did. So much so that Kevin Boyle shrugged and said, "It's definitely not impossible that we could lose."

Mike spearheaded the late surge, which paved the way for a too-close-for-comfort 56–43 win, and finished with 23 points and 14 rebounds to complement another twenty-plus-point outing by Derrick Gordon.

Three nights later, St. Patrick put away Elizabeth High School with a sizzling 22–8 run in the second quarter and walked away with a 76–44 victory that inflated its record to 19–0. Dakari Johnson posted 11 points and 10 rebounds, further proving the freshman center climbed over the rookie wall that hampered him for a short stretch after the team's first trip to Florida.

As Chris Martin returned from a nine-game absence since suffering a concussion during a win over Bishop Gorman at the Hall of Fame Invitational in Springfield, Massachusetts, it seemed as if the rich were getting richer.

Boyle's boys felt Chris's presence right away; it was like he hadn't missed any time. Arguably the best shooter in the state, Chris drilled four three-pointers and registered 14 points in a game during which the Celtics got off to a 16–3 run and stretched their lead to 52–20 at the half of a blowout victory over Union.

Surviving without Chris was the most difficult hurdle the team had faced yet, signifying the road to a national championship was smoothly paved.

"It's wonderful what's being accomplished," Principal Joe Picaro said. "The pressure put on a team to be number one in the country, I wondered if, sooner or later, it was going to get to them."

At that point, the guys kept a level head and adhered to Boyle's one-game-at-a-time reminders. It also helped that St. Patrick players, budding celebrities in the high school basketball universe, never had the chance to inflate their egos during school hours.

"It was pronounced this year, but we always tried to stay even-keeled," Picaro stated. "I bet 50 kids in this school don't know we have a good basketball team. I went to Sacred Heart Academy and averaged something like 40 points a game whenever we played St. Patrick. I thought I was popular. Meanwhile, I was nothing. You've got (players now) signing autographs. But we try to keep the kids from feeling it. I think the players like it because it makes them feel like just one of the boys. There's no special treatment."

That may have been the case, but the Celtics certainly were looked upon as a special team across the country, perhaps more so than any other under Boyle's direction.

♣

Blowback Productions, the company that chose to film the St. Patrick basketball team throughout the 2010–11 season for a spot on HBO, was created by Marc Levin, along with Daphne Pinkerson, in 1988.

The company had made more than 20 films, which won Emmys and many other awards.

Over the years Blowback developed a reputation for producing hard-hitting documentaries, including one entitled *Mr. Untouchable* about LeRoy "Nicky" Barnes—the New York drug lord who snitched to government officials and put Guy Fisher, Corey Fisher's great uncle, behind bars for life.

Another was called *Triangle: Remembering the Fire*, about the 100th anniversary of the Triangle shirtwaist factory fire of 1911, which turned out to be the deadliest disaster in New York City until two planes flew into the World Trade Center buildings 90 years later.

September 11, 2001, had a direct effect on the Boyle family. Kevin Boyle's wife, Kelly, was part of a family that consisted of Irish cops and firemen from New York. Her uncle, Tom Kelly, a member of Engine 4 Ladder 15, was killed on that fateful day inside the World Trade Center, the same building in which he proposed to his wife while he was an iron worker.

"The FBI contacted us a year later because they found the tapes of Port Authority and he was the last voice on the tape," Kelly said. "He was transporting people from elevators downstairs. Moments later, the building collapsed."

Kevin and Kelly met at a T.G.I. Friday's on a Sunday night. Kevin's close childhood friend Jerry Hobbie and his parents had lived next to the chain restaurant, and it was "kind of a happening place for us," according to Boyle. Their pal Mike Brown had left for the night, but Kevin decided to stay because he was working up the courage to talk to a pretty girl he scouted out across the bar.

"I took a shot," Kevin bashfully said with a smile.

Fast-forward 23 years later and Kevin and Kelly had built a wonderful home for three children who understood the importance of family—just like his father Neil taught his children when they were at young ages. Becoming a father was an accomplishment that made Boyle more proud than any Coach of the Year award ever could, and that feeling heightened when he got the chance to coach his own son, Kevin Jr., in high school.

Kevin Jr., ironically, wasn't a spitting image of his father on the court; he measured several inches shorter than him but usually maintained his spot as one of the quickest and most athletic point guards on the floor during any given game. He was a pass-first player, a creator who understood his team increased its chances of winning if his teammates—several All-State candidates—were taking the shots instead of him. As Kevin Jr. grew up, it was evident he'd translate into an athlete with plenty of potential to help the nationally ranked school on the varsity level someday.

"My dad's been coaching there since before I was born, so my life has always revolved around it," Kevin Jr. said. "I've always had such a sense of pride for it."

But one year before Kevin Boyle Jr. enrolled at St. Patrick, his father welcomed three freshmen into his program who worked harder than any other players who put on a Celtics uniform and ultimately walked away with the most sterling legacy in St. Patrick history.

Paris Bennett could've enrolled at Linden High School in his hometown, but he knew he wouldn't get the same education—on the court and in the classroom—had he not opted to choose St. Patrick.

"I thought about St. Pat's and its history," he said. "Those guys are always able to showcase their talents at a high level. I wanted that."

The six-foot-six forward also recognized he was about to embark on a journey in which the best high school basketball coach in America would guide him along the way.

"He's a straight-faced tough guy," Bennett said of Boyle. "You can see he's tight when he's coaching. But off the court, he goes out of his way to help kids. He gave me the opportunity to work with little kids by letting me work at his camps."

Boyle was always an advocate of getting his own players involved with his camps during the summer. It would enable his teenagers to gain some work experience and learn lessons about helping others; he also figured it would give them more time on the court and prepare them for becoming better players themselves.

"He would say, 'You need to do this, and you need to do that to get to the next level,'" Bennett said. "He always had his hand in helping me."

Dean Kowalski, meanwhile, never forgot his first impression of Boyle. The tiny point guard attended the Kevin Boyle Basketball Camp as a young kid, hoping to learn from one of the most prominent coaches in the country and improve his skills enough to quell the disadvantage of his lack of height.

Dean came from a great family and grew up in the affluent suburb of Westfield, a stark contrast to the city in which Boyle coached. After getting past the culture shock of the Elizabeth area—an experience he called, "unbelievable; it was really something else"—he also absorbed the feeling of being in the presence of a true hoops guru.

"The first time I ever saw him was when I went to his camps in elementary school," Kowalski said. "In front of the whole camp he was doing drills, dribbling series, and he'd be sweating. His energy excited me, and he brought that every day at St. Pat's."

Kowalski had planned on attending Seton Hall Prep for several years leading up to ninth grade. He even earned a scholarship there for accumulating such high scores on his high school entrance exams. But in the summer he would play in a highly competitive league as a member of the Jersey City Boys Club with multiple St. Anthony players. Boyle also ran a team within the same league, and Kowalski got to know the St. Patrick coach and his way of handling players. It was something that attracted the point guard right away.

"Then my dad and I just ran with the St. Pat's decision."

Kowalski received several indicators he had made the right choice. The most glaring sign that he was surrounded by good people came when Boyle offered to pick him up from school because Rahway was in close proximity to Westfield. "Before I started driving, he drove to my house every day to pick me up for school," Kowalski said. "He was always there for me."

Bennett and Kowalski instantly became good friends and helped the Celtics jayvee squad to a winning record during their freshman years. They weren't ready for the rigors of Boyle's varsity practices or national schedule just yet, but they believed their time would come. Little did they know, with the help of a classmate named Dexter Strickland, that their time on the varsity would produce such drastic accomplishments.

Dexter attended St. Patrick Academy, the grammar school one building to the left of the high school, because his mother wasn't happy with his performance in the public-school system.

"She stuck him here to straighten his butt out," St. Patrick Principal Joe Picaro said. "His report card came out here, and she reamed him out because I guess his grades weren't up to her standards. He had great guidance by his parents. His upbringing was great."

During Dexter's freshman year in high school he played on the jayvee squad for Chris Chavannes, a tough disciplinarian who served as the assistant principal. One game against St. Raymond's in the Bronx, Picaro and Athletic Director Red Migliore arrived at halftime and took their seats. On the first play of the second half, Dexter tried dribbling through two defenders and had the ball stripped. Chavannes immediately took his point guard out of the game and pointed toward the end of the bench.

"Dexter was one of the most athletic kids you've ever seen, but coaches made it clear he was going to play the way he was supposed to and not the way he wanted to," Picaro remembered.

The demons inside Strickland's head kept him from maturing into a savvy floor general. As a sophomore in 2007, Dexter was moved up to the varsity because Boyle sensed Dexter would eventually blossom with some encouragement and hard-nosed learning experiences against high-level competition.

However, Dexter's supporters in the stands were always urging him to shoot the ball as soon as he got it in his hands, instead of making wise decisions. Everyone loves a ball hog when that ball hog has the ability to orchestrate something special every time he touches the ball.

"He felt some pressure to satisfy everyone for some reason," Picaro said. "So, I said to him, 'You need to relax and have fun. This is high school basketball. So what if you don't score?' And after that, he played so much better."

Picaro's supervision and Boyle's teachings molded Strickland into one of the best players in the state.

"I'd catch myself in the middle of games just watching him because he was about to do something spectacular," Bennett said.

"Dexter was extremely talented," Kowalski added. "He was extremely athletic, but in the beginning it was kind of up and down for him. Coach Chavannes is a hard-ass; he doesn't take shit from anybody."

It all clicked; just in time, too. By the end of the 2007 season, the Celtics were in a tough spot because Corey Fisher and Jeff Robinson had just played their final game in St. Patrick uniforms. That left a gaping hole in the team, forced to restructure and redefine its core at a time when Bob Hurley's St. Anthony Friars were prepared to trot out multiple Division I superstars the following campaign.

"With all due respect to the other coaches, players, and teams, they are not going to lose," Boyle told ESPN.com during the season. "We had the senior leadership last year, and they have it this year."

Dexter certainly possessed enough pizzazz on the offensive end to anchor a guard-oriented offense. Would it be enough to compete in 2007–08? Certainly, but many wondered if the point guard, Paris Bennett, Dean Kowalski, and a cast of ample supporting-role players comprised a championship-caliber roster.

As it turned out, that campaign ended with St. Anthony squashing St. Patrick's three-peat run by cruising to a 64–52 win in the North Non-Public B title game. The Celtics entered having won four of the previous six meetings, including the 62–46 triumph in the same game in 2007. Boyle still maintained a 7–5 record against Hurley, so the end result of this particular season didn't solve anything; the rivalry just continued.

"People ask me where I went to high school," Bennett said, "and sometimes I get a face that says, 'Oh, yeah, you played real *basketball*.'"

Entering his senior year, Strickland established himself as the Celtics' leader. He was a consensus All-State pick and had a chance of becoming an All-American. His unrivaled way of dealing with the media set him apart as well.

"When the team was playing in a tournament down in Texas, he was being interviewed after the game, and he constantly addressed the guy who was interviewing him, 'Yes, sir. No, sir.' He always said all the right things," Picaro said. "The interviewer even commented on-air about how well Dexter conducts himself."

The 2008–09 season was shaping up to be a year in which St. Patrick would shake off its loss to the Friars and aim for a fifth Tournament of Champions title. Nobody counted the Celtics out, simply because Dexter was Dexter.

"He was a big-moment guy. When they needed him, he was there," Mike Quick recalled. "He was a great teammate because he wouldn't average a boatload of points even though he could've. He was a lot of fun to watch. He was very, very good because he played with a team concept. He's mature, very pleasant, and very respectful. It's this way with many of Kevin's guys, but he was always very pleasant to speak with."

The rest of Boyle's team was filled with admirable kids, too. When Bennett was serving as the unsung hero on the court, he played the lead in the school play, *Willy Wonka and the Chocolate Factory*, and always carried himself as a role model. One piece of concrete evidence of Bennett's character was his voice mail automated message, which ended with, "God bless."

Quick and fellow MSG Network broadcaster Jimmy Cavallo would call Bennett "Willy Wonka" but also respected how he kept the Celtics as a tight-knit group. They all supported each other, no matter the individual talent level, and appreciated Strickland for who he was as a person and player.

"Dexter's like a brother to me," Bennett said. "I've known him ever since we were in diapers. We played AAU together as kids, and what's better than playing high school basketball together? He has incredible drive and a will to win. Every game we lost in high school he would cry. It hurt him a lot. You can still see that to this day. He scraps every day."

Scrapping until the end was the Boyle way, the creed of a nationally ranked high school basketball team about to begin another year with hopes of hoisting another trophy. That goal seemed even more feasible when the Celtics learned of a new transfer about to enroll at St. Patrick, a player who would end up being one of the best in the state's history.

NINE

He took me in even though he never saw me play. Not every coach would do something like that. ... Coach Boyle played a big influence on my career.
—Kyrie Irving

Drederick Irving grabbed a drink and closed the glass refrigerator door. Boston University's hotshot basketball star casually walked toward the counter of the convenience store and stopped dead in his tracks. He had to meet her.

A sophomore who had helped the Terriers reach the National Invitation Tournament in 1986, Drederick was looking at Elizabeth, a Boston University freshman on the volleyball team. After the two spoke, from there they formed an unbreakable bond and eventually paved the way to get married soon after their graduations.

After leaving Boston University as the school's all-time leading scorer at that time in 1988, Drederick was unable to ink a professional contract, so he and Elizabeth moved to Puyallup, Washington. However, he would receive the phone call he wanted as the Bulleen Boomers of Melbourne, Australia, requested his services. With one child in the house, a daughter named Asia, the opportunity to cash in on some more money couldn't hurt.

While living in Australia in March of 1992, the couple welcomed another baby into their family, this time a boy named him Kyrie, which translates to 'Lord' in Greek. By thirteen months, Kyrie was dribbling a basketball. By age three he was shooting on a regulation-sized hoop.

Four years later, Drederick, Elizabeth, Asia, and Kyrie moved back to the States and settled in Tacoma, just outside Seattle. But on

September, 8, 1996, the Irving family was rocked when Elizabeth died suddenly from sepsis syndrome, an inflammatory condition linked to whole body infection.

Mourning the loss of Elizabeth, Drederick, Asia, and Kyrie packed their lives in the Northwest and moved to the South Bronx in New York, the place Drederick grew up, and eventually landed in New Jersey. Drederick was still playing ball, and he would have his little ones watch him play in pro-am or adult leagues, a trip they always enjoyed—especially Kyrie.

By the time Kyrie turned nine, he had taken a strong liking to the game his father loved and used as an enjoyable distraction from the pain of losing the love of his life so tragically. Sometimes Kyrie would play with kids from the city as part of the New York Gauchos AAU program, prompting pep talks from Drederick that sent an important message: don't back down from anyone.

Over time, white sheetrock inside a bedroom closet served as the personal diary for Kyrie, an ambitious fourth-grader.

The two biggest goals, which he wrote in a place out of sight from the doorway, had to do with basketball becoming the biggest part of his life someday. He used notches to mark his height and swore he'd grow to be at least six foot four. He had to beat his father, who stood at six foot three. That was one mission. The other was the only one that truly mattered to him, the only one over which he had full control.

"I'm going to the NBA," he wrote. "Promise."

The never-ending doses of encouragement from Drederick resonated with Kyrie, who grew to be a skinny six-foot point guard about to begin his high school basketball career at Montclair Kimberley Academy, a posh private school.

Athletically speaking, Montclair Kimberley Academy's softball team had been the most publicized sport at the school because it had captured eight Non-Public B crowns from 2000 to 2009. The Cougars basketball team, however, was not nearly as prominent simply because of its standing among rival schools that offered mediocre competition. Let's just say Bob Hurley didn't toss and turn in bed thinking about MKA.

Nevertheless, Kyrie brought attention to the hoops program in leading Montclair Kimberley Academy to the Prep B championship by defeating Collegiate Prep, 82–59, on February 19, 2008, as a sophomore. He had scored 11 of his game-high 32 points over the final three minutes, 22 seconds of the third quarter, finished with 14 rebounds, and totaled five steals. The school's only 1,000-point scorer, Irving was accomplishing in two years what many couldn't in four during their high school tenures.

"Kyrie beat us on a fallaway jumper at the buzzer in the state playoffs," said Sandy Pyonin, who had coached Solomon Schechter and trained Irving in the offseason throughout high school. "I saw the potential right away."

Kyrie's was an interesting case in which arguably one of the best players in the state was hidden in the shadows of a meek institution with little to no chance of piquing the interest of newspapers or other media outlets.

"We're a small school," Cougars coach Chris Jones told the *Star-Ledger* after the Prep championship game. "The kids understand what they have to do to win. Kyrie is a pretty special player and there's no jealousy."

Still, the eyes he drew to the small school didn't compare to those more interested in watching Hurley's St. Anthony Friars run away with the 2008 Tournament of Champions title.

Kyrie, along with Drederick, saw he had a future as a possible high Division I player. That much was certain, considering Kyrie's slender and athletic build, knack for scoring at will, and making the men of varsity basketball in the Garden State look like boys.

In order to maximize his potential, though, Kyrie would need to play against the best competition—not just locally, but nationally. He had been working out with Pyonin, a basketball guru who operated out of a small gym in Union, New Jersey. Pyonin had previously helped the likes of Al Harrington, Bobby Hurley, and Randy Foye. Irving decided on another drastic alteration: leave Montclair Kimberley Academy and its Ivy League image for a basketball mecca.

Despite a roster that had already included All-American senior point guard Dexter Strickland, a Mr. Everything forward in Paris Bennett, and freshman sensation Michael Kidd-Gilchrist, Kevin Boyle welcomed Kyrie to the St. Patrick family.

"He took me in even though he never saw me play," Irving said of transferring before his junior year. "Not every coach would do something like that."

The transfer opened the eyes of tristate hoops junkies and even surprised some media members. Could St. Patrick really become any more stacked with superstars?

"I played on the same AAU team as (Irving), so I knew who he was," Bennett said, "but I was hearing how good he was. I didn't see it. I didn't see it until he got here. I knew, with the team we already had, we were going to end up on top. I figured there's no way we'd lose very much with Dexter, Kyrie, Gilchrist, Dean (Kowalski), and everybody else."

Corey Fisher and Jeff Robinson had graduated the year before, leaving gaping holes in the lineup. Boyle had also gone through a 2008 season in which the Celtics walked away with just a county championship and no three-peat trophy when it came to the state playoffs and Tournament of Champions.

Kyrie was a breath of fresh air, an All-State candidate with dreams of playing college basketball one day. Those types of athletes always seemed to walk through the doors of St. Patrick, mostly because they realized their potential and asked Boyle to harness their skills in time for the next level. This was always a beneficial give-and-take for both parties. Kyrie, meanwhile, knew his part. He was to help Boyle keep the team among the best in high school basketball across the country, while anchoring a Tournament of Champions title run.

It turned out he did that and so much more. For those who weren't familiar with Kyrie, they soon would hear the name over and over. The Kyrie Irving Show was no longer New Jersey's best-kept secret.

"I said there is no way this kid can be as good as everybody was saying he was," Mike Quick had said. "All those people were wrong. He was better."

Irving was forced to sit out the first 12 games of the 2008–09 season, a campaign that couldn't come quick enough for Boyle and the Celtics program. St. Anthony ran away with the Tournament of Champions the year before and crushed the three-peat quest for St. Patrick, which had won back-to-back championships in 2006 and 2007. The sooner a chance came to override a black spot in the program's history, the better.

Given the plethora of talent the Celtics possessed, the 2009 Tournament of Champions crown was Boyle's to lose once again. Dexter Strickland, the All-American point guard, was to be the straw that stirred the drink, but since Corey Fisher graduated and moved on to Villanova in 2007, St. Patrick had lacked a surefire, big-time finisher to complement its North Carolina-bound star. Irving seemed skilled enough to possibly fill that void, judging by his increase in height—he grew to six foot two, still two inches shorter than his childhood goal—and his track record at Montclair Kimberley.

To the credit of Strickland and Irving, a point-guard controversy didn't present itself in the early stages of the season, even with fellow floor generals Kevin Boyle Jr. and Dean Kowalski on the roster. Both future Division I recruits were pure point guards, and North Carolina coach Roy Williams was under the impression his prized jewel, Strickland, would be manning that role as a senior under Boyle.

However, Boyle opted to shift Strickland to the shooting-guard slot, a cerebral experiment that paid dividends once Irving was eligible to step onto the court and make his long-anticipated St. Patrick debut.

"(Strickland) struggled to be that second guy, I think," Kowalski said. "I think it was tough for him to be behind Corey (Fisher). But then when Corey graduated, (Strickland) became the man. Even when Kyrie transferred in, it was Dexter's team. He was in the driver's seat.

"It took a while to get him to understand that he didn't need to score to be successful. He learned that if we were winning, he'd end up getting his shots. Then it wasn't an issue. But above all, he was the most athletic player I've ever played with."

Such athleticism was needed from the guard positions, considering this team was dramatically undersized for a national juggernaut. Paris Bennett stood all of six foot six, a nice height for a small forward, but stepped into the center slot.

"I've always been more of a leader," Bennett said. "My last two years I was captain, and (center) is what I had to be. It wasn't a position thing. (Boyle) doesn't see positions, just five guys on the court. Everyone had the opportunity to make plays for other people, and that was my role."

"Paris was the ultimate glue guy," Kowalski said. "He always wanted to be the big-time scorer, but Dexter took the spotlight. We had Ky, Mike Gilchrist, Dexter, and Paris. We had some great players.

Paris was never that vocal, but he played center at six foot six for us. He would go against guys a lot bigger than that, but he was able to do all those little things to help us win."

Without Irving, though, the Celtics underwent a rigorous string of tests to open the 2008–09 season. In the City of Palms Classic, they cruised past Word of God (North Carolina) and its star point guard John Wall thanks to a breakout performance from a little-known sophomore named Derrick Gordon, trying to fight for significant minutes. Gordon, among the other role players, helped quell the absence of Strickland, who was suspended by Assistant Principal Chris Chavannes for disciplinary reasons.

Then they edged Winter Park (Florida), 59–54, despite being handed an unpleasant introduction to how talented a sophomore named Austin Rivers truly was.

Boyle's streak of falling short at the nationally recognized tournament continued as his team lost to Mater Dei, 52–45. St. Patrick's first loss was more or less erased by an ensuing 4–0 stretch at the Beach Ball Classic in Myrtle Beach, South Carolina, during which Strickland and the boys recorded victories over Mullins (South Carolina), in-state rival Paterson Catholic, Pennsburg (Pennsylvania) and Wheeler (Georgia).

The Celtics improved their record to 7–1 with a win over Lakewood back in New Jersey, but were punched in the mouth by Life Center Academy of Burlington, which stole a 59–57 thriller. Strickland took it upon himself to label that as a wake-up call and made a strong impression on the team's psyche.

After three straight wins over inferior in-state programs, Irving finally put on a No. 24 Celtics jersey and sparked a winning streak that ultimately spanned over 13 games—including one eye-popping blowout against rival St. Benedict's Prep—and helped St. Patrick reach the top spot in the *USA Today* rankings leading up to the biggest matchup of the year, a date with national powerhouse Oak Hill Academy.

Located in Mouth of Wilson, Virginia, the Warriors basketball program had become synonymous with achievement on the level of high-stakes high school basketball. Head coach Steve Smith had produced dozens of big-time college players as well as several NBA stars, such as Carmelo Anthony, Rajon Rondo, and Brandon Jennings, who owned a shining title as the top prep player across the country by several outlets as a senior in 2007–08.

Boyle and Smith maintained a cordial relationship and often carried conversation before and after games. Since the departure of Shaheen Holloway, both national powerhouses annually engaged in a proverbial three-way wrestling match along with St. Anthony for the distinction as the most storied program in the country for approximately the last two decades. Such is why when both teams stepped on the court, a lot more than a regular-season win against an out-of-state opponent was on the line.

This time, though, the fight went in favor of Oak Hill by a score of 73–64. The first loss Irving absorbed as a member of the Celtics turned out to be the last of his junior year but still cost them the national crown in the end.

"We didn't finish on top. It was the most devastating loss of my life," Bennett said. "It was the first time I couldn't stop crying. I just sat there and couldn't stop. There was nothing (Boyle) could've said. It just got away from us. We fought, but somebody had to lose."

It was also an emotional time off the court for the Boyle family, as Kevin's older brother, Neil Jr., had just passed away from a two-year batter with cancer.

"After his brother died, the team was devastated, and they all came to the wake," Red Migliore said. "To get kids to go to a wake, it's not easy. But they wanted to be there."

Neil was a huge St. Patrick fan who also understood his brother's love for the game.

"At their wedding," Migliore chuckled, "Kevin's brother Neil said to Kelly, 'you may be his wife now, but basketball is his love.'"

The passing of Neil Jr. brought the team together. St. Patrick ran the table the rest of the way despite a myriad of nagging injuries to Strickland, Bennett, and Kidd-Gilchrist. The Celtics blew through the postseason like a violent tornado, and in the process they captured the Union County title, the North Non-Public B crown with a 79–54 win over Paterson Catholic, and the overall Non-Public B championship by moving past Trenton Catholic, 76–52.

"It's always like that with St. Pat's," Bennett said. "If you lose, you hear it everywhere. You're supposed to win. That year it wasn't like we ever fought from behind, but there was a lot of joy in it."

By recording a 66–40 triumph in the Tournament of Champions semifinal, Boyle was headed back to the last game of the Garden State's basketball season. The opponent was Science Park, a small school based out of Newark that rallied around its hoops squad en route to clinching the North 2 Group 1 sectional title in 2008. Entering this contest with a 30–1 record supplied some poise, but the underdogs quickly learned puffing out your chest in vain doesn't translate into a win over a heavy favorite like Boyle's team, armed with an All-American such as Strickland and a probable future All-American in Irving.

For St. Patrick, a five-point lead after the first quarter grew into an eight-point cushion by halftime. The advantage swelled to 15 points after the third, and by then, Irving and Strickland had buried Science Park en route to giving Boyle his fifth Tournament of Champions title in 11 years.

"It's tough to describe," Kowalski said. "Obviously it's a great feeling, but it was always expected of us to win it every year. So when you do it, it's not like a miracle feeling. But you feel like all the hard work paid off, and it's great.

"Coach Boyle always used to say we're the Yankees. We're the Evil Empire. We always had a ton of people who supported us, who loved us, and who would always be in the stands. But there were also naysayers, people on the outside who hated us for everything we were and everything we did. They hated everything about us."

However, there was a lot to love about the final act of the 2008–09 run. Irving led the way with a team-high 26 points, Kidd-Gilchrist— the New Jersey Gatorade Player of the Year as a sophomore—posted 16 points and 15 rebounds, and Strickland contributed 14 points in the 73–57 victory. Bennett, the George Mason-bound unsung hero all year, who played with a broken nose, chipped in nine points and four rebounds, but his most impressive statistic came from a four-year tenure of hard work and maintaining a winning attitude. Bennett, Strickland, and the Columbia-bound Kowalski had accomplished the rare feat of winning three Tournament of Champions titles in their high school careers.

"It's a winning environment," Kowalski said. "Practices are extremely competitive, and you just know, when you put that jersey on, you have to go out there to win it. It didn't matter who we had on the team. We were St. Patrick, which meant we were expected to win."

Kowalski remembered on several occasions Boyle would have

some of his former stars—Paul Williams and Jhamar Youngblood, especially—scrimmage the jayvee squad during practice.

"We were thinking, 'How the hell are we going to win?'" Kowalski recalled. "We played them once, and we lost. We then had to run laps around the park outside, and we were just bitching to each other. We ran, came back, and, believe it or not, we won. All along, he was teaching us that no matter what, you have to find a way."

That was an important lesson Bennett took away from his time with Boyle, too.

"He's a great guy, a great father, and he treated us like his own kids," Bennett said. "He's one of the best coaches in America. And I wouldn't be surprised if he is one day voted in (the Naismith Memorial Basketball Hall of Fame). Hurley did it, and (Boyle) has picked him off lots of times over the years. Why shouldn't he?"

The Celtics finished the year fourth in the last edition of the *USA Today* Super 25 poll. Strickland, Bennett, and Kowalski punctuated their time with Boyle in storybook fashion.

"In my four-year stretch, we won three state titles and three county titles," Bennett said. "Some guys were better than others, and some of the other St. Patrick teams were better than ours, but that's basketball. At the end of the day, we have a legacy. I wouldn't trade those teammates for anybody. We learned how to fight together."

Meanwhile, Irving's tale had just begun.

That following summer Kyrie turned into one of the most talked-about recruits in the nation, alongside Jared Sullinger of Northland (Ohio) and Enes Kanter, a big man from Turkey who played his high school ball at Stoneridge Prep in Tarzana, California.

St. Patrick was destined to produce another championship run and perhaps a national title chase in 2009–10. Despite the graduation of Strickland and the other two senior role players, Boyle welcomed back Irving and rising junior Michael Kidd-Gilchrist, considered the top player in the class of 2011. The Celtics also prepared to give Derrick Gordon more minutes, while relying on seniors Josh Daniell—a six-foot-seven forward who gave a verbal commitment to Wagner College—and Kevin Boyle Jr., who would assume the starting point-guard role.

Taking in a six-foot-nine freshman named Austin Colbert added depth and concrete evidence that the program's future remained bright.

Even before his senior year began, Irving was a walking celebrity on campus. He would often attend his friends' baseball games throughout the spring in Roselle but couldn't find time to enjoy them because he was too busy signing autographs. By September everybody figured he would be the next St. Patrick player to crack the rotation of a big-time college and garner plenty of face time on CBS or whichever network aired NCAA basketball games.

Kyrie was also a model student at the high school, proving that some kids could find refuge in various extracurricular activities aside from running on the basketball court. He took pride in being cast in the school play; he helped pull off a successful rendition of *High School Muscial*. He was an overall success story similar to that of Drederick, now a bond analyst at Thomson Reuters.

Irving never had the lead role in the school plays like Al Harrington or Paris Bennett, but it was refreshing, nonetheless, to watch a budding superstar try to broaden his horizons. "He was a backup player in the plays," Joe Picaro joked. "He wasn't a backup player on the court, though, by any means."

That backup in the school play turned into coach Mike Krzyzewski's favorite recruit. Irving verbally committed to Duke University in October, knowing he'd be headed to a program with a rich tradition and a reputation for developing NBA players. He also knew he was inching closer to achieving the goal he wrote and underlined several times inside his bedroom closet as a fourth-grader.

"Promise," it said.

He wasn't kidding.

Kyrie was the main attraction in the Garden State, a guard who never stopped improving from the day he left Montclair Kimberley and stepped through the doors at 221 Court Street in Elizabeth.

His reputation as the most dangerous scorer in the area grew even more when the Celtics put a 78–52 hurting on Trenton Catholic, a talented team with aspirations of going far in the state playoffs, on January 10. Kyrie posted 22 points in the third quarter and finished 30 for the game in front of a sellout crowd at Kean University as part of the Scholarship Fund for Inner-Children Festival. Boyle's son, Kevin Jr., scored 10 points, dished out seven assists, and held the Iron Mikes' best player scoreless. Austin Colbert started in place of the injured Kidd-Gilchrist and netted a season-high 11 points.

Still, it was Kyrie who made this much-anticipated game turn into a laugher, one that showed why the Celtics—and their point guard, himself—were in a class of their own.

"He's the best high school basketball player I've ever seen," Picaro stated. "He did such spectacular things and made them look ordinary. He was a great shooter. He was just spectacular, and I've seen many a great player in 69 years."

The All-American candidate helped the Celtics start the 2009–10 campaign with a perfect 11–0 record before falling at the Hoop Hall Classic in Springfield, Massachusetts, by one point to Findlay Prep of Henderson, Nevada. This squad, like the previous year's, was inspired by playing for Boyle's father, Neil Sr., who had passed away on December 16. Coach's boys were always there for him.

Ranked among the top five in the *USA Today* poll throughout the early stages of the season, Irving and his team would lose only three games that year—all by one point to teams among the best in the country.

However, the most devastating basketball defeat that winter came in a courtroom at the New Jersey State Interscholastic Athletic Association headquarters in Robbinsville, New Jersey. It was one that not only dissipated the program's national crown hopes but rocked Boyle's world in a way that nobody saw coming.

Ten

He's always been a great coach and a great guy. When it comes to basketball, he's all business. He's helped a lot of kids through school and hiring him was the best decision I've ever made.
—Red Migliore

Kelly Boyle was not afraid to admit that her husband's demeanor, attitude, and mental state completely transform as the winter begins to expire. Of course it does; it's playoff time. One would think, though, that after two decades Kevin Boyle would have used his excellent resume and vast experience to help quell the jitters of the county and state playoffs. Instead, his competitive edge, the chronic hunger for another trophy, consumed every moment of every day.

"Nope," Kelly said one day after practice when asked if there were any calm moments once the calendars are about to flip from February to March. "Every year around this time, I feel it. I see it. He can't sleep, which means I don't sleep, and we end up just laying there on our backs staring at the ceiling."

Winning is everything to Boyle. That is why the chance to capture a fourth Tournament of Champions title in five years having been taken away toward the end of the 2010 campaign crushed him.

Back in the early fall of 2009, the New Jersey State Interscholastic Athletic Association began investigating St. Patrick after Executive Director Steve Timko received a call from former NBA player Chris Washburn Sr., who expressed concern about the transfer of his two sons, Julian and Christopher, to the Elizabeth school, according to the initial report by the *Star-Ledger*. Washburn's wife, Michelle Washburn, from whom he was separated, and her sons moved from Texas to the

Garden State during the previous summer. Timko told the committee Chris Washburn questioned how his wife could afford the relocation.

Washburn told Timko that Michelle did not have employment there or the savings to live in New Jersey and send the children to a private school, firing the smoking gun. "All things in my opinion that sent up a red flag that required investigation," Timko said in the transcripts, which were originally obtained by the *Star-Ledger* after a January 26, 2010, hearing before the Controversies Committee of the NJSIAA.

The NJSIAA, which would eventually find itself in the headlines during the 2011 season for wasting millions of dollars on extravagances, used an undercover investigator hired in 2007 to increase its stranglehold over alleged recruiting. According to the *Star-Ledger*, that person secretly videotaped six practices at St. Patrick.

No recruiting violations were found despite Chris Washburn's account, but as a result of what some called a "witch hunt," Boyle admitted during a state athletic association meeting to violating out-of-season practice rules when his players worked out in front of college coaches in October 2009—about eight weeks prior to the official start of that winter season, which was November 27 that school year.

In the wake of those occurrences, St. Patrick Athletic Director Robert Migliore was suspended for three months without pay for failing to properly educate his coaches on the rules.

"The state contacted me and when I found out, I was furious," he said.

Nevertheless, the Controversies Committee recommended a hefty suspension for Boyle and recommended that the Celtics, the state's top team and favorite to win the upcoming Tournament of Champions, be disqualified from the state playoffs.

"It's a sore subject," Kelly Boyle said. "At the end of the day, it was a terrible punishment that affected my family. It was devastating to my family and my son's senior year. It was a kick in the gut. They hired a private investigator who lied his way into the school and then found nothing wrong. It was horrible."

On February 12, 2010, the NJSIAA Executive Committee in Robbinsville, New Jersey, voted unanimously to ban St. Patrick from the state playoffs and suspend Boyle for three games for being present during workouts before the official start of the season.

Boyle's attorney, Kevin H. Marino, stood at a podium during the hearing and sternly addressed the committee for nearly an hour to question the motives of the organization and how it decided to go about exposing Boyle and his program, both of which had clean records in the eyes of the state.

"For the past 22 years, 22 years, St. Patrick basketball and St. Patrick student athletes have achieved success under the guidance and the direction in no small part due to the love and the dedication of Kevin Boyle," Marino said in a statement videotaped by the *Star-Ledger*. "Mr. Boyle is present here today. He is standing in back of the room. Twenty-two years without a single disciplinary infraction of any kind."

NJSIAA President James Sarruda sat alongside Timko at a table and listened to Marino's heated deliberation, in which he called committee member Michael Herbert a liar and threatened further legal action, according to the *Star-Ledger*.

"After all was said and done, and after two hearings, they were apologetic," Migliore said.

Still, St. Patrick suffered its bruises. The best high school basketball team in the nation would not be able to participate in the tournament, and that was that. The night of the hearing simply made the day as a whole even worse for those saddened by the puzzling news.

Hours after being stripped of the chance to reach their expectations of winning yet another state title, the Celtics, then boasting an 18–2 record, faltered in the fourth quarter of a 79–78 loss to Oak Hill Academy in the 2010 PrimeTime Shootout at Kean University.

Derrick Gordon hit one of two free throws to forge a 78–78 tie with 54 seconds remaining, but McDonald's All-American Doron Lamb, a future star at Kentucky, converted his second free throw with 9.4 seconds left to put the Warriors back up. The Celtics were then put in position to tie or win as Derrick was fouled while driving to the basket with 0.4 on the clock. He misfired on the ensuing free throws, fittingly ending the school's day of despair.

"I feel heartbroken," said Kyrie Irving, who finished with 28 points for St. Patrick. "All three of our losses have been by one point. We just need to come together as a team."

Ranked fifth in the country according to the *USA Today* poll, the Celtics had already absorbed one-point losses to Findlay Prep of

Nevada and St. Benedict's Prep earlier that season. No doubt, this one stung the most.

"There's mixed emotions," Taylor Plummer's older brother, Chase, said afterward, knowing his senior year before heading off to University of Maryland-Baltimore County was drenched with disappointment. "We're not playing in the state tournament, but, on the other hand, we can look at different ways for a resolution where we can compete for the national title.

"We're going to review our options and have a team meeting about what to do from here, and we're going to take it step by step. At least if we win the county tournament we can go out on top for something."

St. Patrick played with plenty of pride, matching Oak Hill's ferocious offensive attack basket-for-basket throughout the entire game. Sparkling efforts by Kyrie and Michael Kidd-Gilchrist—who poured in 13 of his 28 points in the third quarter—were just not enough against the seventh-best team in the nation, though.

St. Patrick eventually scored a victory over Union High School in the Union County tournament championship game, its last of the 2010 season. Kyrie's conspicuously brilliant high school career ended because of dramatic unforeseen events that rocked Boyle's world.

That didn't sour the consensus of Kyrie. He was one of the best players to ever play in New Jersey.

"He was in the Kenny Anderson stratosphere in high school basketball," Mike Quick said. "The highest compliment I can say to a kid is, 'Great player, better person.' That was Kyrie. He's up there with Felipe Lopez and Elton Brand."

While Trenton Catholic, the team that was handled easily by St. Patrick, went on to clinch the Tournament of Champions title by defeating Camden Catholic, the Celtics still were named as the top team in the *Star-Ledger*'s final Top 20 for the fourth time in five years. Highly respected reporter Mike Kinney wrote: "There is no precedent for awarding The *Star-Ledger* Top 20 Trophy to a team that did not play a single game in the NJSIAA Tournament, but we feel strongly about making an exception here."

Irving was off to Duke University as one of the biggest recruits in the nation, perhaps second to only Ohio State's Jared Sullinger. Meanwhile, the goal for the 2011 Celtics had already been set: let the black eye heal and bring back glory to the streets of Elizabeth.

♣

On February 9, 2011, the St. Patrick community was robbed of watching two of its finest alumni square off in one of the most heated rivalries in sports. As No. 21 North Carolina made the short trek to Cameron Indoor Stadium to face No. 5 Duke, Dexter Strickland and the Tar Heels knew they had a chance to alter order in the ACC because Blue Devils all-world freshman Kyrie Irving was about to miss his 16th straight game with a toe injury.

Strickland scored six points and played a solid point guard, turning the ball over just once in 22 minutes, and teammate Tyler Zeller recorded 24 points and 13 rebounds, but Duke ran away with a 79–73 victory.

Four days later, however, Boyle and his Celtics had their own big-time matchup to worry about. St. Thomas More, an all-boy boarding school as scenic as its address presumably suggests on Cottage Road in Oakdale, Connecticut, was coming to Kean University looking to knock off the top team in the country, and the team was bringing its star center with it.

The six-foot-eleven Andre Drummond was considered the best player in the class of 2012 by the majority of recruiting outlets and already had more Division I offers than he could count. Kentucky, Connecticut, North Carolina, and Duke seemed to be the front-runners to eventually gain his services, as those programs usually are with young players already dubbed future NBA All-Stars.

St. Patrick saw Drummond go for 13 points, 10 rebounds, and four blocks in a losing effort against Hargrave Military Academy at the Hoop Hall Classic in Springfield, Massachusetts, several weeks prior. Boyle had spent the majority of practices talking about isolating the behemoth opponent, knowing freshman Dakari Johnson and his equally large frame weren't enough to contain the most talented center around. Even having welcomed back Chris Martin, who scored 14 points and sank four three-pointers against Union in his first game back since suffering a concussion in Springfield, didn't mean the Chancellors would end up like the rest of St. Patrick's opponents: on the losing end.

The night before the Saturday afternoon showdown, which would certainly draw a sellout crowd, Boyle wrapped up practice earlier than usual because the Blowback Productions documentary crew needed at least an hour to film certain clips of Dakari, Derrick, Mike, Jarrel Lane, and Chris Martin.

The crew asked for each player to stand at midcourt and dribble the ball in a variety of ways. They could bounce the ball through their legs, behind their back or from side to side. Jarrel chose to show off his superb ball-handling skills and even performed some tricks. It was all in good fun for both parties.

"For the kids, I bet it was hard to act normal," Principal Joe Picaro said of the documentary. "Maybe they're thinking, 'Is my hair in place?' I'm sure they were okay with it, but I just think it'd be especially hard for teenagers because they're so self-conscious about everything."

Actually, the kids loved it.

Several players not involved in the shoot were clogging the locker-room doorway in Public School 28's gym, hoping to make a dash toward their bags and dress quickly to watch the scene. Tyrone O'Garro and Taylor Plummer were the first ones out and began offering their sarcastic critiques.

"Don't dribble it off your foot," quipped Taylor, sporting a gray peacoat and a red and blue SpongeBob SquarePants backpack while standing beside Tyrone, whose excessive laughter brought about a coughing attack.

One crew member pushed the other with the camera on a sliding dolly toward Jarrel, holding the ball at his chest and wearing a stone-faced look.

"Good job, Jarrel. Next!"

Derrick's turn.

The shooting guard took the ball and bounced it back and forth while swaying his body.

"Yo, do something else," Dana Raysor joked.

"Chill. You're going to mess me up," Derrick embarrassingly snapped, trying to keep his stoic expression and dribbling groove intact.

Rae Miller looked on with the rest of the assistant coaches, trying to juggle his time between enjoying the laughter and making sure his Duracell battery of a three-year-old son, Dianhi, didn't run out of the gym.

"Hey! Stay in here! Go run from there to there," Rae scolded, pointing from baseline to baseline on the full-sized court. Decked out in jeans and an extra-small St. Patrick basketball shirt, the tiny ball of energy sprinted from end to end 12 times without slowing down.

"He just doesn't stop," Rae said, shaking his head with a smile.

"He'll be one hell of a basketball player, though," fellow assistant coach Jyron Brooks shot back.

Meanwhile, the laughter grew louder when Chris wrapped up his set and flipped the ball to Dakari. There's no way a six-foot-ten center handling the ball will look smooth and coordinated, everyone figured. He did just fine. Mike asked if he could push the dolly toward Dakari for the final moments of filming, an odd request one crew member happily honored.

Mike got behind the cameraman and slowly brought the platform toward a smiling Dakari, palming the ball at his side.

"Man, if this basketball thing doesn't work out, I'll be a producer," Mike exclaimed.

Right. John Calipari and every NBA executive would've loved to hear that one.

The Celtics were hours away from putting their perfect record up against the top player in the class of 2012, who would eventually skip his final year as a post-graduate at St. Thomas More and commit to UConn for the fall of 2011. If there were any nerves or cause for worry lurking in the minds of Boyle's team, it was impossible to see. Twenty wins, zero losses and smiles all around. The next day at Harwood Arena, though, it was back to business.

Jimmy Cavallo and John Celestand set the scene for this 2011 Prime Time Shootout megamatchup between two of the top players in the country, Andre Drummond and Michael Kidd-Gilchrist.

Kicking off the MSG Varsity broadcast, Celestand praised Drummond for being "a traditional big guy. He can post-up, he has soft hands, he can rebound, and he is a big-time shot-blocker."

A former Villanova star who won a championship with Shaquille O'Neal, Kobe Bryant, and the Los Angeles Lakers in his only NBA season one decade earlier, Celestand warned, "He's going to be a handful for the Celtics of St. Patrick."

Cavallo, a veteran sportscaster, did not need to say much about Mike, who entered the game with averages of 19.6 points, 11 rebounds, four assists, and 2.5 blocks. "Here's all you need to know about him: he's a McDonald's All-American."

Among the thousands of fans finding their places in the two opposite sets of multirowed bleachers, Kentucky coach John Calipari sat courtside next to Camden High School legend and former NBA player Dajuan Wagner, former Chicago Bulls point guard and five-time NBA champion Ron Harper, and one of the most influential figures in basketball, William Wesley, also known as World Wide Wes.

Wesley served as a consultant for Creative Artists Agency and was a client of LeBron James's agent, a Philadelphia attorney named Leon Rose. Wesley was also a former star at Pennsauken High School in southern Jersey, where he played the roles of best friend and rival to Dajaun's father, Milt Wagner, who went on to star at Louisville and eventually reached the NBA.

In a 2010 issue of *GQ* magazine, Alex French wrote an in-depth piece trying to decode the mysterious man with the hoops universe in the palm of his hand entitled "Is This the Most Powerful Man in Sports?"

According to the article, "Wes's big break came in the late 1980s or early 1990s, when Milt Wagner put him in a room with Michael Jordan. Jordan ended up giving Wes a job at his basketball camp."

Since then, Wesley has been everywhere. For example, he was the individual on the court holding back Ron Artest during the melee at the Palace of Auburn Hills in a 2004 game between the Indiana Pacers and Detroit Pistons.

On this day, though, he chose to take in a game involving the best high school team in the country and two NBA hopefuls putting on a show in front of thousands packed inside a small college arena. Some joked about whether one could even call this event a high school basketball game. It seemed more like a matinee at Madison Square Garden.

The Prime Time Shootout is a three-day event in which 34 teams from around the country face off at multiple venues. Louisville coach Rick Pitino once said, "It's the best-kept secret. It's like one-stop shopping." Yes, this truly was a recruiting gift shop.

Calipari and Rutgers coach Mike Rice shook their heads in

amazement as Drummond recorded a steal, drove coast to coast, and drew a foul by plowing over Jarrel, a guard about 11 inches shorter and 100 pounds lighter than the train coming at him. On the next play, Drummond showed off his soft touch and drilled a three-pointer.

Derrick scored seven points during a two-minute span in the final minutes of the first quarter, but St. Thomas More stayed within three points after eight minutes of play. The Chancellors weren't used to this game format, as they played two 20-minute halves instead of four eight-minute quarters. Some felt it was an advantage because they were conditioned to play for 40 minutes as opposed to the Celtics, who had always played 32. Others felt it could disrupt the flow of Drummond and the rest of his teammates.

Either way, Mike was breaking down the first line of defense atop the key. St. Thomas More coach Jere Quinn, who had recorded more than over 800 wins in 33 years, had no answer for the All-American forward, making Calipari feel like a million bucks.

Mike made a driving layup, converted two free throws, and put St. Patrick ahead 19–12 just 50 seconds into the second. "How do you stop a guy that has that quick a first step? I don't have an answer," Celestand surrendered. "I'm just glad I'm behind a microphone here instead of holding a clipboard."

While Quinn had his hands full with learning firsthand just how explosive Mike truly was, Boyle had his own problems. Drummond was doing whatever he wanted in the paint and even spread the floor with several short jumpers. Off an inbounds play midway through the quarter, he accepted a pass, took one dribble, spun around, and stuffed a two-handed dunk over Dakari.

Two more baskets from Drummond and a clutch three-pointer by Indiana Faithful, a sharpshooting guard who had been named the Gatorade Player of the Year in Maine before enrolling as a postgraduate at St. Thomas More, put the Celtics in a one-point hole with 1:11 remaining. Dakari hit two free throws and Mike capitalized on another fast-break layup before the buzzer, however, and Boyle and his team led 29–26 at the half.

The conclusion of the back-and-forth third quarter didn't go as favorably for the Celtics, who fell victim to a three-pointer as time expired. The last-ditch prayer of a shot caressed through the net, causing

Boyle to roll his eyes in disgust even though his team maintained its level of play and held a 49–45 lead going into the fourth.

By the 2:45 mark of the final quarter, St. Patrick constructed its largest lead of the game, holding a 60–50 advantage. Derrick flushed a minirun by Drummond and St. Thomas More by breaking free from a double-team and catching a lobbed inbounds pass from Chris in the open court. Derrick flew by two other defenders near the three-point arc and found Dakari, who accepted the feed and threw down a dunk for an eight-point cushion.

Dakari capitalized on the free-throw line with 17.5 seconds remaining to ice the 73–61 victory, making sure the Celtics improved to 26–0 since their last defeat, which occurred 366 days prior to this game.

Drummond finished with 17 points, six rebounds, and two blocks, but this was all about Michael Kidd-Gilchrist, the kid who posted 28 points on seven of 11 from the floor and 13 of 15 from the line.

Boyle mentioned in his postgame interview how the Celtics lost by three in a preseason scrimmage against Point Pleasant Beach, causing him to believe they'd lose "one or two" in the City of Palms Classic. Obviously, the eventual outcome had no resemblance to Boyle's fear. Since then, he said, "Things just started clicking."

That clicking hadn't ceased. The St. Patrick Celtics conquered Drummond the Giant and rallied past yet another opponent the way they had all season. The only things standing in the way of finishing atop the national rankings were the county tournament and state playoffs.

Eleven

You have to respect what he's done over there. Every year it seems his program is right up there with the best of them.
—Danny Hurley

The Celtics kicked off the 2011 Union County tournament by producing their highest-scoring game of the season, thumping Scotch Plains, 100–62. Chris Martin drilled seven three-pointers en route to scoring a game-high 25 points and leading five St. Patrick players in double figures.

It was an easy win that sent Kevin Boyle's team into the semifinal matchup against Roselle Catholic three nights later beaming with confidence.

That game, however, turned out to be the furthest thing from a microcosm of how the Celtics' season had gone. Instead, it was a bit nerve-racking, a tad frustrating, and certainly not the prettiest display of basketball execution.

Chris looked nothing like he did in the first-round contest, clanking one shot after another off the rim. Several people in the crowd made it a point to chuckle about how even the best shooter in the state was forced to suffer the agony of an off night. Even more puzzling, Michael Kidd-Gilchrist had a difficult time taming his counterpart, junior forward Jameel Warney.

Clinging to an underwhelming 32–24 lead at the half, Boyle's first bullet-point of discussion was about Warney, who had dodged the Celtics' post players for seven points on three wide-open layups and six rebounds through two quarters.

"He's down on the block, and he's doing whatever he wants," Boyle complained to Mike. "You have to do a better job with him."

"But it's all those screens," Mike contested.

"Well, then fight through the screens!"

"And when we get to the foul line, do your routine," Boyle bellowed, obviously irritated at the lack of success at the charity stripe. "We're giving away points on the foul line. We can't do that. Not in a playoff game. It's not only that. We've got to get up and pressure them."

"It's true, man," assistant coach Rae Miller offered. "He's stepping right around us …"

"Dakari, you and Mike have to do better," Boyle interrupted. "He's a good player, but not an elite athlete. You've got to play smart, play with your feet, and stop the flash. I told you guys before the game, it's how hard you want to work. We're in trouble of losing the whole thing right now. Seniors, it's on you. Do you want the chance to win a national championship to end here tonight?"

Nobody had to answer. Everybody already made it their mission to put away the pesky opponent and find a way to play for the county title. As the players were walking out, Frank Peralta walked alongside Mike, saying, "His feet are always moving. He's like a running back."

"He was just strong," Mike said, shaking his head. "That was it, man."

Mike was never one to scream after a big play or wear his emotions on his sleeve. It would be tough to notice from the bleachers if he was angry or focused, excited or content. He was always the first to break out into a dance after the game or kick off any prolonged joke in the locker room, but he never strayed from being a closed book on the court. At this point, though, Mike's bloodthirsty nature when it came to competing was kicked into another gear.

He was not letting Warney get the best of him. He opened the third quarter with a jumper from atop the key and completely silenced Warney after he netted nine more points. Enough was enough. Warney converted a layup to cut Roselle Catholic's deficit to 47–36 with 7:42 to go in the fourth. He did not score again.

With his mother and grandmother proudly watching from the stands behind one basket, Mike finished with 27 points, 17 rebounds, seven blocks, three assists, and two steals as St. Patrick pulled out a 63–50 win. Warney had slightly exposed St. Patrick defensively by registering 20 points and 11 rebounds but did not walk away from the gymnasium knowing he would get a chance to play in front of a raucous crowd at Kean University for the county crown.

"I think you know what I'm talking about now when I keep saying that Gill St. Bernard's is better than this team," Boyle said to the team in the locker room. "They're not as big but better. (Roselle Catholic) played a good game, but we necessarily didn't play bad."

Boyle was not the only one to notice Chris's difficult evening, in which he scored eight points, all on layups. It was the first time that season he had not drilled a three-pointer.

"I watched you take seven, eight, nine shots," Boyle said. "That's what I want. I want you to keep shooting. If it's a close game we have to be mature (with shot selection). But I thought we ran stuff pretty well tonight. We didn't shoot the ball well enough, and we kind of let the big kid body us down low. But that's what (St. Anthony forwards Lucious Jones and Jerome Frink) will be like. You don't get too many of these games. If we play this way against a national team, we probably lose.

"We didn't do a bad job," Boyle continued. "I believe if we make a couple more foul shots, and they miss one or two of theirs, it's a 20-point game. It's a tribute to you guys that you're having a great year, and people are ready to give you a standing ovation."

The following night Linden disposed of Plainfield, 66–53, in the other semifinal game, setting up a third meeting between the Tigers and Celtics in just over a month. By winning those games by 24 and 13, respectively, St. Patrick collectively felt good about the team's chances, even if it was facing a probable sectional championship winner yet again.

Chris, in particular, was excited simply because he believed karma in the sports world came in waves.

"The last time I had a bad night shooting I had a terrific night in the next game," he said after the semifinal victory. "The game has its ups and downs. We always have good team chemistry, though. Guys are always going out and showing how tough they are. We just have to hope we come out ready again. We can't be looking too far ahead."

St. Patrick would treat the Linden game like any other—with a serious businesslike approach that catered to the team's style of in-your-face defense and ball pressure. So Boyle opened his pregame speech in the basement of Kean University's Harwood Arena with a reminder of his wish to come out and make the first punch a knockout haymaker.

"It all starts with ball pressure," Boyle said. "In the first two games (of the county tournament) we did a really good job with that. We've got to be great defensively and great on the glass, okay? It'd be heartbreaking to lose this game just because we didn't play defense or rebound."

"We've got to decide to put them away early," Miller offered. "Take care of shit early, okay, guys?"

"If we fall behind 14–4 or something in the first few minutes, we're still in the game," Boyle promised, perhaps to give the starting lineup a dose of assurance because Jason Boswell was given the nod over Mike to start at small forward. Mike arrived in uniform just 15 minutes prior to game time because he and his mother were stuck in traffic on the always-clogged Garden State Parkway. "But if we're ahead 14–4, we're walking out of here with a 25-point win. Let's go."

Derrick took the opening tap and cruised in for a quick layup four seconds in and drilled a long three-pointer 36 seconds later. Acclaimed Linden coach Phil Colicchio already was pacing on the sideline. Coming out hot was his squad's only realistic chance of putting Boyle and company on the ropes, and that opportunity was already vapor. Things were going so well for the Celtics that even Austin Colbert, the power forward who had been building a strong reputation as an inside force rather than a shooter, connected for a three-pointer. Chris, who everybody in attendance expected to light it up from beyond the arc, followed suit, and St. Patrick eventually went ahead 14–0 halfway through the first quarter.

Mike and Da'shawn Suber checked in for Jason and Jarrel with 2:20 left in the opening quarter and their team comfortably leading, 17–8. While the packed crowd snickered about Mike not starting, Derrick was busy slashing through the lanes and finding a way to the hoop. He drew one foul and converted just one of two shots from the line. Da'shawn launched a three-pointer, and Derrick drove into the paint and earned two more shots from the charity stripe on the ensuing play.

"C'mon, DG, follow through," Boyle shouted at Derrick, whose troubles at the free-throw line throughout the entire season bordered on maddening. He missed both. Dakari Johnson got those two points back, though, by working for a layup with 11 seconds left, to balloon the Celtics' lead to 23–8. Boyle got exactly what he needed, while Colicchio had already pushed the panic button.

Inspired play from reserve Tyrone O'Garro helped St. Patrick stay the course in the second despite minimal contributions from Mike, who entered the locker room with just one point. Jarrel hit a three-pointer with one second remaining before the half to increase the advantage to 32–19, one Boyle felt was not enough for him and his boys to relax.

"This game is far from over," Boyle cautioned. "We've got to put it away the first four minutes (of the third quarter). As long as we stay in this game, we're in a good position. Don't make it a possibility for them. The most they can score now is 42 or 44."

It was a tactful way of viewing things, especially from the driver's seat. Even if Linden turned it up and outplayed St. Patrick in the second half by a significant margin, Boyle's team would need to score 20 or so more points to squeeze out a win. Such is life with eight-minute quarters and no shot clock, an often debated characteristic of high school basketball that clearly favored the Celtics—especially in this instance.

"Keep their big guy off the glass," Boyle offered, speaking about Linden freshman Quadri Moore, who stood just as tall as Dakari and was the only member of the Tigers lucky enough to successfully puncture the St. Patrick defensive scheme. "Somebody apparently woke him up and told him he was six foot ten and athletic right before game time."

Boyle reached for a black marker and clasped onto his trusty whiteboard. "Let's go Tyrone here, Derrick here to start the half," he snapped, establishing the spots the two wing players would station themselves in the first half-court set of the third. "Let's go with Mike over here," he added before explaining how a quick slash from Mike at the far side to the paint should result in a quick layup, similar to Derrick's at tip-off.

Sure enough, that play worked to perfection as Derrick crossed Mike in the paint and caught the ball right under the basket for an easy layin to start the second half. Mike followed with an emphatic dunk, his first field goal of the game, and Austin converted after snaring an offensive rebound just 87 seconds into the third for a 39–19 lead. It appeared Linden was near flatlining in the biggest game of its season, but somehow managed to wake up and construct a 16–5 run to close the quarter.

The closest Linden would come was 59–50 with 3:30 left. Chris put the dagger in the opposition's heart with another three-pointer, and Mike scored six points—including a thunderous slam dunk that sent the crowd to its feet—in a three-minute span to punctuate a 70–58 victory and third consecutive Union County championship.

Under Boyle's direction, the program had now won 13 county titles. Many would suggest cruising past Linden and adding yet another year to the team's dominance in Union County was simply routine—almost boring, perhaps—to Boyle because it was far from being his main goal this season and every previous one. That wasn't the case. Boyle happily made himself available to a crowd of reporters standing around the jubilant players posing for dozens of pictures in front of their bench.

His quotes more or less promoted Union County as being the state's deepest in terms of pure talent and went as far as predicting that there could be five Union County representatives in the six-team Tournament of Champions.

"You can look several places with the seedings," Boyle said. "Roselle Catholic was 16 or 17–1 when they had all their players eligible. You got Plainfield and Linden; both are two of the top programs in the state. You really could have five in the TOC. They all could be a one- or a two-seed if you're picking objectively and not by records."

The players of St. Patrick had no interest in offering their predictions for the Tournament of Champions, a single-elimination format in which the winners of New Jersey's six sectional championships square off for all the marbles. No, this moment was about celebrating a big step in their journey toward national glory.

Even the newcomer, Chris Martin, who had not experienced having a chance to compete for a fourth Tournament of Champions ring in five years taken away, recognized the significance of getting to play another day. "This feels great," he told reporters. "My teammates are hungry. I wasn't here last year, but I could feel the pain. Now, we just have to keep working hard."

Once the flashes from cameras ceased and fans decked in green and white began filing out of the arena, players took the long walk down two flights of stairs and through the narrow corridor into the locker room.

Boyle kept his evaluation short and to the point. "Towards the end there, those kids started shooting and got hot. We were atrocious from the free-throw line; this would have been a 25-point game if we were good at the free-throw line. Guys, we are the best team here. I'm not being cocky, just honest. Any basketball person can see that. This was a great accomplishment. For us to have this kind of success in that tough environment, it's a tribute to the coaches and players."

Players excitedly clapped with approval. Boyle left his players by shouting over the applause: "No practice tomorrow. Take the day off, okay?"

Taylor Plummer jumped up and kicked off a frenzy that included plenty of cheering and dancing from Mike and Dakari, while Diozy Mathos joined Da'shawn in waving a towel over his head while standing on top of the bench.

Cindy Richardson, Mike's mother, and Makini Campbell, Dakari's mother, stood outside the locker room wondering what the hell happened behind the closed door to trigger the ruckus.

Boyle just smirked and joked, "I thought they are supposed to be upset when I say no practice."

Indulging in what was the sweetest part of the season, Derrick, outside the locker room after getting dressed, dropped the first hint that he and the rest of his teammates were already thinking about facing St. Anthony and Naismith Hall of Fame coach Bob Hurley.

"To be a county champ, that's good," he said, shrugging his shoulders, "but they want us, and we want them."

No translation needed. Everybody knew who 'them' was in the St. Patrick basketball circle.

St. Anthony, meanwhile, was busy winning game after game, too. Hurley's Friars were undefeated the same way Boyle's Celtics were, entering the state playoffs. Fanatics that lived on high school basketball forums began begging for a matchup of the country's two best teams for an unofficial national championship game.

The only way that would happen was in the North Non-Public B championship, which was more of a glorified semifinal game for the overall Non-Public title, scheduled to be played at the Rutgers Athletic Center. It didn't matter. The hype was picking up steam—and fast.

The Celtics had to win two games before they could take the court against their rival in what was projected to be the biggest high school basketball game the state had ever seen.

TWELVE

Kevin Boyle is the most passionate, dedicated, and respectful person I've ever met. He is a great coach, father, and teacher. No one puts time in like he does. It's the only way he knows how to do things.
—Mike Nardi

Kevin Boyle had his arms in the air, quickly gliding his feet across the painted rectangle inside the foul line while wearing wingtip black dress shoes that would've likely sent the school janitor into a tizzy if he saw the kind of scuff marks the basketball team's larger-than-life coach was making on the hardwood surface. His white buttoned-down shirt, once tucked neatly into his slacks, began puffing out. The only article of clothing missing from his corporate-like getup was the red tie he yanked off before engaging in a heated practice filled with game-like scenarios just several days before the state playoffs began.

"Chris, you're coming through here, coming through here, and then boom," Boyle bellowed as he ran into Chris Martin, who keeled over in pain upon absorbing a hit to the solar plexus by a man that looked like he belonged in a boardroom filled with investors from Wall Street rather than running on a basketball court with the best high school team in the United States.

"That hurts, right?"

Boyle jogged back up toward the foul line and asked for the ball from Jarrel Lane, the half point guard, half assistant coach who was the only player in the gym with enough cajones to catch the eye of anybody looking at him and offer a playful, twisted grin that suggested he damn well knew his coach was comically obsessive at times. "The dress pants and everything, man. KayBee don't care," Jarrel chuckled after practice. "But we feed off that. He does whatever is necessary to prepare."

So evidently lost in the whirlwind of a busy day that left him no time to change into his usual nylon warm-up pants and dry-fit St. Patrick basketball polo shirt for practice, Boyle continued his explanation for curling at the foul line and running into Chris. "Too many guys don't do that (defensively), and let the guy blow right by him and do whatever the hell he wants in the paint. Move your feet under the basket and in front of the basket and don't let that guy come down here!"

St. Patrick was scheduled to face Marist High School in the first round of the New Jersey State Interscholastic Athletic Association playoffs. Boyle's practices for the week preceding that game were not focused so much on Marist, but on Gill St. Bernard's, which would be the opponent in the semifinals.

"I talked to the Linden coach, and he was so mad that we beat them by attacking players," Boyle said after switching the focus over to reviewing some offensive schemes. "He had no idea we'd be so quick on that play off the tip. Remember, Mike's throwing it, and we're taking off."

Derrick Gordon and Michael Kidd-Gilchrist eyed each other, remembering the tip-off play Boyle built to perfection. Running and gunning was such a huge factor in St. Patrick's ability to outhustle, outrun and outsmart teams by the third and fourth quarters during most, if not all, of its games. It was also very rare for an in-state opponent to boast a center as tall as their own six-foot-ten freshman Dakari Johnson. Qaudri Moore of Linden was one. Andre Drummond was the other.

A freakish athlete with NBA superstar written all over him, Drummond's presence gave St. Thomas More of Connecticut a fighting chance to upend the Celtics at Kean University a couple weeks prior to this practice session, and Boyle reminded his team Gill St. Bernard's made its engine run off strong guard play and shooting, not height and interior power.

"St. Thomas More is very similar to (Gill St. Bernard's), but they don't have the big guy," Boyle said. "They had their time when they saw us come out with the (full-court) press. We will full-court press again, but in certain spots, okay?"

"I know this is a tough week," he continued, after instructing his team to congregate near the stage under the basket. "We're going fast and slow in practice, stopping and going, playing and then listening more than we have all season. But I want to make sure we don't lose our focus, and we can bounce back. I'll see if we can get into the big gym (Public School No. 28) this week. That way we can have a little more size. Also, we have big tests coming up. We have deficiencies coming out, so please make sure you are where you need to be. Just remember, it's time for scholarships. Some guys have the choice between two or three schools, and some of you might be lucky enough to choose between nine or 10."

It was wise advice that each player already knew. Aside from Mike, Derrick, Jarrel, and Chris, others were getting their feet wet in the rough waters of recruiting. Sophomore forwards Austin Colbert and Jason Boswell had been generating interest from several Big East schools. Da'shawn Suber, a junior serving as Jarrel's backup at point guard, already received offers from West Virginia and Quinnipiac, while Georgetown, Oregon State, and Marquette were also in the picture. Boyle always made it clear that school work came first because without the grades, basketball at the next level couldn't be a reality.

At that moment, though, reality was showing the Celtics that the scrutiny they had faced all season, having their every step filmed by the HBO documentary crew, was nothing compared to what the next week would present. Reporters from dozens of outlets began showing up at more practices, causing the players to learn that life with a camera or tape recorder in your face day after day wasn't exactly comfortable.

"Stay humble; stay hungry," Boyle cautioned. "People are talking about St. Anthony already, so you just have to say that we respect them, but we'll be able to talk about them more when the time comes."

As Boyle adjourned the two-hour workout, a busy scene that mirrored the calm, cool, and collected feeling amongst the Celtics was on display. Their first state playoff game was just a day away. Gill St. Bernard's and a future Division I sharpshooter named Jaren Sina were waiting in the wings. Above all, Bob Hurley and St. Anthony were preparing in their own gym just over ten miles away in Jersey City for the apocalyptic showdown everybody in the state and country was hoping for. Above all, Boyle could sense a meeting with his archrival was looming.

Trevis Wyche, a chiseled six-foot sophomore point guard, snatched a ball from the side of the gym and asked his boisterous teammates to clear a path. He took two dribbles and elevated his body toward the rim.

Slam!

"You see this? I didn't know he could do that," marveled Dakari, beside himself with laughter.

"Stop it," Rae Miller snapped. "You'll break your goddamned leg or something."

"Fine, fine," Trevis playfully succumbed. "You like that, though, right?"

Meanwhile Boyle was on the other end of the gym holding a minifootball, pointing to Jarrel.

"If you don't catch this, you can't play in the next game," he joked.

"C'mon, coach!"

Boyle whizzed a perfect spiral into the hands of his senior floor general standing approximately 50 feet away.

"Touchdown!"

For the man who had spent all season crafting a team-wide businesslike approach, this light moment of fun disguised the effects of a cluttered mind, saturated by the racing thoughts about a new opportunity that would possibly change his life forever.

The Kevin Boyle Basketball Camp had developed into one of the most respected destinations for young kids trying to improve their skills in time for the high school scene. Boyle and his wife, Kelly, started the camp at the beginning of his tenure at St. Patrick, hoping to generate some extra income and further promote Boyle's image as one of the top clinicians in the area, who had also taught at the Nike Camp littered with future NBA stars. According to the camp's website, which prominently displayed a picture of Boyle and LeBron James with their arms around each other, 85 percent of campers returned each year.

"It's gradually improved," Boyle said. "The first year I did it, we had 24 kids. Now, it's grown into one of the most attended camps in the state."

Boyle's basketball IQ and gentle way of connecting with children with a budding love for the game made the camp a roaring success. But when his youngest son, Kevin Jr., graduated from St. Patrick in 2010 and went on to Emerson College, while his daughter Kelscey was at Villanova, Boyle began feeling the financial constrictions that so often sting the families who have multiple kids enrolled in college.

"Those bills come in, and it's like I have to do several camp sessions just to pay one of them," Boyle once admitted.

For several years, there had been whispers of St. Patrick High School near flatlining due to so little funds circulating in the Archdiocese of Newark. That year, in particular, the talks became louder. A merge with St. Mary's of Jersey City was rumored, which would ultimately serve as a costly solution for the two institutions that were apparently hemorrhaging money. Still, the prospect of the school closing scared Boyle and the dozens of teachers, administrators, and employees of St. Patrick.

"There's not a lot of pay from working that day-to-day job," Rae said. "And just to support the St. Pat's program, it was a challenge. It's the little things, too. Some kids can't get lunch every day, or some kids can't afford bus fares. It becomes a costly proposition. The cost is enormous."

Too many of these hindrances often led to Boyle keeping his finger on the pulse of potential opportunities at the college level. In today's market, it's common for Division I college coaches to pull down fat six-figure salaries. Some even make millions. For Boyle, though, stability was the key perk.

"I talk to Kevin three or four times a day," Rae said. "I actually talked with him for the last four or five years about how the time may come where he would have to consider his options and weigh everything for his family. At some point, he needed a new challenge. He had the same challenge for 23 years, so he needed a new one just to test himself.

"Kevin and I are like brothers. He is always more open with me, and I am always more open with him. I sometimes would tell him how I'd handle things; give him good advice—what's a good idea, and what's not a good idea. Our relationship transcends basketball. We're there for each other and each other's families."

When word got out that Dave Calloway resigned as Monmouth University's head basketball coach on February 27, the high school basketball forums lit up. Will the Hawks pursue Boyle? Will Boyle pursue the Hawks?

When Boyle and Jarrel finished running their football patterns and players filed out of the gym for the night, Boyle spoke about the opening very candidly. "I'm focused on this (season), but afterward, if someone showed interest, I'd explore and see if it's the right fit," he said, while making it clear he was happy where he was and would not leave St. Patrick for something that wouldn't shine on his resume.

"I wouldn't be disappointed if something wasn't the right fit, and I was here for another three, five, or ten years," Boyle said. "I love these kids, and I love this school. The thing with me is I'm 48 years old. Obviously I've had my hand in at St. Pat's for a long time. I've had great relationships with (school Principal Joe) Picaro and Robert Migliore, our athletic director.

"But you have concerns. Our school, like a lot of Catholic schools, has had to do a lot of fund-raising and different types of things to survive (financially). It's an issue everybody thinks about. If the situation presents itself, when you think they have interest, it's worth evaluating."

Truth be told, he was quietly well past the first stages of evaluating a potential exodus from the place he called home.

Brendan Boyle held a small silver microphone as his voice cascaded off every wall of the Public School No. 28 gymnasium.

"At forward ..."

"*Forward, forward, forward ...*"

"Number 31 ..."

"*One, one, one ...*"

"Senior, Michael Gilchrist!"

Brendan, Boyle's youngest son, who had just wrapped up his freshman season on the St. Patrick jayvee team with a heartbreaking loss in the Union County championship, was announcing the starting lineup for the Celtics as they were about to tip off against Marist in the first round of the state playoffs. He had been emceeing the varsity games since 2007, when he was 11 years old.

Before he developed this interest, he used to run around with a giant basketball costume on his head and "was our little mascot," team trainer Karen Magliacano said, trying to hold back laughter. "Someone came up to me and said, 'Is that the same little kid who used to run around like that?' I'm just like, 'How in the world do you remember that?' The picture is in my father's office. It's legendary."

Every fan cramped in the two-level bleachers along a side wall next to the court knew how much Brendan loved owning the night with a microphone and rosters for each team. They also understood how special Senior Night was, especially for Diozy Mathos.

Diozy was a senior who rarely played in games and only saw the court if the Celtics were up big on a much inferior foe in the fourth quarter. He never complained, though. On a team littered with future Division I prospects and NBA hopefuls, it was a bit surprising to find someone of his ilk stitched into this group.

Diozy often led the locker-room dance parties after big victories and was a team favorite. A muscular guard no taller than five foot eight with several tattoos planted on each of his cut biceps, Diozy dove for a loose ball and gained possession several seconds into the game.

"Let's go, Oze," Taylor Plummer screamed, waving a towel at the end of the bench.

Diozy continued his stellar play, dishing an assist under the basket for an Austin Colbert dunk that gave St. Patrick a 20–5 lead with 5:29 left in the first quarter. Derrick and Mike led the offensive charge that enabled the team to explode for a 41–9 cushion by halftime. Marist, however, was creating opportunities on several fast breaks after forcing a handful of turnovers.

"We started well, but we didn't do a good job of getting back," Boyle snapped in the locker room. "We've got to wake up and find guys on defense. If I was on their team I'd be looking downcourt for my streaking guy and throw a touchdown every time. You've got to listen and pay attention to the details out there. You've got to adjust and know who you're covering the whole time. That's a big thing for Sunday."

"We can't take plays off," Boyle continued. "If we do that, all of a sudden, they get in the zone and start making shots they only make once every ten games. Sunday's game is going to be like the Linden game. They're good for two spurts in the game. You've got to put them away, because you don't want to look up and all of a sudden it's a four-point game in the fourth quarter. We need to play hard until the horn sounds."

Boyle kept his speech short and simple because he was due on the court to help orchestrate the Senior Night ceremony before the third quarter began.

Steve Mango, a teacher at St. Patrick, first introduced Diozy, who was escorted by his father, Mike Mathos. The guard, who was having the time of his life as a starter on the best high school basketball team anywhere, stopped dead in his tracks and graciously extended his arm while bowing his head as if to usher his smiling father onto the court. The crowd broke into laughter.

Scorekeeper Naji Shabazz was introduced, followed by Jarrel, who walked onto the court with his arms around his father, Martin, and his mother, Joy, next to his grandmother. Chris Martin hugged his mother and best friend, Janice, with his right arm the whole way across the court. Derrick followed with his parents.

Mango said, "Our last introduction, but certainly not the least, is Mr. Vincent Richardson and Mrs. Cindy Richardson and Grandma Rene McLeary with Michael Gilchrist." Mike walked with his closest family members to center court, but ran back to greet another family with a bouquet of flowers: the Plummers. The Plummer family graciously opened their home to Mike—and any other player who called home far from Elizabeth—during the season. They were the team parents who everybody adored.

Boyle then walked to the court and took the microphone to hand out some awards. Jarrel, Chris, Derrick, and Diozy were elated to receive plaques from the school, and Mike looked like a child on Christmas morning when he was given a basketball with "1,000 Career Points" inscribed on it.

"We appreciate all your hard work, seniors," Boyle gushed. "Thank you all so much."

As the players walked back to the bench right before the second half tipped off, Taylor laughed at Dakari and DaQuan Grant for sitting on the floor because not enough chairs had been set up prior to the contest to accommodate the 15 players and five coaches.

"Y'all shit out of luck."

Dakari's mother, the guys' favorite teacher at school, walked over with two cushion chairs that looked like thrones compared to the flimsy fold-up chairs the rest of the team sat on.

"What?" Taylor playfully shouted in disbelief. "C'mon, Mrs. Campbell! Get me one of those!"

Light moments littered the evening, signifying all was right in the Celtics' universe. Diozy enjoyed more playing time in the third quarter and got on the scoreboard by hitting a jumper from the right side with six minutes remaining to extend St. Patrick's lead to 68–39, sending the bench into a state of jubilation.

Boyle spoke so often, especially at the beginning of the season, about becoming a team. He begged his players to trust in one another and pull for each player for the greater good of the group. It was working. The culture of a squad that consisted of so many individual superstars transformed into a unit that only cared about the success of the program as a whole. What a Senior Night it was.

After the Celtics wrapped up an 84–48 victory in the first round of the state playoffs, Diozy was delighted to know he contributed in a game the program was unable to reach the previous season due to the NJSIAA ban. "I felt good because it was my first time starting and getting some real playing time," he said. "I found out earlier this week I was going to start, and I thought about all the ways I could contribute. Now we're ready for Sunday."

The kid who was so used to watching Mike, Derrick, or Jarrel get interviewed after games treated his interview like a professional. He knew how it was done. After all, he made it known he would be interested in studying media or film in the future. He admitted he even observed how the Blowback Productions crew conducted its business around the team with hopes of soaking in a tip or two.

There were smiles all around the locker room after the game, especially as the team sang "Happy Birthday" to Chris and Dana Raysor. On this night, though, the mothers of the players were beaming the brightest.

"It feels like this long journey and chapter in our lives is closing," Janice Jackson, Chris's mother, said. "He's crossing over into becoming a man. We've been really close, and he's been my best friend. He's been a real motivation."

Janice, more than anything, was relieved to see that her son made a home for himself at his new school. "Especially because he's only been here one year, I was concerned that he wouldn't know how to fit in. But this was like a fairy tale. He loves these guys so much. He told me he's probably going to cry at graduation. Hearing that, I just couldn't ask for more.

"I couldn't believe he landed at a place like St. Pat's. St. Pat's has been so great. I never knew that they would receive him this well, and Coach Boyle is such a great person and a phenomenal coach. It's hard to put into words how happy and proud I am."

Chris, meanwhile, admitted it was the best birthday he ever had. Getting a win in the state playoffs and setting the stage for a showdown against Gill St. Bernard's in the semifinals was great, but having his mother there to watch was even better.

"It meant everything that she was here," Chris said. "She's my best friend, so it meant a lot. I don't get to see her a lot now, so this really was the best birthday present ever."

Cindy was just as proud of her son, Mike. "I can't find the words to describe how happy he makes me," she said. "He's such a great kid and a great human being."

"I don't let it," Cindy said when asked if the influx of attention on Mike and the family tended to become overwhelming at times. "There are a lot of things that take precedence over basketball, and family is one of those things. Here at St. Pat's, everyone is a family."

Even with the state championship three wins away, it was like everyone in that family made it already.

St. Patrick's track record against Gill St. Bernard's—ranked third in the *Star Ledger*'s statewide poll—was comforting for those who felt an upset was an attainable feat for the underdog Fighting Uggs. The Celtics had run away with a 75–58 victory in the most recent meeting thanks to a 23-point performance by Kyrie Irving in late January of the previous season. The upcoming game had a little more juice, though. It was the state playoffs, after all, and a win would mean a showdown with St. Anthony later in the week.

Stopping sophomore sharpshooter Jaren Sina was the key to victory, and the Celtics did just that. Jarrel and Derrick shut down the sophomore, holding him to single digits for the first time the entire season and did not let him sink one three-pointer.

An eight-point lead at halftime swelled in the second half; Mike and Derrick combined for 37 points, and St. Patrick used a 20–6 fourth-quarter run to thwart Gill St. Bernard's, 69–41. In winning his 32nd consecutive game, Boyle had punched a ticket to the NJSIAA North Non-Public B title game at the Rutgers Athletic Center.

As for the showdown of all showdowns, the Celtics did their part. Bob Hurley, the man who won his 1,000th career game on February 2, had to coach his St. Anthony Friars to just one more triumph to complete the wish and set up high school basketball's dream matchup.

Thirteen

That game took on a life of its own. It was like something out of Hollywood. That's what made it so incredible.
—Mike Quick

For the entire high school basketball universe, March 8, 2011, turned into Christmas Eve once word got out that St. Anthony upended Oratory Prep in the North Non-Public B semifinals.

It was a normal Tuesday at school for the St. Patrick players, but their minds weren't on biology or trying to make sense of the latest Shakespeare book being read in Makini Campbell's English class. After all, facing their rival in the sectional championship and mythical national title game at the Rutgers Athletic Center the following evening would provide more drama than any scene in *Macbeth* or *Julius Caesar*.

Basketball columnist Dave D'Alessandro wrote an article in that Monday's *Star-Ledger* about Kevin Boyle and his chance to cast away the demons of being banned from the state playoffs a year ago. More than anything, the reader walked away with a distinct understanding that the memory still ate away at the coach's core.

In actuality, this date with Bob Hurley and his Friars transcended the prospect of erasing the lone blemish on Boyle's sterling resume; furthermore, it was the golden chance to finally close the gap between the two powerhouses in the eyes of those who held St. Anthony well above St. Patrick in the Garden State totem pole.

Boyle told D'Alessandro that finishing ahead of St. Anthony nine times in the last 13 years in the *Star-Ledger*'s poll was the greatest of all the Celtics' achievements. Winning the upcoming round would likely turn the tide, and not just numbers-wise.

Hurley had earned unanimous respect in the high school hoops circles after nearly four decades of helping kids get off the streets of Jersey City and into a gym that housed his own basketball boot camp, inevitably putting them on a positive life path. He had won 25 state championships and three national titles and was the subject of the TeamWorks Media documentary *The Street Stops Here* and a best-selling book by Adrian Wojnarowski entitled, *The Miracle of St. Anthony*.

He says his best accomplishment was sending all but two of his players to college.

A retired probation officer, Hurley has two sons who helped build a reputation as New Jersey's basketball royal family. Hurley's oldest, Bobby, was a senior who averaged 20 points and eight assists on the undefeated 1989 St. Anthony's team that captured the first-ever Tournament of Champions title and finished No. 1 in the *USA Today* national rankings.

After playing alongside two fellow first-round selections in the NBA draft—Terry Dehere and Rodrick Rhodes—and star Jerry Walker, Bobby became a four-year starter and All-American at Duke University. Bobby, Christian Laettner, and Grant Hill orchestrated one of Mike Krzyzewski's finest spurts when the Blue Devils won back-to-back national titles in 1991 and 1992.

Bobby's No. 11 jersey was retired at the famous Cameron Indoor Stadium in 1993, and nine years later he was named to the Atlantic Coast Conference 50th Anniversary Men's Basketball Team as one of the 50 greatest players ever in college basketball's historic conference.

Selected seventh overall by Sacramento in the 1993 NBA draft, Bobby was seen as a beacon of hope for Kings fans, who suffered through watching their team drudge through a miserable 25–57 season in 1992–93. Bobby was averaging 7.1 points and 6.1 assists in 19 games as a rookie, but a house painter named Daniel Wieland changed the course of what promised to be a long career.

Wieland was driving without his headlights on the night of December 13, 1993, the night Bobby turned into Wieland's station wagon after a Kings game and was tossed from his vehicle while not wearing a seat belt. He suffered several life-threatening injuries but was rescued by teammate Mike Peplowski, who was driving minutes behind the rookie point guard.

Bobby spent the rest of his rookie season rehabilitating in a hospital. He returned the next season but was never the same. He played four full seasons with the Kings and spent half of his fifth and final NBA year in 1997–98 with the Vancouver Grizzlies.

Bob Hurley's youngest son, Danny, also starred for the Friars and went on to play point guard for P. J. Carlesimo's Seton Hall University Pirates in the early 1990s, shortly before Shaheen Holloway arrived on campus. Danny enjoyed a stint as an assistant coach at Rutgers before taking the head job at St. Benedict's Prep in Newark, turning the Gray Bees into a national powerhouse and triggering a three-way rivalry between his school, his father's, and Boyle's.

"When I was burying my head on my desk at Rutgers, I didn't realize what I was missing," Danny said in *The Miracle of St. Anthony*. "I didn't realize the feeling you got when one of your high school players calls you from college and tells you how great it is, and how much maybe you've affected his life getting there."

At St. Benedict's, Danny amassed a 223–21 record over nine seasons and groomed NBA player J. R. Smith, among many other Division I players. He and Boyle engaged in an ongoing battle year after year, trying to strong-arm each other on their respective sidelines whenever the two squads met. Though the two didn't have a friendly relationship, Danny always respected Boyle's work and vice versa.

"You have to respect what he's done over there," Danny said. "Every year it seems his program is right up there with the rest of them."

Since Danny's St. Benedict's team was always right up there with the best of them as well, he was afforded the opportunity to make the rare leap from the high school level to Division I when he was named head coach of Wagner College, a small school in the Northeast Conference stationed in Staten Island, in April 2010.

As fate would have it, Danny asked Bobby, who at the time was involved with thoroughbred racing in Florida, to become one of his assistants. Bobby gladly accepted, and the two helped Wagner go from a dreary 5–26 team to one that went 13–17 overall and 9–9 in conference play.

Since the two were in the area—Danny and his family never moved from their Freehold, New Jersey, home in the wake of taking over the Wagner job—they were able to be in attendance when their father notched career victory No. 1,000 on February 2, 2011.

"It's an unbelievable accomplishment," Danny said that day. "To win as many games as he has, to coach the amount of years he has, it's amazing."

That milestone further validated Bob Hurley's induction into the Naismith Memorial Basketball Hall of Fame in 2010, joining Morgan Wootten and Bertha Teague as the only high school coaches to be enshrined. The 62-year-old Jersey City native was in a class that included Jerry Buss, Cynthia Cooper, Karl Malone, Scottie Pippen, the 1960 USA men's Olympic team, and the 1992 USA "Dream Team."

This season Hurley had a "Dream Team" of his own, one that boasted Rutgers-bound point guard Myles Mack and highly recruited junior forward Kyle Anderson. Thanks to the pair of Paterson Catholic defectors, St. Anthony had won 29 straight games leading up to the showdown with St. Patrick. Many of those victories finished similarly to the 92–32 thrashing the Friars gave to Oratory Prep in the semifinals. No mercy. No contest.

After 43 years, Paterson Catholic, the alma mater of Tim Thomas and many Division I players, closed its doors in June due to a mountain of financial problems, forcing 186 underclassmen to find a different school to attend for the following year. In turn, that left the school's nationally ranked basketball program's players without a team.

Anderson, Mack, Reggie Cameron, Kavon Stewart, and Jhamir White were all key contributors to a squad that won its third consecutive Passaic County Tournament and started 28–0 before falling to St. Anthony in the North Non-Public B title game in 2010.

Anderson and Mack joined forces with Hurley at St. Anthony, conjuring up playful comparisons to LeBron James and Chris Bosh fleeing their former teams for South Beach to suit up with Dwyane Wade. Meanwhile, Cameron and Stewart both landed at Hudson Catholic. White, meanwhile, decided to spend his senior season at John F. Kennedy in Paterson.

Mack was a speedy guard no taller than five foot eleven, but he instantly became a favorite of first-year Rutgers coach Mike Rice. During warm-ups of any St. Anthony game that Rice attended, the future Scarlet Knight and his future coach would lock eyes, jerk their heads upward, and smile.

At six foot eight, Anderson was a hybrid player with a boatload of talent inside and outside the paint. His handle and athleticism even prompted many scouts and coaches to project him as a point guard once he landed at the college of his choice.

Mack and Anderson headlined a core of players that bought into Hurley's system. Guards Jordan Quick and Lucious "Lucky" Jones were defensive specialists known for playing baseline to baseline for four quarters, much like the undersized, yet fearless, center Jerome Frink.

Amid a myriad of lopsided results against inferior New Jersey teams, that group helped St. Anthony post convincing wins over out-of-state foes such as DeMatha (Hyattsville, Maryland), Mount Vernon (New York), Boys and Girls (Brooklyn, New York), and Long Island Lutheran (Brookville, New York).

"There's some really good teams, the same suspects," Hurley had said. "But our room for growth is as high as any team we've had in a long time."

Based on other quotes in the newspapers, though, the Friars shied away from speaking outwardly about the matchup with St. Patrick. Boyle told his players it was because "I don't think they think they can win." Perhaps it was Hurley's way of controlling his public relations. Regardless, many thought the Celtics had enough juice to run the table and finish undefeated, but if there were one team with enough talent to shatter that dream, it was St. Anthony.

Mike Kinney, Dave D'Alessandro's veteran colleague at the *Star-Ledger*, spoke with Adam Zagoria of SNY.tv about this much-anticipated showdown and called it the "biggest game" of his 28-year tenure covering Garden State high school basketball.

"As far as quality teams, as far as national exposure," Kinney said on the zagsblog.com posting, "this has to the biggest game because one and two in the country has never happened before."

By the time school had ended and Boyle met with his players for practice on Tuesday, tickets were already being sold at Rutgers. The event staff was expecting a sellout, which would mean nearly 9,000 people would be in attendance.

In a February 25 article, *Star-Ledger* columnist Steve Politi, who commended Boyle's fight against the NJSIAA and its ruling to ban the Celtics from the 2010 state playoffs, had petitioned this game be moved to the Prudential Center because it would accommodate more spectators.

Politi wrote: "And did we mention that The Rock would let the cash-strapped NJSIAA use its building at a significantly cut rate, without charging a facility fee and capping expenses below normal levels?"

Ultimately, this plea went in NJSIAA Executive Director Steve Timko's one ear and out the other. "Well, we've been going (to Rutgers) for the last ... I can't tell you how many years," he told Politi. "I can't back out on them after I said we're a go."

The Game, a tad too big to give its title lowercased letters, ultimately would be scheduled at the RAC. Fans were well aware of the capacity, kicking off a frenzy to obtain tickets. By 10:00 a.m. on Tuesday the Friars and Celtics sold out the home of the Scarlet Knights.

"Parking is going to be ridiculous because of the type of event it is," Boyle said to his players, who were crowding around him in front of the stage in the compact St. Patrick gymnasium. "If you're going to go home and rest or whatever, fine, but we leave here at 5:30. Before that, we're going to go over the plays, so go get taped if you need to. Then it's time to get focused. If we guard the way we did against Gill St. Bernard's, they'll have a tough time scoring."

Boyle made it clear he was hell-bent on his guards contributing on the glass. He mentioned St. Anthony's ability to rebound, and promised his team, if it outdid the opposition on the rebounding side, things would be fine. With several reporters waiting patiently for interviews near the back corner, a court's length away from the stage, Boyle urged Derrick, Chris, and Jarrel to get 12 rebounds combined. He drafted that number with full certainty if the trio of guards reached the goal, the Celtics would walk away with a win. An addition to the wish list was made once the three guards accepted the challenge.

"Let's get a block from Mike early," Boyle said, asking his All-American to deny Frink his first shot attempt with hopes it would silence him the rest of the evening. "The magnitude of that for Frink will be huge. He'll have the ball, and if he gets blocked once, he'll be like, 'Where's Gilchrist?'"

"Also, Austin, Dakari, Derrick, and Mike, you guys need to get offensive rebounds," Boyle urged. "We're clearly the better team. We just need to calm down and hit our free throws. It should be a 15- or

20-point game. It should be double digits, guys. We've beaten better teams. We have to play every possession. Guys on the bench, you have to be ready. Hakim, you did a great job in practice taking charges. If you get in, you have to get one on Mack."

Boyle recognized this was an all-hands-on-deck approach. Sure, the Celtics were the favorites, but the 23-year head coach was smart enough to know it was Hurley, and Hurley always finds a way. Always.

"I told you guys before, what you do in the next ten days, you will carry with you for the rest of your life," Boyle softly offered. "We've been doing it all year. This is just another game. You guys have been working hard. I've been coaching basketball for 30 years, and no one has ever worked harder than you. Remember that, okay?"

Derrick and Jarrel sat on the stage several minutes untying their sneakers after Boyle ended practice and walked away to address the waiting reporters nearby.

"The whole state is ready," Jarrel said, ready to hop into his Lexus and drive to his home in Rahway with hopes of relaxing. "It's a major game. It's great for the state; it's great for the country. It's great for high school basketball in general. But this season we've been taking it one game at a time. Now, it's finally here."

Yes, it was time. The countdown was over; the final grains of sand slithered down from the top of the hourglass to the bottom. St. Anthony was all theirs.

"I'm anxious, not nervous," Derrick said. "We're all used to playing on the big stage, and this year we could be national champs. We've definitely got a little bit of an advantage playing a bunch of out-of-state games. Now we just have to prove ourselves again. They don't like us, and we don't like them."

Back when Hurley's documentary was about to air March 31, 2010, on PBS, producer Jay Sharman told ESPN.com: "I knew we were going to have a great documentary when I sat down with him and said 50 percent of the people are going to say, 'Gosh, this is just great, we need this kind of coach,' and 50 percent are going to say, 'I can't believe he yells and screams at kids like that.' And he said, 'I don't give a blank what people think about me. I just care about my kids getting into college.'"

Boyle, meanwhile, was the focal point of his own documentary. The crew reveled in its fascinating subject, knowing the project was blessed with a bevy of strong elements backed by a man with the strongest of personalities. Truth be told, Blowback Productions couldn't have drawn up a better climax than what was about to unravel the next day, on March 9, inside a rowdy arena where the Celtics stared at a fork in the road.

They could finish their job by winning the mythical national championship and taking over for St. Anthony as the powerhouse of all powerhouses, or they could let the walls crumble.

A man who identified himself as Phil walked away with his young son from the middle ticket booth at the Rutgers Athletic Center shaking his head.

"All sold out," he grumbled.

Phil wasn't the only basketball junkie turned away from the doors with hopes of watching Boyle and Hurley duke it out for the North Non-Public B title and mythical national championship. Some who weren't lucky enough to score a ticket could have approached one of the coy scalpers selling them for $75 a pop, but paying more to see a high school game than a Knicks game at Madison Square Garden was far from justifiable. Some swayed the other way and coughed up the insane asking price for a chance to witness history.

"They could've put the damn things on StubHub," one St. Patrick insider remarked.

"In 23 years I had never covered a national championship, and if I do this for another 23 years I don't think it would happen again," gushed Mike Quick.

While St. Peter's Prep and Seton Hall Prep were engaging in a tight battle for the North Non-Public A crown in a game that started two hours before the main event, the half-empty arena began to fill out. Soon, the place was stuffed with fans of all ages waiting for the appetizer portion of the evening to conclude.

"(This) game took on a life of its own. It was like something out of Hollywood. Both schools have had better teams; it's not even close. But there was a giddiness about this game. It was like, here it is," Quick recalled. "With Paterson Catholic closing, this was a death-and-taxes game, but you didn't know which team (would win). That's what made it so incredible."

Boyle joined Rae Miller and Jyron Brooks in standing next to the first tier of seats in the back left corner of the court just outside the entrance way to the locker rooms. The roped-off area adjacent to the media room, filled with dozens of reporters and camera men, quickly transformed into a cocktail hour of big names.

Jason and Devin McCourty and Tiquan Underwood—all former Rutgers football stars in the NFL—scoped out their front-row seats while standing among Steve Kroft of *60 Minutes*, Caroline Kennedy, Senator Richard Codey, and Kentucky coach John Calipari. It was even rumored Jay-Z planned on arriving in time for tip-off.

Chris Martin had asked several of his teammates if Carmelo Anthony and Chauncey Billups would show up, only to be shot down when he was told the Knicks were in the middle of a midwestern road trip and had a game in Memphis that night.

Conversations drowned the mild cheers from those involved in the current game, but Boyle stood silent. The chatterbox who was known to have 20-minute conversations with strangers was stone-faced, staring at the court. He was alone with his thoughts, silent in a public forum.

"Bob Hurley was as loose as he's ever been, but Kevin Boyle seemed as tight as can be," said Quick, sitting two rows above the crowded area at the time. "He is all about holding court and talking. The whole thing was just so bizarre. During that Non-Public A championship game, Kevin Boyle was not Kevin Boyle. When is he ever quiet? He was silent before that game."

Several minutes went by and Boyle retreated under the tunnel. As thousands of people eventually watched Texas-bound point guard Sterling Gibbs rally Seton Hall Prep to a 55–47 overtime victory by scoring 25 points, Boyle was alone in the dimmed locker room drawing up plays on the marker board.

He looked up from his trusty Five-Star Basketball coaching handbook and paused before adding to the scribble. Watching the thrilling end to a game that consisted of teams his Celtics would potentially face in the overall Non-Public B title game spawned no interest in Boyle. He was a man possessed, with one thing clouding his mind: St. Anthony.

Da'shawn Suber and Jarrel Lane sat next to each other bobbing their heads to the beats blasting out of their headphones. Assistant coach Frank Peralta walked over to Chris, who was sitting on the ground with his legs spread and leaning over to touch his shoes, stretching his hamstrings.

"This is what you came here for, right?"

"Yes sir, I did," Chris answered with no hesitation.

Boyle clapped three times, quickly licked the index and middle fingers of each hand and rubbed his palms together. He paced around and picked up a cup of water. Anxious as can be, he called his players over to the seats where the Rutgers women's basketball team reviewed game tapes.

With a deep breath, he began a pregame speech different from any other in the 2010–11 season.

"We worked extremely hard all year for this," Boyle said. "You've worked harder than anyone in the country. I don't know about you, but I feel extremely confident. We're prepared. When we focus, we play incredible defense.

"There are different moments in life that are significant—when you get married, when you have your first child, and, unfortunately, experience death in the family. Those memories are very vivid forever. They are there for the rest of your life. Guys, this is one of the moments. This is it.

"Nine of the last 13 years we've been the better team. If we beat them tonight, there's a new sheriff in town. When you're older, when you have grandkids, they'll want to hear about this day one more time. We can control that. Next year when you're in college, when you're at Kentucky, or wherever you're going, you're going to make friends. But you won't have friends as close as this group. We're here right now. We control this. Let's come together and make it a good one."

After the final words of the Hail Mary were said in unison, the glass door swung open toward a winding corridor that led to the open arena filled with more than 8,000 screaming onlookers.

Fourteen

There was never a normal day, ever. There were always cameras and reporters, and ... it seemed like there was always something. It was crazy. It was crazy every day. It was always one situation or another. We just wanted to get through the season unscathed.
—Rae Miller

It worked again.

The tip-off scheme which called for Derrick Gordon to break from the circle and sprint straight to his team's basket with hopes of receiving a pass from Michael Kidd-Gilchrist, Jarrel Lane, or Chris Martin turned into one of Kevin Boyle's favorite trick plays. It was an ace up the sleeve of a basketball chemist, the guy with that big Five-Star Basketball handbook at his side.

Austin Colbert stood five inches taller than Jerome Frink, St. Anthony's burly—yet undersized—center, and he used that excess height to his advantage when the referee cautioned the two players to have a good, clean game before lobbing the ball upward in between the kid in the white and green Celtics uniform and the kid with the black uniform trimmed with gold and maroon.

Game on.

Austin won that battle, tipping the ball over an outstretched arm of Frink and enabling Mike to gain possession for a millisecond before firing a one-handed bullet to Derrick, who was streaking down court and aware enough to catch a quick outlet pass and score the first basket of the contest just five seconds in. The play had worked against St. Thomas More back in February and again in the Union County championship against Linden. Boyle liked his odds with that scheme and went with it.

It gave credence to Boyle's philosophy of carrying out execution every second of every game—literally. Most high school basketball teams who win the jump ball waste about 30 or 40 seconds before attempting a first shot. St. Patrick lived and died with an attacking mind-set, a characteristic that went from being a perk to a necessity the night the Celtics faced Hurley and the Friars.

Lucious Jones, a feisty guard with a passion for defense who everybody called "Lucky," answered back with a wide-open layup, and Myles Mack, the Rutgers-bound point guard who more or less made this all possible for Hurley and his camp, stole the ball from Jarrel and converted another point-blank attempt for a 4–2 advantage.

The next two minutes looked like the kind of basketball Boyle craved so desperately on this night. Crisp passing. Suffocating defense. Smart, high-percentage shots. It was all working.

Derrick drilled a three-pointer for a 5–4 lead, and Chris followed suit by draining a wide-open three for an 8–4 cushion. Time-out St. Anthony.

The cameras of *60 Minutes* swarmed the Friars bench to capture Hurley, the subject of a future segment on the CBS television show, in his first stage of discomfort of the night. The man who was cool as a cucumber prior to tip-off turned beet-red in the face and urged his players to clamp down defensively, but to no avail.

After the stoppage, Chris hit another shot from beyond the arc for an 11–4 lead. There was no such thing as full relief in this type of game, though, and Boyle understood that. For St. Patrick, it still was nice to have some breathing room.

Derrick drove the lane for a pair of finishes, and Mike responded to Mack's layup and long three-pointer by hitting his first shot of the game to put St. Patrick up, 17–11, with 1:40 left. The Celtics would finish the opening quarter of the mythical national championship carrying a 19–13 advantage.

Kyle Anderson finally got involved by hitting on two shots to open the second. The junior made a name for himself as a sophomore who played so well in Paterson Catholic's deep playoff run, which turned out to be the school's last. With Mike, arguably the best player in the nation, covering him this night, he knew it'd be difficult to steal the show like he had so many times throughout the regular season.

It was a foregone conclusion that Mack and Anderson needed help from their supporting cast, and that's exactly what they were getting as the second quarter unraveled. Jimmy Hall converted a put-back after grabbing several offensive rebounds. A fuming Boyle called timeout as his team squandered its lead and enabled St. Anthony to even things up, 21–21, with 4:30 remaining in the first half.

Boyle expected Mack and Anderson would make shots, but getting outrebounded signified his team was getting completely outworked. Boyle stormed onto the court before his players reached the bench. "Are you kidding me?" he snapped with a snarl on his face.

The timeout served as a wake-up call for the Celtics, who mustered up another spurt of effectiveness. Mike rejected a shot from Frink—a play Boyle asked of his superstar to alter the confidence of the opposing center—and Derrick hit another short jumper. Mike converted a pair of free throws after forcing a turnover and then drilled a three-pointer two possessions later. It was the Michael Kidd-Gilchrist that 8,057 came to see. You could even say those who paid the $75 for scalper's tickets were getting their money's worth.

Mike's presence shook the Friars, who were at a standstill; they didn't seem comfortable on offense one bit. Chris, who already had eight points, and Derrick had cooled off but still were creating shots. St. Anthony couldn't even cash in on some ill-advised fouls, as Anderson missed two free throws with 28 seconds left before halftime.

Chris got another open look and launched a three-pointer that went awry at the buzzer. Hurley breathed a sigh of relief and escorted his team to the locker room trailing, 28–23.

Rae Miller walked into the Rutgers women's basketball team locker room, a plush space filled with leather couches, framed pictures, a big-screen television mounted to the wall, and a movie theater-type section for film viewing. These surroundings were certainly different than what St. Patrick was used to. Usually the team would congregate at halftime and before and after games inside a cramped, nondescript area with rusted lockers and a single wooden bench.

As a whole, the extravagant Rutgers Athletic Center dwarfed Kean University's Harwood Arena, a beautifully well-lit place where the

Celtics played their home games because St. Patrick's gym looked more like an open storage area.

With the Celtics clinging to just a five-point lead, even the game's situation was unlike any other. Boyle so often pointed out that his team was never threatened during the season. "There would be games where we'd only be up ten or 12 or whatever, but you never once thought we were in any trouble," he would say.

This was a bit different.

Amid all this change, Rae internalized his fears. He wondered if this game was winnable, wondered if St. Patrick had enough gas in the tank to make it home. Why? He got the sense of the needle approaching empty the evening before.

"I worried about it the last practice on Tuesday before the Wednesday game," Rae said. "That practice scared me. Everything was changed. The focus changed. There were cameras showing up in the middle of practice, from MSG to News 12 to HBO. There were reporters everywhere. And I just saw in (the players') faces, they were tired. They needed a breather from all of it.

"We needed to muster up all this energy. Throughout the year it wasn't that teams were ever afraid of us. Most teams wanted to play us because they wanted to see how tough we were and how tough they actually were. It was draining. With all those types of distractions, it took a lot out of us."

True or not, his speculation received some concrete evidence once Boyle chose to pinpoint what he felt was the biggest problem of all through two quarters of play.

"They have three offensive-rebound baskets," Boyle said. "We've got to rebound better. Use two hands and be aggressive. Derrick and Chris, I haven't seen either of you grab a rebound. Meanwhile, you're watching Mack fly out of nowhere and getting one!"

Yes, Mack was showing a type of energy completely absent from everyone on the Celtics roster.

"We're settling for way too many long threes," Boyle continued. "We have to execute things better because we're settling for too many jump shots. Let's get some movement going. We have two minutes left. You want it? Let's go!"

Meanwhile, Hurley preached down the hall about how his team was right where it needed to be. The Friars were enjoying a game that consisted of four long quarters; they had nothing but time to chip away. On the night of the Friars' Tournament of Champions victory over Elizabeth in 1989, Hurley told the *New York Times*: "If we didn't win the Tournament of Champions, the season would have been considered a failure. We had to win so we wouldn't be the Rodney Dangerfields of the national polls."

St. Anthony was rid of such a burden this season; all eyes were on the favorite, the new sheriff in town, St. Patrick.

The Celtics, on the other hand, seemed squeamish and wanted the night to be over. If they were going to win the mythical national championship and cast away the program's demons of playing second fiddle to Hurley, they would do it by escaping.

By the end of the third, that stomach-turning feeling heightened. Jordan Quick opened the third with a pair of three-pointers and Kyle Anderson capitalized on a steal by converting a wide-open layup. A five-point deficit at the half turned into a seven-point lead in a matter of minutes. Boyle stood still on the sideline with his arms folded. Hurley's team had a pulse; Boyle's was near flatlining.

But just as he did in the City of Palms Classic, Derrick rose to the occasion and anchored a short comeback that saw his team regain the advantage, 39–35, with two minutes to go in the quarter. Derrick was the subject of a front-page story in the *Star-Ledger* that morning involving the heart-warming tale of the senior keeping his incarcerated brother in thoughts and prayers every day. In many ways, the day was about him. It was only fitting he was carrying a sluggish St. Patrick team on his back.

The Western Kentucky-bound guard netted nine points in just over three minutes, and the Celtics were back in business. Lucky Jones found a way to escape the opposition's defense and made his third layup or dunk of the game, while Mack hit a circus-like layup over Jarrel's outstretched body in midair. In the waning seconds of the third, Derrick—the kid whose lone bugaboo was being successful at the foul line—made one of two free throws, and St. Patrick closed the third with a slim 40–39 lead.

In fitting fashion, the most hyped high school basketball game New Jersey had ever seen was shaping up to be a dandy. One question, however, that blanketed those rooting for the Celtics caused a stir in the stands.

Where was Mike?

The Kentucky-bound senior who was listed as the probable No. 1 pick in the 2012 NBA draft was struggling mightily, thanks to a brilliant defensive effort by Lucky Jones. Mike scored seven points in the first half but was held scoreless in the third. If it weren't for Derrick and his 10 third-quarter points, the game would've been way out of reach at that point.

Earlier in the season, after cruising past Plainfield at Teaneck High School in the New Year's Jump-off Tournament, Hurley borrowed a philosophy from Dwyane Wade, one the Hall of Fame coach believed applied to his team. In fact, the Miami Heat superstar's statement conveyed how confident St. Anthony's basketball program was.

"Dwyane Wade said this week that his team is not a championship team right now, but is developing championship-team habits," Hurley said that night. He then went on to comment on how the arrival of Mack and Anderson spun St. Anthony into a transitional period of adjustment.

"It's very strange because they transferred in and right away were the best players on the team. So, our guys who are returning are adjusting to them. The chemistry is starting to develop. They're both unselfish to a fault, and there's a lot of potential here."

Hurley's assessment turned into prophecy, as his team was engaging in a heated battle for the national championship. Only, the Friars were ranked second and the Celtics were first. Eight minutes were left to alter that calculus.

As Jones made a layup to open the fourth and hand the Friars a two-point lead, Boyle and his team were dangling. With a pivotal steal by Anderson and another layup from Quick, St. Patrick lost its grip completely.

Frink converted a layup.

Derrick missed three free throws in a matter of two minutes.

Frink made another layup, further exposing the Celtics' porous interior defense.

Anderson hit a jumper.

Boyle looked up at the scoreboard, which read: St. Anthony 52, St. Patrick 42; just 3:22 to go.

All of a sudden, tight strands that kept the Celtics together as the top basketball team in the nation frayed enough to put their undefeated season in grave danger. While St. Anthony clasped onto a healthy lead despite going one for five at the charity stripe (the Friars finished seven for 21 for the game) in the fourth, Chris and Derrick made three of four from the line to keep the deficit from ballooning any more.

Jones and Frink scored again, but it was Mack who delivered the death blow. With Mike Rice sitting in the stands just hours after his Rutgers team fell to St. John's in the Big East Tournament at Madison Square Garden, the future Scarlet Knights point guard drove the lane, weaved past two defenders and drew a foul before releasing an off-balance shot that kissed off the glass.

The arena exploded. Hurley raised both arms in the air, clenching his fists, while looking up at the sky.

Glory in Jersey City again.

It was over.

Mack stood in front of a crazed section behind the basket and saluted the fans with a boyish smile on his face. As Mack made the ensuing free throw, giving St. Anthony a 59–45 advantage, the fans who expected a changing of the guard in the national high school basketball realms began filing out.

Michael Kidd-Gilchrist made his final steps as a high school basketball player onto the bench upon being called for his fifth foul. His night was over before the buzzer sounded, and the All-American, who walked away with just seven measly points, buried his face into Rae Miller's chest with hopes of hiding the tears that soaked his face.

Seconds before St. Anthony clinched a 62–45 win in the North Non-Public B title game and afforded itself the chance to win the overall championship and then in the Tournament of Champions, Hurley took his starters out. Mack, Anderson, Frink, and Jones exited to a raucous ovation. As the four stood at the end of the bench, Mack took a seat and wiped tears of happiness from his eyes. He was sobbing; the relief was pouring out of him, knowing he took down the best team in the country and, in turn, was now *on* the best team in the country.

Rae's worst fears came true. St. Patrick, as valiant as it was, was mentally, physically, and emotionally spent. In other words, there was a direct explanation for being outscored 23–5 in the final quarter of the program's most magnified game.

"It was different for them because of all the attention on the team," he said several weeks later. "There was never a normal day, ever. There were always cameras and reporters, and the situations with Mike and then Derrick's family and his brother being in jail. It seemed like there was always something. It was very difficult. It was our first time winning the City of Palms; it was the first time we were number one that early for so long.

"Then we had Chris Martin get knocked senseless on television, and we were traveling to Florida and back from Florida and then back again only to then go to Massachusetts. It was crazy. It was crazy every day. It was always one situation or another. We just wanted to get through the season unscathed. But we came up short, which was disappointing because of all that work that we put into it."

St. Anthony was ready to claim another state title under Hurley when the Friars would face Cardinal McCarrick in the overall Non-Public B final in three days. From there, they would move on to the Tournament of Champions, which consisted of all the sectional winners, for all the marbles. If the school from Jersey City made it through that obstacle course, Hurley would have a fourth national title and a fifth undefeated season added to his resume.

A celebration kicked off amongst Hurley and the all-new No. 1 team in the country, while pain filled the air in the solemn room across the hallway.

Boyle stood in front of his dejected players in silence.

Mike and Da'shawn, finally somewhat composed after spending several minutes sobbing on the red couch against the wall near the entry hallway, were escorted to the seats in back of the room along with the rest of their teammates, where the Rutgers women's basketball team conducted its film viewing.

For over two hours, the Celtics were on the hardwood below a nonstop blitzkrieg of shrieking, screaming, cheering, booing, shouting, and the distinct buzz of the scoreboard, which filled the air with noise at a sonic-boom level. At this moment, this period of regret, sporadic sniffles and coughs interrupted an eerie silence.

Austin, Jarrel, and Derrick sat in the front row wiping their drenched eyes and staring at their coach, who was at a loss for words.

Adjusting his stance and slowly stroking his chin, Boyle looked down.

Many would say, after 23 years as a coach, Boyle was never one to struggle with conveying his thoughts because he would use those prolonged sentences that often tailed off the subject and found their way back to stating his uncensored opinion. He always was, always will be, a reporter's dream interview—a fascinating figure always armed with something enlightening to say, never absent of zest and color.

A whole minute, an eternity in a wordless forum, went by.

He wanted so badly to tell his guys that everything would be okay, that what just transpired to the dismay of the St. Patrick community would soon blow over, that their dream season, which shattered into fragments of despair, was salvageable.

Boyle tried his damndest to make sense of all the painful thoughts that ran through his mind. He folded his arms and stared at the floor, keeping his emotional and reflective disclosure to himself.

Sometimes basketball is like life in general. Sometimes things are not fair. Sometimes dreams take an alternate route, for reasons you cannot understand right now. I have been doing this for a long time, and I wonder if I'll ever understand.

All I know is that I wanted it just as badly as you did. I was there for every practice, every moment, every time we were together. We went through a lot. It seems like just yesterday we began practice, hoping for a chance to win it all. Hell, we were all daring enough to firmly believe we could do the unthinkable, run the table and become the toast of the country without any bumps in the road. We almost did. Isn't that incredible?

Remember when I told you guys you can't achieve personal success unless we achieve what we want as a group? You all listened to me. You all trusted me that if we stuck together as a team, we'd get there.

Boyle's bottom lip began to quiver.

Remember when we welcomed the new guys to our family? Chris Martin, Hakim Saintil, Jason Boswell, Dana Raysor, Dakari Johnson, I knew right away each of you was special.

Chris, I'm so proud of you for becoming a man during your tough journey. I know it must not have been easy to fit in as the new kid for just one year. But you had an open mind, you worked hard, and you became one of our best players. Without you, we aren't here. Without you, this team isn't the one that took an entire nation by storm.

Hakim, remember when I yelled at you so much for being too aggressive and, in turn, making irresponsible decisions in the heat of the moment in games or practice? You learned. You listened. I have such high hopes for you. You're going to be great one day.

Jay and *Dana*, like Hakim, you quickly showed me potential. I can't wait to see your faces when you realize it's all coming together on the court.

Dakari, with your size, your great attitude and eagerness, you're going to be someone special. I still can't believe you are just a freshman. I remember when you hit that rookie wall. I had faith that you'd figure out how to push through and become a player that learned on the job and realized the kind of future that is ahead of you. Well, you did just that. You have an awful lot to be proud of.

Da'shawn Suber, I know why you are crying the hardest out of everyone in this room. You care. I know you do. All those times I watched coach Rae order you to run outside as punishment, I couldn't help but laugh inside because I know we have an understanding, as a family, we want you to become better. I know you probably think the window closed. It hasn't. I'm going to challenge you to become as good as Jarrel was at the point guard position for next year. I know you can do it.

Taylor Plummer, you and I have known each other for a while. I coached your older brother and saw him become our unsung hero so many times. I get the impression you're destined to do the same next year for this team. People always comment on how our program is a tight-knit group. We joke, we laugh, and we truly enjoy each other. You've always been the staple when it came to that. You're the most charismatic kid here. I know I have scolded you for taking jokes too far sometimes. Inside, I always appreciated it.

DaQuan Grant, one of my only regrets this year was not finding more minutes for you. You were always a team player. I want you to know that I noticed all those times you finished first in sideline-to-sideline relay races during practice. I never took for granted how unselfish you were.

Trevis Wyche, it's always a rewarding feeling when a coach sees one of his young kids grow up. I was so glad to see you blossom as a contributor. I remember when Chris was out with the concussion and I was forced to trust you in tight situations during important games. You made me believe you have one hell of a future as a basketball player. Don't stop improving.

Tyrone O'Garro, whether you played 20 minutes or two minutes, you made it count. I truly believe this team is not a national force without you. I loved how you embraced it when we all made fun of your extraordinary intelligence. Trust me, that will make you a great man one day. You always got straight As on your report card, but also aced your junior season, too.

Austin Colbert, last year when you were a freshman I saw a kid destined to dominate on the court. This year I saw you go through some struggles and adapt for the better. The second half of the season showed everybody just how talented you are. Remember all those times when I got on you for not switching on defense? I hope you hear my voice when you play at a big-time college someday. Helping you mature as a person and a player has been an honor.

Jarrel Lane, you were so much more than just my floor general. You were my assistant coach with a ball in his hands the whole game. You can say that bond started when you were six years old and attending my camps. Remember those days? I sure do. I still have pictures. Don't dwell on this. Don't let this define your career. You added your name to a list of all-time great St. Patrick point guards. Take that thought with you to college. I know you'll be great. You'll always have a fan in me.

Derrick Gordon, maybe you don't know this, but I always told reporters that you were a worthy candidate for the All-American team. I meant every word of it. You were one of the few guys I ever coached who was a true threat on offense for more than two years. I've gotten to know you; I've come to admire your driven demeanor. Don't ever lose that. If Western Kentucky is on television, you know I'll be watching.

Mike Gilchrist, I understand. I understand this isn't fair. I know you wanted more. You gave me everything. You sacrificed it all. And guess what? You are one of the greatest players I will ever coach. For the rest of your long basketball career, people will just see you as a gifted athlete on the court. Millions upon millions of people will be deprived of actually getting to know you the way I have. You're more than just a superstar. You're a great person. Don't change for anybody.

Coaches, maybe I don't say it enough, but this team is nothing without you guys. I've known you all for a long time. A head coach is not much of a leader without his supporting cast on the sideline. I never forgot that. I never will.

I don't know what to say about this game. It just wasn't meant to be. Someday we'll look back at this season and forget this pain we're all feeling. We'll remember our trips to Florida, you guys hating me for taking your *phones in Massachusetts, the feeling of invincibility, secretly loving every second of cameras following our every move, Jarrel's shot at the City of Palms that made this all possible, and all the wins in between.*

I'll never forget this. You'll always be my boys.

And I love you all.

Boyle composed himself and cleared his throat, giving way for Principal Joe Picaro to offer a much-needed icebreaker. "I'm proud of you for conducting yourselves as gentlemen," Picaro said. "You're all winners. I'm very proud of you, and I want to thank all of you."

"Um, I want to thank the seniors," Boyle started, clearing his throat to hide the cracking of his voice. "It's been a great year up until tonight. It's definitely crushing for you guys, as well as the rest of us. I don't really want to rehash about the game right now, but in that second half we had some sloppy handling that led to that quick run. Obviously this is very disappointing, but all you guys have to find a way to get back to work so we can win a title."

He ran his hand across his cheek and exhaled.

"Man, this is tough."

"Younger guys, part of this is looking forward," Rae jumped in to offer some relief. "We need to take care of our bodies. They pushed us around tonight. You guys just aren't ready, and you've got to get ready to do it next year. We're in this together. We need to accept this hell. Don't hang your heads, because we're coming back next year. And seniors, we appreciate you. You've done so much. I love you guys so much."

Those seniors were too overcome by emotion to think about the spectacular things they had accomplished. Mike, Derrick, Jarrel, and Chris, along with their coach, had taken the good St. Patrick reputation and made it even more pristine. This group opened the eyes of everybody across the nation, who wondered whether it was even possible for a team filled with teenagers to pull off such an incredible run. They enabled their leader to win his third National Coach of the Year award and gripped wide audiences by blowing past other national powerhouses on ESPN television networks.

Even in falling short of their short-term goal, even in losing the chance to dethrone Hurley's big, bad Friars as the cream of the crop in the Garden State, they achieved something broader. It was a dream of Boyle's some 23 years ago: find a way to the top of high school basketball.

Who knew this group was capable of such a feat despite tasting a heavy dose of pain.

"The sign of a good team is how it responds to adversity," Boyle said. "How do you want to come back? You work hard academically because that's what going to get you far in life. The key is how we react to all of this. Thank you for trusting me and for making this magical season happen."

Boyle and Rae embraced in a drawn-out hug in front of the players, who were too distraught to even console one another.

Leaving his players in the comforting hands of Rae and the other assistants, Boyle stepped to the podium in front of several dozen reporters in a cramped media room down the hall that looked more like a press conference following the Super Bowl.

"We looked a little fatigued," Boyle opened. "We got the lead back in the second half, but it looked like we wouldn't have enough energy to sustain it. In the first half when it was 28–23, I think they had three offensive rebound baskets, and we had zero. They should have been up nine or ten, and we were up five. We had some turnovers, so you can credit them for pressuring the ball.

"It's been an emotional rollercoaster. We had an emotional win over Gill St. Bernard's the other day, and we had a good practice on Monday, but our kids were too hyped. Our energy was sapped on Tuesday."

One local reporter asked about Mike's outing, one that saw the All-American grab 14 rebounds but score just seven first-half points before fouling out in his final high school game.

"Obviously, with Mike, they were packing it in," Boyle said. "For us, sometimes you want to win so bad you force it a little bit. He always filled the stat sheet. Obviously he's one of the greatest players in New Jersey history. This doesn't define his career. This was a big game, but he was great for the whole year."

An expressionless Boyle concluded his final statement of the 2010–11 season: "You had an atmosphere where there was such a buzz. Unfortunately, we didn't play off the energy. It's a tough loss."

Hurley, meanwhile, did a remarkable job disguising his elation by downplaying the significance of a victory in the biggest game in his native state's history.

"I'd hate to burst your bubble, but this was a North Jersey semifinal game," Hurley said. "We need to win our game on Saturday. This was a monumental win, but it'd be responsible for the team that won today to go and win again."

"We've been a work in progress all year," Hurley continued, with flashing lights illuminating his sweaty face. "We've come to know it's been a difficult situation, but they adapted well."

Adapt.

That was something the Celtics were unable to do once the pressure mounted in that fateful fourth quarter. Truth be told, even as the dust was far from settling, opinions as to why St. Patrick folded were being formulated in the eyes of every credentialed media figure.

"Kevin was wound up too tight. The thought of the national title consumed him," Mike Quick figured. "It was all about the national championship. For the first time, and maybe this is why they didn't win, he took his eyes of Hurley and focused on the national championship. He took the competitiveness that had fueled him all those years, took the 'I've-got-to-get-what-Hurley-has' and lost it in his bid to win a national championship."

Derrick was the last to leave the locker room. Mike had just exited with Cindy, who congratulated Dakari on a fantastic freshman season as the six-foot-ten boy was consoled by his mother.

On the other side of the arena, Boyle hugged his daughter, Kelscey, who was home from studying abroad in England, and he waited for Kelly to finish her conversation with several people in a group not far away.

"C'mon, let's go," Boyle softly urged his wife.

With that, Kevin Boyle walked through the doors and into the offseason, unknowingly taking his final steps out of a gymnasium as head coach of the St. Patrick Celtics.

Fifteen

I wanted him to stay at St. Pat's forever and get 1,000 wins there, but this is a business, so I understand. It takes a special type to coach to win with or without talent. He should be in the Hall of Fame.
—Shaheen Holloway

Dave Calloway received the fateful phone call on a Sunday night in late February from Athletic Director Marilyn McNeil. After fourteen years at the helm of Monmouth University, Calloway's run was over; he was informed the Hawks intended on hiring a new coach upon completing their fifth consecutive losing season in the Division I Northeast Conference, a respectable league that often serves as a punching bag to top-seeded teams in the first round of the NCAA Tournament.

"It wasn't my choice," Calloway said in a telephone interview with the Associated Press. "Everything has been great. Coaching at Monmouth has been terrific. You always like to win more. I have nothing but good things to say about the university and everybody involved. This is just how the business works. They made a decision."

Now McNeil had another decision to make. Which candidate would propel Monmouth back to the top of the conference, where it had finished under Calloway in 2001, 2004, and 2006? Following a 9–21 season in 2010–11, a big splash needed to be made.

Through the early stages of the interviewing process, McNeil declined to comment on the standing of any candidates. The *Asbury Park Press* reported that Jeff Ruland, a former NBA All-Star and coach at Iona, who was currently coaching at Division II University of the District of Columbia, was in the running.

At the time when the first quarter was put in the collegiate coaching carousel, when Providence had just hired former Fairfield coach Ed Cooley, the names of possible candidates for the Monmouth opening began to emerge on a daily basis. Notre Dame assistant Martin Ingelsby, Bowling Green's Louis Orr, William Paterson's Jose Rebimbas, Vanderbilt assistant King Rice, and Temple assistant Dave Duke were all listed. Some felt Calloway's right-hand man, assistant Kevin Murphy, was the likely front-runner.

Two names on the list, though, caused a stir in the high school universe: Christian Brothers Academy Coach Geoff Billet and the newly named Naismith National Coach of the Year, Kevin Boyle.

Billet was an interesting option, considering his deep roots in New Jersey as the leader of a prominent Catholic high school. Perhaps those ties would deliver an advantage when it came to in-state recruiting. Boyle, on the other hand, had a glistening resume that proved he had the hands to build a program from the ground up and maintain that status year after year.

Sure, it was a long shot for any high school coach to make the jump to a Division I level. Danny Hurley had done it a year ago, going from St. Benedict's Prep to Wagner. Why couldn't Boyle?

Before the state playoffs began, Boyle had said on record he would explore an option if it was worth looking into. This was definitely worth looking into.

One report claimed if St. Peter's College coach John Dunne left his post to take the same position at Monmouth or Manhattan, Boyle could step in. Boyle later said that was never an option he truly considered.

Plus, anyway, coaching a Division I program armed with a beautiful arena worth $57 million, which had just been completed after seventeen years of its original planning, and which was also close to his Rahway home seemed too good to ignore.

Boyle threw his name in the Monmouth hat.

During a school day one week after the loss to St. Anthony, Elizabeth Mayor Chris Bollwage visited St. Patrick and bought the entire basketball team pizza and soda to be enjoyed in the tiny library in the basement under the gym. Bollwage expressed his delight and appreciation for the Celtics, of whom he had become an avid fan.

Outside the doorway Boyle spoke about the Monmouth job. Its possibilities, its perks, and why he'd be thrilled to become a Hawk were topics he causally touched upon while wearing a green Jordan-brand zip-up. His interview was scheduled for sometime the following week, so he was hard at work in preparing his updated resume and a presentation that highlighted all of his lofty accomplishments.

Boyle was not anxious to leave the place he had called home for 23 years as a coach and teacher. He was simply shaken by the prospects of the school eventually closing due to financial reasons, and he was lured by the possibility of a fatter paycheck for the sake of his family's well-being. A merge with St. Mary's of Jersey City was rumored, but Boyle jokingly said he wouldn't be a fan "because then we might have to change our colors. I'll tell you, if that happens I'm making sure our color remains green, and the backs of our jerseys still say Celtics."

He followed up with a loud laugh, but knowing him, he was somewhat serious, too. St. Patrick was still his baby, no matter the outcome of his interview.

Boyle's name was in the news every day, it seemed, so the possibility of St. Patrick's heart and soul making an exodus on his own terms reached the eyes and ears of proud alumni. Still, it was better than reading about how St. Anthony completed its undefeated season and ran past Plainfield, 61–49, on March 21 at the IZOD Center to hand Bob Hurley his eleventh Tournament of Champions crown and fourth national championship.

Mike Nardi, the former Villanova guard who had spent four years of high school with Boyle and helped the program capture the 2003 Tournament of Champions crown, was one who was surprised but supportive.

"To be honest, I thought, sooner or later, he'd look for another challenge," Nardi said. "He's such a great coach, and he was so great for so many years at the high school level. But he made a decision. He had to be selfish for once, look out for himself and his family. He's amazing at what he does, so he had to take advantage of it. St. Patrick is a great place, but it isn't the greatest place for resources or pay. This is a business."

This business was one that could include a six-figure salary, a job with plenty of opportunity, and a new so-called office still close to home. It was the perfect fit.

Marilyn McNeil, however, later determined Vanderbilt assistant King Rice was the perfect fit for her broken boys basketball program.

Rice's credentials were superb. The former standout point guard at

North Carolina from 1988 to 1991 under legendary coach Dean Smith had been an assistant at Vanderbilt for the previous five seasons. He also served as an assistant at Illinois State, Oregon, and Providence. Acting as former NBA player Rick Fox's personal trainer for five years was a cherry on top of the sundae.

Boyle, meanwhile, shrugged off the disappointment and turned his attention to enjoying the rest of the school year and preparing for another run at Hurley, or possibly another college opening.

"He was never upset about the Monmouth situation and not getting chosen for that," Rae Miller said. "That went on for about three or four weeks. He was probably one of the last guys interviewed, and, by that time, when you're looking at seven or eight different guys, it kind of becomes yesterday's news. He had already prepared to look at other options. He also always knew St. Pat's would still be there. He knew we'd have a very good team returning to make another run at it. He was never nervous.

"The Monmouth thing wasn't a surprise. I know how difficult it is to get to that level. Very few high school coaches will be able to move directly to Division I. There's so much pressure in the tristate area, too, that Monmouth would've had to take a chance on a guy like Kevin. But it was probably a blessing in disguise."

A blessing in disguise it was. Boyle needed just another week to see why.

Kevin Sutton had served as athletic director and head coach of the boys basketball team at an international boarding school located just outside of Orlando, Florida, for eight seasons. In a mission statement written on Montverde Academy's website, he wrote, "My coaching reflects Luke 12:48 ... "To whom much is given, much is expected."

Ironically enough, his performance did not meet the high expectations of school headmaster Kasey Kesselring. Sutton was forced out, and the reasons were kept internally. The initial report by Bright House Sports Network stated Boyle and Findlay Prep coach Mike Peck were expected to interview for the job.

Montverde Academy is known for its fine educational system and growing athletic programs. The Eagles' boys soccer program was among the nation's best, while the basketball team had completed a 22–4 season in which it was ranked No. 15—13 slots below St. Patrick—in the final *USA Today* Super 25.

Under the direction of Sutton, the Eagles had produced two NBA players—Luc Richard Mbah a Moute of the Milwaukee Bucks and Solomon Alabi, a seven-foot-one Florida State product selected by the Dallas Mavericks in the second round of the 2010 draft.

The night before Boyle's interview with Monmouth, he checked his e-mail before going to bed. He found a message from Montverde Academy, but passed it on to Kelly.

"There's an e-mail you might want to see," Boyle said. "I'm going to bed. I have to focus on tomorrow, but let me know what you think."

After Kevin and Kelly expressed their interest in the Florida school, they soon flew down to Montverde Academy, all 1,095 miles, and met with Kesselring. Boyle ultimately blew him away with his win-at-all-costs attitude and grandiose resume.

"I always told Kevin you don't owe us anything, and we don't owe you anything," St. Patrick Principal Joe Picaro said. "We gave you the opportunity, and you made us the best team in the country. It was a great trade-off, so to speak. He was putting in for the Monmouth job, so I knew what was going on. I'd always pull for him to do well, whether it is at St. Patrick or not.

"He told me about Montverde (pronounced Montverd)—I say Montverdy out of spite—and I said you have to take this job; you don't have a choice. We're a little Catholic school. We don't have any money. So I did the opposite of what you'd think I would do, and I encouraged him to take it. I want success for him."

In an emotional, private meeting with the players at St. Patrick the morning after he arrived back home, Boyle broke the news he was going to accept Kesselring's offer.

"We all flew down together because we wanted to decide together," Kelly said.

"It was very sad because they all loved Kevin and Kevin loved them," Red Migliore admitted about the moment he heard the news of his basketball coach telling the players he was moving on.

Jarrel Lane, one of the seniors in the shocked room who wouldn't be affected by the change because he had played his final game at St. Patrick, was happy for his mentor. He kicked off a frenzy of back-and-forth banter between teammates on Twitter by posting: "KB is taking his talents to South Beach!"

Not long after Rae had confirmed the change to me via phone, every media outlet imaginable posted a story on this huge alteration in the DNA of high school basketball. ESPN.com had an image of Boyle slapped onto the front of its Preps page. The local newspaper reporters were busy tapping away on the keyboards to launch a breaking-news story for their respective sites and for the next morning's editions.

"The biggest hurt was leaving the kids," Kelly said. "Kevin's always made it a point to stick to his word. He'd always say how he'd be around for their whole high school careers. He stopped saying that about four years ago."

Meanwhile, Rae was the first to speak on behalf of his close friend and the talk of the town. "He was never upset about evaluating certain situations," Rae said. "He's now elated to be at Montverde Academy."

Mike Quick, who developed a bond with Boyle over the years, reached for his cell phone and dialed the coach who sent media outlets scurrying for facts, quotes, and confirmations of this developing story. Quick was the only media member for whom Boyle picked up.

"My question was, 'Is it true?' He said, 'Yeah, it's time.' I had done this with other guys I consider friends. You build relationships with these guys, and while I was happy for him and his family, I was sad because he made covering St. Pat's fun," Quick said. "When it comes to St. Patrick and St. Anthony, that dynamic has changed forever. It'll never be the same, and that's a shame."

Recruiting analyst Tom Konchalski echoed those thoughts, telling Adam Zagoria of SNY.tv, "There will be a huge hole in Garden State high school basketball. I just hope the school stays open. One of the great rivalries in New Jersey in the last 30 or 40 years has just dissipated."

Since St. Patrick was to retain key returners such as Austin Colbert, Dakari Johnson, Da'shawn Suber, and Tyrone O'Garro for the following season, the gap of talent levels between the Celtics and Hurley's Friars didn't appear to be extraordinarily wide. Without Boyle, though, the heated rivalry that captivated so many people across the state and nation was deflated of so much tension and drama.

The ongoing argument of Hurley or Boyle, Boyle or Hurley as New Jersey's prime basketball sage was vapor. Hurley stood alone.

Boyle reluctantly bowed out of the blood war for greener pastures, and understandably so. Twenty-three years of maintaining a steadily growing dynasty and garnering three National Coach of the Year awards earned Boyle a financial incentive that reportedly exceeded the salaries of four current Division I college coaches, a new house across the street from the school, and a car.

"I'm disappointed, in a sense, that he wasn't offered to be a college coach because he'd be an unbelievable college coach," Sandy Pyonin said. "As a high school coach, you couldn't have asked for anything more from him. He works hard; he loves the game. He loved the game as a player, and he loves it as a coach. He always puts in as many hours as needed."

He finally cashed in.

"I had some inclination that the opportunity was his. I had no inclination that the opportunity would be as good as it was," Rae said of the offer. "He had to consider it greatly. What was shocking to me was that there was an opportunity at the high school level worth taking. I never anticipated another high school that would offer the same benefits as a Division I college team."

Montverde Academy got its guy, one of the best in the business.

The next day, Boyle conducted his first on-camera interview since announcing his decision to leave St. Patrick and move down to the sunshine of Florida.

"It was tough because you grow fond of the kids—you care about them—and it definitely isn't an easy thing to do," Boyle told MSG Varsity. "Some of the kids, they came here obviously to play for St. Pat's, possibly for me, and you always try and do what's right for the kids here. But in this case, I had to do what's right for my family."

Meanwhile, Picaro fielded phone calls to express his sincere adoration for Boyle. He also put a bandage on the temporarily bleeding program, whose wounds of falling to St. Anthony about four weeks prior to that had just begun to heal. By naming assistant principal and jayvee coach Chris Chavannes the "interim program head coach" the Celtics were hoisted by some stability again.

While Picaro, Red Migliore, and Boyle shared some laughs over dinner that night at a pizzeria near the Menlo Park Mall, Chavannes was left to begin his regime at a time of distress.

"The kids won't see too much difference in anything," Chavannes said. "We'll have the same philosophy. How we go about accomplishing those things might be a little bit different. A lot of the kids here have already played for me. They know me very well. I've spent a lot of time with them in school and out of school, so, again, the transition won't be difficult for both parties."

Perhaps, but playing for St. Patrick without Boyle was like watching the New York Yankees play without Derek Jeter.

Still, it was time to face facts. Kevin Boyle was moving on.

♣

The green balloons darted back and forth in the wind, being held down by strings wrapped around the stairwell banister. The St. Patrick annual basketball banquet in a church hall down the street from St. Patrick was moments from beginning, and Kevin and Kelly Boyle arrived just in time before all the 50–50 tickets were sold.

Trays of catered food were sizzling over flames; it was the only sight Taylor Plummer and Dana Raysor could keep their eyes on. Joining Taylor and Dana at the L-shaped table area reserved for the Celtics were Dakari Johnson, Chris Martin, Michael Kidd-Gilchrist, Jarrel Lane, and DaQuan Grant. Soon after, Trevis Wyche, Derrick Gordon, Austin Colbert, and Tyrone O'Garro filled in empty chairs.

"Everybody in the country knows about St. Pat's," one guest speaker told the crowd seated around him. "Anybody that loves basketball, really, knows about St. Pat's. In life we learn to appreciate taking steps up the ladder. Right now, you guys are high on this ladder. It's remarkable what this little school has done."

The speaker received a round of applause for his 15-minute monologue, and Migliore then grabbed the microphone.

"In all the years I've been at St. Pat's, this had been the longest we've been number one in the nation. Everybody in the nation knows St. Pat's. We had the greatest coach we've ever had in Kevin Boyle, and I'd be remiss if I didn't say good luck, and, Kevin Boyle, you will always be a part of St. Patrick."

Migliore went on to speak about each individual player, saving Mike for last.

"He's everyone's hero," Red said.

"Actually I think Kyrie was the best," Boyle quipped with a laugh that livened up the crowd.

It was the man of the hour's turn. Decked in a striped button-down shirt and dark jeans, Boyle cleared his throat for a few words certainly less dreadful to utter than those said weeks ago in the lonely locker room in the Rutgers Athletic Center.

"First of all, congratulations to our cheerleaders," Boyle said pointing to the corner where the cheer team sat. "They wanted a shout-out, and they got one!"

"Karen does so much for us behind the scenes," he said when the cheering ceased, "and I probably talk to her five times a day. All the parents of the seniors, when I first got here we had kids in tough situations, but recently we've had great parents who support the kids and the program. Today's parents are incredible. Just look at Mrs. Plummer and how many people she's helped in all these situations.

"I always say as a coach you're only as good as the staff around you," he continued. "Eric was in his first year and was a tremendous help. We were fortunate to have Ed Leibowitz with us. Jyron Brooks has done a terrific job. Pete Mairston works 14-hour days at his warehouse, and he's at every practice on time. Coach Frank Peralta, a phenomenal salesman, is an example of success. We've got a great group.

"But in over 20 years of coaching, there was one guy who dealt with the parents—good, bad or indifferent—and he's just a great person. He's developed a relationship with every kid, and those relationships are long-lasting. Rae is always the first guy there for anyone. Someday I hope to be as good a person as he is.

"Mr. Picaro, Red—there are just so many special people, and hopefully you can keep it going for years to come. There will be a time when you guys will have a big game against St. Anthony again. I'll be smiling from Florida if we get some revenge."

Every person in the room stood on their feet and offered a minute-long ovation for Boyle. The man who gave his life, time, and effort had made his last public speech as the head coach of St. Patrick.

After it was announced that Boyle was the lucky winner of the 50–50 raffle, he blushed and handed the wad of cash to Picaro. He had to give back one last time.

Kevin Boyle's last day at St. Patrick was a steamy, hot Friday. He spent the majority of the morning of June 11, 2011, sitting with me for the last of his interviews and then went on to cover his last classes.

The Blowback Productions documentary crew members were present, this time without cameras, to see their project's subject off. Boyle turned down a night of dinner and drinks, citing his pending early rise the next morning to catch a flight to Orlando.

He and Kelly had been traveling back and forth several times to begin moving their belongings into their brand-new house in Montverde with hopes of being settled by late July. Boyle shook hands with the members, promising he'd be around sporadically throughout the summer to run some of his camp sessions.

School was dismissed, and Boyle had the majority of the coach's office in the basement cleared. He walked out to his car in the gated parking lot behind the school building, holding a cardboard box under his right arm filled with the memories of 23 years.

He placed the box in his truck, slammed the door and fiddled with his keys while pausing for one last gaze at the place he called home. After backing out of the parking lot, he turned on his right blinker and drove away.

Kevin Boyle's job there was done.

Epilogue

NBA Commissioner David Stern approached the podium on the stage inside the Prudential Center in Newark, warning the thousands of rowdy fans in attendance that the Cleveland Cavaliers were on the clock.

The shattered franchise suffered through a tumultuous 2010–11 season defined by its hometown hero taking his talents to South Beach, ultimately causing the Cavaliers to go from a top-seeded Eastern Conference team to a 19-win laughingstock.

Ping-Pong balls at the lottery decided Cleveland's original draft position would be No. 4, but a February trade that sent Baron Davis and a 2011 first-round pick from the Los Angeles Clippers to the Cavaliers for Maurice Williams and Jamario Moon gave the LeBron-exodus victims and their uncensored owner Dan Gilbert hope. Despite a mere 2.8 percent chance of that future pick becoming the No. 1, the basketball gods showed compassion for a city in desperate need of a new savior.

Much to dismay of the Clippers, the top selection in the 2011 NBA draft belonged to Cleveland, which became the first team since the 1983 Houston Rockets to own two top-five picks in one year.

Kyrie Irving opted to leave Duke University after his freshman season to enter the draft. His choice to forgo three years of college eligibility was highly criticized because he played in just eight regular-season games before suffering a torn ligament in the big toe that kept him out until the NCAA Tournament. Irving averaged 17.7 points over three games in the Big Dance, but Duke was eliminated by Arizona in the Sweet 16.

On the eve of draft night, Irving sat at a round table inside the Westin hotel in Times Square with dozens of reporters and cameramen inquiring about his decision. Clad in a black suit and red tie, the six-foot-two point guard said being able to play in March Madness and the glamorous opportunity to reach the NBA level swayed his decision. He wanted to become the next St. Patrick alumnus to excel on basketball's biggest stage.

Irving made it a point to sternly shoot down anyone asking if he would welcome the pressure of replacing LeBron James in Cleveland. He glared at one reporter and said, "I'm not the next LeBron; my name is Kyrie Irving."

One year removed from graduating St. Patrick, Irving was holding court on NBA draft media day, wowing reporters with his professionalism and poise.

"Back then I really wasn't thinking that far," he said about NBA dreams at a young age, "but knowing now that I'm at this point, it's a special thing for me. The life lessons I extracted from St. Pat's were how to be tough all the time; tough in a sense that every night we had to play against guys who wanted to kill us.

"It definitely feels good that I'm still projected to go number one. Honestly, let's see how it goes, but it's an honor. It feels surreal, knowing all that hard work is coming to fruition. I'm achieving my dream, and it's an experience I'll remember for the rest of my life."

Knowing the draft would be held just ten minutes from his West Orange home, Irving smiled and said, "It's just the perfect situation for me and my family. It hasn't resonated yet, but it will tomorrow night."

Potentially, Irving would be the third point guard in four years to go No. 1, joining John Wall (Washington, 2010) and Derrick Rose (Chicago, 2008). He could also be the sixth point guard to be selected No. 1 over the last 35 years. In addition to Rose and Wall, the others were John Lucas, Magic Johnson, and Allen Iverson.

Nevertheless, he maintained he had not gotten any hints as to whether he was Cleveland-bound. After all, Arizona forward Derrick Williams and Turkish big-man Enes Kanter were nice options, especially because the Cavaliers could pick Kentucky's Brandon Knight at No. 4 to cover a need for a point guard.

"They're keeping their cards closely, as they should," he shrugged.

The very next night, a Thursday, at seven thirty, the Cavaliers were prepared to show their hand to the world.

Stern reappeared from behind the stage, walked to the microphone, and smiled, waiting for the cheers to subside.

"With the first pick in the 2011 NBA draft …"

Irving, sitting at his table alongside his father, sister, agent, and two best friends, clenched his hands together.

"… the Cleveland Cavaliers select …"

Kevin Boyle, the man who welcomed Kyrie as a junior at St. Patrick and watched him become one of the greatest players he would ever coach, sat at the edge of his seat wearing a red golf shirt just several rows up from the player seating area.

"… Kyrie Irving …"

Irving stood up in conjunction with his family and friends to the sounds of applause, grabbed his father, and embraced him for several seconds, gift wrapping for photographers a beautiful image that became the front page of the *USA Today* sports section on Friday morning.

"To be the number one overall pick as a small guard who played just 11 games in college, I'd have to say it was something that would never happen," said Sandy Pyonin, who trained with Kyrie for more than five years leading up the draft.

He accepted his Cavaliers fitted hat, slowly walked up the stairs on the right side of the stage, and held out his hand to greet Stern. The two posed for pictures, and Irving exited the left side and into a pit for his first interview. He then trotted down the walkway and sat down for another interview with ESPN radio.

Guided by a female Cavaliers official, Irving went into one Prudential Center corridor with a cluster of NBA Entertainment cameramen and reporters following his steps.

Entering a large press-conference area, he sat down at a white table with the NBA draft logo plastered onto the backdrop behind him.

"I want to thank everybody for coming," he started. "When David Stern came up there and said the Cleveland Cavaliers have five more minutes on the clock, that felt like the longest five minutes of my life. It's a great feeling being drafted, knowing that all of my hard work has come to fruition now, and I'm just really looking forward to getting to go to Cleveland and making a quick contribution whenever the NBA season starts."

He answered 14 questions before mentioning Boyle. "I didn't get a chance to talk to Coach Boyle yet. He texted me earlier and congratulated me on this opportunity of mine. I'll probably talk to him a little later, but he played a big influence on my career."

By this time, the Minnesota Timberwolves took Derrick Williams, the Utah Jazz selected Enes Kanter, and the Cavaliers chose former St. Benedict's Prep forward Tristan Thompson with the fourth pick.

A University of Texas standout as a freshman, Thompson played for Danny Hurley at St. Benedict's before transferring to Findlay Prep in Henderson, Nevada, for his senior year of high school. On media day, Thompson recalled referring to St. Patrick as "the enemy" and decided one of the things he wanted to do in the NBA was dunk on Kyrie.

"Tristan is a great friend of mine," Irving said after looking over at the television screen to notice Thompson shaking Stern's hand with a Cavs hat on. "Just having another fellow freshman being drafted to Cleveland, I'm really looking forward to it. Playing with him, I'm really excited. I was looking over there while I was trying to listen to the question at the same time. Having somebody alongside you that will go through the rookie ups and downs with you, it will make the transition into the NBA that much easier."

His fourth interview in about 20 minutes wrapped up, and he was asked to enter a makeshift television interviewing area. The room consisted of several booths created by black curtains with every major news network waiting to interview the man of the hour. Irving made his way down the line, starting with ABC and NBC. After finishing up the 30-minute process, he hugged Enes Kanter in passing and congratulated him on going to Utah.

Irving's father, Drederick; his sister, Asia; his agent; and two best friends—Eli Carter, a former player for Bob Hurley in high school, and Kevin Philemon—met their shining celebrity outside in the hall before walking over to a photo shoot behind the stage together. Irving just finished up a conversation with Cavaliers coach Byron Scott on a BlackBerry the Cleveland official handed him, a brief exchange that went like this:

"Whatever you say, coach. ... I'll be ready every day at practice. ... Oh, I will. Don't you worry. ... Okay, thank you. ... Sounds great, coach. I can't wait."

Waiting for the photographer to finish her preparation, Irving hugged Eli and Kevin. The three looked like little kids again, laughing and playfully punching each other's shoulders.

Kyrie was about to grow up fast, though, as he entered a whole new world of NBA stardom.

♣

Despite swirling rumors of closing its doors because of financial reasons, it was announced St. Patrick High School would remain open for the 2011–12 academic year.

"When Kevin Boyle announced he was going to leave, I heard the school was going to close," Joe Picaro said. "All I can say is no one man can determine what happens to an institution. No one is the end-all, be-all."

HBO aired the Blowback Productions documentary about St. Patrick's basketball team, titled *Prayer for a Perfect Season*, in October 2011.

Winston Smith was serving as the coordinator of basketball operations at Drexel University. During his time at UMass, he was the team captain as a senior and earned the Top Defender Award and the Mr. Hustle Award. The Minutemen made three postseason appearances with Smith on the team, including a pair of trips to the NCAA Tournament. After graduating with a bachelor of science degree in sociology in 2001, he had stints as an assistant coach at Hofstra, St. Francis (Pennsylvania), Youngstown State, and Fairleigh Dickinson. He and Rae Miller speak every day.

Shaheen Holloway continued to serve as an assistant coach to Kevin Williard at Seton Hall University. He and Kevin Boyle speak often.

Al Harrington signed a five-year contract with the Denver Nuggets worth $34.5 million prior to the 2010–11 NBA season. He completed his 13th year in the league, averaging 10.5 points and 4.5 rebounds for the Nuggets, who finished 50–32 in the regular season and were eliminated by the Oklahoma City Thunder in the first round of the Western Conference playoffs. According to basketballreference.com, Harrington has earned over $68 million in his career. He and Kevin Boyle do not speak regularly but remain on good terms.

Samuel Dalembert completed his ninth NBA season in 2010–11 with the Sacramento Kings. He averaged 8.1 points, 8.2 rebounds and 1.5 blocks over 80 games. Dalembert, who has earned over $68 million in his career, continues to contribute to the Haitian earthquake recovery. He and Boyle do not speak regularly.

Mike Nardi had been playing professional basketball in Italy for the last four years. His team didn't make the playoffs in the 2011 season, so he returned home to New Jersey and prepared to weigh his options.

Grant Billmeier stayed as an assistant at Seton Hall University and was enjoying his time coaching at his alma mater.

"When Kevin Williard was hired at Seton Hall, Grant got the assistant coaching job because he would volunteer to show up at every practice," Picaro said. "He was there before everyone else and left after everyone else. Williard asked Shaheen about him, and Shaheen just said that's the way Grant is."

Billmeier's devotion to Kevin Boyle still stood firm.

When approached about an interview for this book, Billmeier replied: "I'd do anything for Coach Boyle." He later added, "He taught me how to manage kids. It's not just about the yelling, but developing relationships. You find out how to get each individual kid to run through a wall for you. You can't scream at every kid. You have to know which ones you need to put your arm around and which ones need a kick in the ass time to time. More than anything, he taught me how to build a team, build a program, and bonding."

Derrick Caracter began his college career at Louisville but transferred to the University of Texas-El Paso in the 2008–09 season upon withdrawing his name from the 2008 NBA draft. He was selected by the Los Angeles Lakers with the 58th pick in the 2010 draft, but averaged just two points and one rebound in 5.1 minutes over 41 games while being shuttled back and forth from the NBA Developmental League as a rookie.

Corey Fisher graduated from Villanova in the spring of 2011. He was not among the 60 players selected in the NBA draft but signed a one-year deal with Antalya B.B. of the Turkish Basketball League in July.

Dexter Strickland completed his sophomore year at North Carolina averaging 7.5 points, 3.1 rebounds, and 2.1 assists over 37 games. His improvement in 2009–10 helped the Tar Heels reach the NCAA Tournament's Elite Eight, where they fell to Kentucky.

Paris Bennett was getting ready to enter his junior year at George Mason, while Dean Kowalski was still working toward becoming a force at point guard for Columbia.

"The position I'm in both academically and athletically is 100 percent attributed to Kevin Boyle and St. Patrick High School," Kowalski said. "I wouldn't trade anything about my experience with him for anything. We played so many great players in high school because of our schedule Coach put together. I turn on the television now, and I say, 'Oh, we beat him, we beat him, and we beat him.'"

Chris Martin signed a national letter of intent with Marshall University in April. After the basketball season concluded, he frequently visited his mother in Washington, DC. The morning of his first summer class at Marshall in early June, he woke up wearing a St. Patrick shirt.

Derrick Gordon took his excitement for attending Western Kentucky to the next level by creating a catchy nickname for his recruiting class, "Team Reset," which instantly made him a fan favorite among Hilltoppers fans on Twitter. He often visits his brother in prison.

Jarrel Lane was the last of the four scholarship seniors to leave New Jersey for college. He walked onto the University of Maryland-Baltimore County campus in mid-June and was looking forward to playing alongside former Celtics teammate Chase Plummer.

Austin Colbert, listed as one of the top 20 rising juniors in the country by many media outlets, was named captain of the Celtics for the 2011–12 season. Over the summer, he left St. Patrick and enrolled at the Hotchkiss School in Connecticut.

During the early summer, Dakari Johnson competed on the Under-16 Developmental Team but was left off the Men's Under-16 USA National team roster. In late July, he transferred to Montverde Academy. He was excited to continue playing for Kevin Boyle.

Jason Boswell transferred to Trinity Catholic in Stamford, Connecticut.

The rising junior felt it was a beneficial move because instead of traveling two hours from the Bronx to Elizabeth, he'd commute 30 minutes to play for a school that had won the Class M title in 2010–11. The transfer did not affect his Division I scholarship offers.

Hakim Saintil transferred to Roselle Catholic, and Tyrone O'Garro passed up serving as a tri-captain for his senior year at St. Patrick and left for St. Peter's Prep. Taylor Plummer chose to enroll at his hometown Plainfield High School, while Da'shawn Suber switched to Lincoln High School in Brooklyn.

Trevis Wyche, Dana Raysor, and DaQuan Grant decided to weigh their options and see if transferring out of St. Patrick would be the best fit for them. Kelly Boyle said all the transfers and lost tuitions are "something the place can't afford. It's scary."

Michael Kidd-Gilchrist scored 16 points and grabbed 12 rebounds in helping the East defeat the West, 111–96, in the McDonald's All-American Game in Chicago. He was named co-MVP with North Carolina-bound forward James McAdoo. He also shined at the 2011 Nike Hoop Summit in Portland, Oregon. In May, he was featured on the cover of SLAM magazine alongside Austin Rivers and Anthony Davis, who was poised to join Mike at the University of Kentucky in the fall of 2011. As of early June, his No. 14 Wildcats jersey had been a popular item in sports retail stores throughout Kentucky.

Assistant coach Jyron Brooks left the St. Patrick staff to coach at St. Peter's Prep. Rae Miller, Rich Biddulph, Frank Peralta, Ed Leibowitz, and Eric Woroniecki were still weighing their options prior to the school year.

Chris Chavannes was looking forward to his first season as head coach of the St. Patrick varsity team. One day into his tenure, he named his captains and opened up to the media about how he has such big shoes to fill.

Kevin, Kelly, and Brendan Boyle moved over the summer into their new house near the campus of Montverde Academy in Montverde, Florida. Kevin Boyle Jr. was thriving at Emerson College, and Kelscey Boyle was set to return to Villanova for her senior year.

Kevin Boyle expressed how excited he was to coach his youngest son, and he felt the Eagles would be ranked among the top teams in the nation for the 2011–12 season.

A picture of the last St. Patrick team he ever coached is displayed prominently in his new, spacious living room.

About the Author

Brian Fitzsimmons is a senior writer and editor at MSG Varsity, the first television, online, and interactive network devoted to high school sports and activities. A graduate of Sacred Heart University, Fitzsimmons previously served as a reporter for the Associated Press, *Connecticut Post*, NHL.com, and PA SportsTicker. He lives in New Jersey. Follow him on Twitter: @FitzWriter.

Acknowledgments

Throughout the process of writing this book, many people asked me if I had developed a friendly relationship with Kevin Boyle. In turn, I always provided the same answer: Coach Boyle, his family, players, and fellow teachers and administrators at St. Patrick High School all welcomed me with open arms. Those wonderful people helped make this book as detailed and accurate as it could possibly be.

Kevin Boyle was an unwavering supporter of this project from the start. A high school coach who was the best at his profession embraced a reporter who was far from the best at his and took a chance to make both of our dreams come true.

That gesture—combined with hours of conversation he didn't have to engage in, e-mails he didn't have to reply to, phone calls he didn't have to pick up, unlimited access he didn't have to provide, and kindness he didn't have to show—only proves what kind of person he is.

Even as Kevin, his wife Kelly, and their three children, Kelscey, Kevin, and Brendan, enjoy their new lives in Florida, I hope to remain close to them. They're the type of people with whom you want to surround yourself.

For months, Joe Picaro took time out of his busy school days to entertain me. And entertain me he did. I don't think I've ever come across a better storyteller. His input was invaluable and much appreciated. Same goes to Red Migliore, the man with fingerprints all over the St. Patrick community's great work.

Michael Kidd-Gilchrist always made sure to say hello and ask how the book was coming along. Jarrel Lane, Chris Martin, and Taylor Plummer became instant friends and offered their critiques for the cover of this book.

Derrick Gordon, Tyrone O'Garro, Dakari Johnson, and Dana Raysor always welcomed me and treated me like one of the guys.

Trevis Wyche, Hakim Saintil, Austin Colbert, Da'shawn Suber, DaQuan Grant, and Diozy Mathos extended their friendship as well, and they never turned down an interview. Of course, their hard work helped make this project a reality.

When it comes to the team staff, Karen Magliacano deserves the MVP award for this book. Ed Leibowitz, Frank Peralta, Jyron Brooks, Pete Mairston, and Eric Woroniecki provided unquantifiable assistance, making me feel honored to be a part of the family all season.

One assistant coach in particular deserves all the credit in the world. He was also one of the first people to hear I was pursuing this project and encouraged me to actually go through with it: Rae Miller. I'll steal a line from my good friend and coworker Mike Quick by saying Rae is a great coach, but a better person.

Without the help of Kevin Boyle's famous former players, this book would not be sitting on shelves today. The assistance and warm friendship of Grant Billmeier, Mike Nardi, Dean Kowalski, and Shaheen Holloway were especially treasured. The same can be said about Marc Levin, R. Binky Brown, Karl Hollandt, Ben Selkow and the rest of the Blowback Productions crew. It was a pleasure spending every day with you guys.

I'd be remiss if I didn't thank the wonderful people at iUniverse, especially Marie Belaneso and Sarah Disbrow, who answered too many of my phone calls and offered their assistance during too many busy days.

My photographer and good friend Adrienne Accardi deserves a ton of credit for providing hard work and an example of what it means to chase a dream. Matt Tarro, a college friend who became a coworker, was a superstar graphic designer, too.

Meanwhile, the crew at MSG Varsity never admitted they were sick of hearing about this book. For that, and so much more, I'm thankful. All of you guys make coming to work every day a blessing.

In addition, Brett Topel, John Quirk, Larry Berger, and Mike Quick were great friends, de facto therapists and editors, while Lou Brogno was the man who gave me the green light at the start and perpetual support until the end.

Back when I first broke into this business, Barry Werner, Bill Bernardi, Chris Palochko, Jimmy Ralabate, Scott Erskine, and Tom Torrisi were there to encourage me. They also whipped my ass into shape, and I'm convinced not one word of this book would've made it to a Microsoft Word document without them. Same goes to my good friend Pat Pickens, a damn fine writer himself, who always told me to keep dreaming big.

So many other people contributed in numerous ways to his project, big or small, and I am indebted to all of those who made this journey a lot easier. Some of those friends and peers include: Adam Kimelman, A. J. Walkley, Adam Zagoria, Alex Kline, Andrew Miller, Bob Klapisch, Bob Phillips, Brad Holland, Cindy Simoneau, Dan DeAngelis, Dan Exter, Debbie Danowski, Fernando Rios, Fr. Michael Fugee, Gary Rogo, Greg Yannalfo, Ian O'Connor, Jim Castonguay, Jimmy Cavallo, Jim Grillo, Joanne Kabak, John Celestand, John Frustaci, John Nestor, Jonathan McCarthy, Jordan Schultz, Keith Idec, Kevin Armstrong, Kevin Kernan, Mario Mergola, Matthew Stanmyre, Mike Casey, Mike D'Avino, Mike Kinney, Mike Vaccaro, Nate Campbell, Nicole Minio, Robert Aanonsen, Steve Conoscenti, Steve Levy, Tom Liodice, Zach Braziller, the Brozyna family, the DeCoons family, the Fitzsimmons family, the Goldsmith family, the Mazzola family, the Mergola family, the O'Neil family, and the Roy family.

A special thanks to Dan Brozyna and Brian Mazzola, my brothers through it all, because it's your constant support and motivational speeches that keep me going, not just now, but since we were little kids.

Finally, a heartfelt thanks to the great family the Lord so graciously blessed me with. Your unconditional love and unflappable encouragement shaped my dream, cultivated it, and eventually made me believe in myself.

Mom, thank you for providing a constant reminder to protect my dream and for too many of the other things you have done as my hero. Megan, it's a blessing to know we're each other's biggest fans. Dad, your encouragement and advice never fail to inspire me. Thank you for bringing me to watch Kevin Boyle and the St. Patrick Celtics when I was a little kid; that's where this passion was born. Dori and Kate, the love and support you have given keep me grounded.

Above all, my family members have always kept me on track, and for that I'm forever grateful.

Author's Interviews and Bibliography

Kevin Boyle was among dozens of sources interviewed multiple times for this book. Some sources requested and received anonymity.

Multiple phone calls to Samuel Dalembert, Dexter Strickland, and Kasey Kesselring were not returned over the span of several months. Access to Al Harrington was denied by multiple individuals.

John Calipari denied an interview request.

Author's Interviews

Adam Zagoria
Austin Colbert
Bob Hurley
Brendan Boyle
Chase Plummer
Chris Martin
Cindy Richardson
Corey Fisher
Dajuan Wagner
Dakari Johnson
Dana Raysor
Danny Hurley
Da'shawn Suber
DaQuan Grant
Dean Kowalski
Derrick Gordon
Diozy Mathos

Drederick Irving
Eli Carter
Eric Woroniecki
Frank Peralta
Frantz Massanet
Grant Billmeier
Hakim Saintil
Janice Jackson
Jarrel Lane
Jason Boswell
Jimmy Cavallo
Joe Picaro
John Celestand
Jyron Brooks
Karen Magliacano
Kelly Boyle
Kevin Boyle
Kevin Boyle Jr.
Kevin Philemon
Kyrie Irving
Luther Wright
Makini Campbell
Michael Kidd-Gilchrist
Mike Brown
Mike Nardi
Mike Quick
Paris Bennett
Pete Mairston
Rae Miller
Rich Biddulph
Robert "Red" Migliore
Sandra Gordon
Sandy Pyonin
Shaheen Holloway
Taylor Plummer
Trevis Wyche
Tyrone O'Garro

Books

James, LeBron, with Buzz Bissinger. *Shooting Stars*. New York: The Penguin Press, 2009.

O'Connor, Ian. *The Jump*. Emmaus, Pennsylvania: Rodale Inc., 2005.

Wojnarowski, Adrian. *The Miracle of St. Anthony*. New York: Gotham Books, 2005; Penguin Group (USA) Inc., 2005.

Magazines

GQ
SLAM
Sports Illustrated

Newspapers/Wire Services

Asbury Park Press
Associated Press
New York Daily News
New York Post
Orlando Sentinel
(Massachusetts) Republican
(Newark) The Star-Ledger

Websites

www.basketballreference.com
www.cfnews13.com
www.espn.go.com
www.maxpreps.com
www.msgvarsity.com/new-jersey
www.zagsblog.com

Television networks

ESPN
Home Box Office
Madison Square Garden Network
MSG Varsity
News 12

Videos/Broadcasts

Adam Zagoria, Mike Kinney interview, ZagsBlog.com, February 16, 2011.

Mike Quick with Kevin Boyle, "A Quick :60," MSG Varsity, 2011.

Game Broadcasts: ESPN2, ESPNU, MSG Varsity.

CPSIA information can be obtained
at www.ICGtesting.com
Printed in the USA
LVHW100218131221
706039LV00031B/1685